Lutheran Theology

Lutheran Theology

A Grammar of Faith

Kirsi Stjerna

t&tclark

LONDON • NEW YORK • OXFORD • NEW DELHI • SYDNEY

T&T CLARK
Bloomsbury Publishing Plc
50 Bedford Square, London, WC1B 3DP, UK
1385 Broadway, New York, NY 10018, USA

BLOOMSBURY, T&T CLARK and the T&T Clark logo
are trademarks of Bloomsbury Publishing Plc

First published in Great Britain 2021

A catalogue record for this book is available from the British Library.

Library of Congress Cataloging-in-Publication Data
Names: Stjerna, Kirsi Irmeli, 1963-author.
Title: Lutheran theology : a grammar of faith / Kirsi Stjerna.
Description: London ; New York: T&T Clark, 2021. | Includes
bibliographical references and index.
Identifiers: LCCN 2020024314 (print) | LCCN 2020024315 (ebook) | ISBN
9780567686718 (paperback) | ISBN 9780567686725 (hardback) | ISBN
9780567686732 (pdf) | ISBN 9780567686749 (epub)
Subjects: LCSH: Lutheran Church–Doctrines.
Classification: LCC BX8065.3 .S75 2021 (print) | LCC BX8065.3
(ebook) | DDC 230/.41–dc23
LC record available at https://lccn.loc.gov/2020024314
LC ebook record available at https://lccn.loc.gov/2020024315

ISBN: HB: 978-0-5676-8672-5
         PB: 978-0-5676-8671-8
         ePDF: 978-0-5676-8673-2
         eBook: 978-0-5676-8674-9

Typeset by Integra Software Services Pvt. Ltd.

To find out more about our authors and books visit www.bloomsbury.com
and sign up for our newsletters.

I dedicate this book to my students at Pacific Lutheran Theological Seminary of California Lutheran University and at the Graduate Theological Union, Berkeley.

CONTENTS

PREFACE

The Horizons of This Book

This book arises from my teaching of Luther and the *Book of Concord* in a seminary setting over the last twenty years. Today I teach them in the West Coast in classrooms with individuals with different backgrounds and traditions and involved in different degree programs. I cannot take many things for granted. I cannot give authoritative statements, and nor would I want to. I teach as a European-born and -raised theologian who has studied and taught history and theology in university and seminary settings and who is familiar with the confessional divides between Lutherans globally speaking, while not interested in being tangled in them. I participate in international Lutheran scholarly collaborations, am grateful for the ecumenical agreements, and covet for more mutual understanding between different Lutheran constituencies. While it is clear from these pages that I personally and professionally stand with the Evangelical Lutheran Church of America and the Evangelical Lutheran Church of Finland, my approach with the texts and topics aims to imagine a path that is walkable on theological grounds for individuals from a variety of home bases.

Luther studies have been the core of my theological scholarship, and Luther's theology remains the main lens for my hermeneutics. In my observation, Luther is not only historically interesting but can also be a theologically and spiritually engaging conversation partner in contemporary constructive theological discourse. As a reformer, he reacted to urgencies of his world and took a theological stand where he considered it needed. Regardless of how one relates to the content of his theology, one can resonate with (at least some of) his pondering on the rationales for theological action and recognize the courage he demonstrated with his commitment toward a Scripturally informed and contextually illumined theology that promises to have a liberating and a grounding impact in people's lives.

In conversation with my students who have brought their rich life experiences and fresh questions to the study of the Lutheran sources, I have sought to develop an approach of coming together to study the sixteenth-century texts critically and compassionately, with humility and mutual respect, and with openness for new insights. I personally am convinced that Lutheran theology, with warts and all, offers seeds for transformative theologies for the contemporary world, but it needs to be freed, and in part purged, from unhelpful elements and the unnecessary tensions regarding who can offer the most correct interpretation and application. Lutheran history is rich in debate, thus the written confessions in the first place. The sixteenth-century sources express the complexity embedded in Lutheran theological discourse from the very beginning. They also demonstrate an effort of the authors, who did not see eye to eye on everything, to engage in discourse toward at least functional unity, even amid disagreements, on theological grounds.

This book does not aim to solve the inner or intra-Lutheran tensions but rather engages selections from the *Book of Concord* texts, particularly the *Augsburg Confession* and *Large Catechism*, as tools for exploring the promise and challenges of Lutheran faith today. I approach the texts as sources that can assist readers with different starting points in understanding Lutheran identity (and headaches) theologically speaking over the centuries, while testing their relevance for theological languages of faith today. In other words, this book hangs between history and tomorrow: interpreting the materials in light of their historical roots as well as reading them with today's theological questions in mind.

With the above considerations in mind, the chapters in this book are designed to articulate what can be discerned as distinctively Lutheran theological language and approaches, in light of history but with a contemporary theological orientation. For these purposes, the confessional texts are briefly introduced as a foundation for the grammar of a particularly Lutheran faith language. Rather than laboring for a detailed description of past debates and sorting out the multitude of viewpoints presented since the Reformation century or engaging the rich array of doctrinal studies of the texts, my interest is in equipping readers to engage the texts critically for themselves and with curiosity about their practical and spiritual bearing today in order to speak with a distinctively Lutheran voice to matters that matter.

To Whom and for What Is This Book For

This book is not written as an ode to the past glories of the Lutheran tradition. It is not written as a norm book or a linear guide for what to think and believe. It is far from comprehensive in terms of the topics that could have been included. It is written out of appreciation for the tradition and its history, while seeking for the transformative power of the theological principles the Lutheran tradition has to offer for today. The focus in this book is theological and spiritual, rather than historical or descriptive, or philosophical or comparative. I seek to engage Lutheran key teachings not for simple coasting along but as an invitation for a renewed and involved theological and spiritual engagement with new partners. The book is intended as an introduction with imaginary conversation partners' questions in mind, just as it is shaped by the actual questions that have been raised in the classroom.

To whom is this book written for? For individuals and groups interested in engaging the Reformation-era sources that are still shaping the lives of Lutheran Christians today and feeding living theological discourse and spiritual orientations. For individuals and groups desiring clarity for their faith language with a historical foundation with sources that can be read, reread, and reexamined, and debated with. In my mind are first and foremost the students who are encountering these sources for the first time—and with the word "student" I mean not only those enrolled in seminary classes but anyone who wants to take the bull by the horns and look into this pot. I hope this book serves as a friendly welcome and an accompaniment for that journey.

On the anniversary of women's ordination in the
Evangelical Lutheran Church in Finland
March 6, 2020
Berkeley, California

ACKNOWLEDGMENTS

I am grateful to Anna Turton for welcoming this project to the T&T Clark's published works and to Veerle Van Steenhuyse and Rachel Walker, and Viswasirasini Govindarajan at Integra for their assistance with the manuscript through the many stages. I offer warmest thanks to Jill Disbro, my graduate assistant in 2019–20, who contributed with her diligent work with the sources and different pieces of information, as well as managing varied other tasks, freeing thus my time for this project. I owe deep gratitude to my students at the Pacific Lutheran Theological Seminary in Berkeley, whose curiosity and questions with the materials we studied together fundamentally shaped the heart of this book. I am grateful to California Lutheran University, my employer, and my colleagues there, for the essential sustenance and for the place around the table. My children, Kiki Kirsikka and Kristian, with their compassionate inquiries and sparkling conversations on faith and religion have in many ways fueled my thinking, as I have sought for a language that would make sense beyond the seminary and church spaces. Last but not least, my husband and fellow scholar Brooks Schramm, who has encouraged me over the years to follow this dream of mine, to write exactly this book, who provided multidimensional assistance with the Luther sources and with obscure words, who contributed substantially in sections on Jesus, the canon, and biblical interpretation, and who with endless scholarly interest has engaged in discussions on topics of our shared interest, he deserves my deepest thanks and affection, always.

I thank the Fortress Press for their gracious permission to use quotations from the following texts:

- *The Book of Concord*, eds. Robert Kolb and Timothy J. Wengert et al. (Fortress Press: Minneapolis, 2000).
- *The Annotated Luther*, Vols. 1–6, gen. co-eds. Hans J. Hillerbrand, Kirsi I. Stjerna, Timothy J. Wengert (Fortress Press: Minneapolis, 2015–17).

1

Introduction

Reorientations in the Junction of Past, Present, and Future

Students on our Berkeley campus are invited to study Martin Luther's theology and the Lutheran confessional texts from the sixteenth century as building blocks for their fresh constructive theologizing, courageous proclamation, and compassionate spirituality. Be it their first encounter or not, students are often pleasantly surprised how relevant they may find these sources and many of the questions elaborated in them. Theological time-traveling can be enthralling! With first-hand engagement with historical texts, they can experience the benefit of maintaining intellectually and spiritually stimulating conversations across the centuries. With the commitment to free Lutheran theology to be a transformative power in the world today, critical and creative engagement with the historical works in informative and free conversations can powerfully equip new voices to contribute, in their turn, to the layers of Lutheran theology and hermeneutics.

In the twenty-first-century contemporary context, many of the haunting problems of the Western Christian theologies have been amply identified, e.g., the past predominance of white and male voices, prioritizing heteronormative and binary thinking, Christian theologies' role in different forms of oppression and unjust distribution of resources, the anti-Semitic elements imbedded in biblical hermeneutics and Christian proclamation, and human-centered ideologies and practices that endanger the entire creation. There would be a plenty of reasons to reject the past, start afresh, and pursue entirely new paths in theological discourse and spiritual seeking. Some feminist scholars have chosen this path, to the point of suggesting an entirely new vocabulary even. Another temptation is to stay with the old shoes and not get the blisters with trying new ones, to use a mundane metaphor. Yet another is to look into the theologies of the past with a clinical descriptive or historical analytical lens, without attempting to connect with contemporary questions too much, to avoid the terrible sin of anachronism! It makes a difference whether one aims to read historical sources as something strictly belonging to the past, or to hold onto them as guiding documents today, or to explore them as worthy of live engagement for developing historically respectful yet forward-looking faith talk for the present. In this book, the main interest is in Lutheran theological language and how it resonates today, in conversation with the sixteenth-century documents.

In this book, I wish to invite the readers to engage Lutheran faith talk with their feet in both worlds, history and today, and with eyes toward the future. Without attempting to develop a brand-new faith language with no roots, but rather responding to the need to communicate, critique, and reconstruct particularly Lutheran theological language in ways that respond to contemporary questions and experiences, I have chosen a middle path: to look into the roots of Lutheran theological language and its sources, to honor the work of the faith ancestors, but to do so in the spirit of reforming theology, to identify in the inherited legacy the ingredients that are still helpful and worth further kneading, as well as to note the unhelpful—or tainted—ones.

The title *Lutheran Theology* identifies the specific historical roots of the tradition and the sources addressed here. It also indicates my conviction and hope that there is space, material, and a rationale for a theology called Lutheran. The book is prepared especially keeping those readers in mind who are preparing themselves to lead Lutheran faith communities or speak Lutheran language in their vocations, but also those who wish to explore the dimensions of Lutheran theological language on their own and find support in their desire to clarify their own positions. Assuming very little previous knowledge, and drawing from the lively classroom, I have crafted the book as an accompaniment for those in the beginning stages of their journey.

The texts in the *Book of Concord* are an obvious start to explore the foundations of Lutheran theology. The 1580 collection of the confessional texts has served the Lutherans over the centuries by giving coherence to their theological voice and their faith communities worldwide. At the same time, most Lutherans would hardly know to speak to its importance, if even able to name it; many have probably never even opened the book. The texts are more familiar for the teachers of the faith and for those interested in the study of the Lutheran doctrine. That said, for any reader they offer a substantial exposure to what Lutheran theology has meant in the past, as well as a springboard for Lutheran faith language for today and tomorrow.

The sources in the *Book of Concord* are still named as the guiding foundation for Lutheran proclamation, ministry, and spirituality globally speaking. By themselves, they serve as a helpful introduction to the Lutheran ways of theologizing and hermeneutics and to understanding how Lutheran Christian expressions of faith in communities and in private lives have been organized and guided since the sixteenth century. For contemporary uses as a source for critical reflection for what the word "Lutheran" means today in theological discourse and spirituality, they are limited if left standing on their own; they need reinterpretation in new contexts and with new readers.

Over the centuries, strong traditions have developed about the accurate interpretation of the Lutheran sources, and Lutherans have found themselves in endless debates about the meaning and parameters of genuinely Lutheran perspectives and practices. This reality manifests itself in the differences between the diverse live Lutheran constituencies around the world. Time has come to break free from such binds and take a fresh look, and not just one but several looks, with new questions and new partners. This book is one such look and an invitation for further discourse.

In terms of understanding Lutheran faith communities and commitments today, the sixteenth-century sources give an orientation into why and how Lutherans got to be the way they are, theologically speaking. They also provide stimulus to constantly reconsider the Lutheran pillars and emphases in theology, as well as to reckon the growing edges of that tradition today, especially in the company of other religious traditions that offer vitally important illumination on shared matters that matter. In this book, I hope to present the historically formative Lutheran texts as helpful sources for developing contemporary faith languages that can equip individuals and communities with theological clarity for themselves and toward developing transformative theologies that can nurture church communities, individuals' spiritualities, as well as theological imagination vis-à-vis the care of the common affairs in the world.

In the following pages, the main texts engaged are the *Augsburg Confession* and *Large Catechism*, both included in the *Book of Concord*. The topics arise from the texts, particularly the *Augsburg Confession*, while their explanation involves Luther's insights from the *Large Catechism* and, to a lesser degree, from his *Smalcald Articles*. Other texts from the *Book of Concord* are included in various places, but only modestly so. The red thread throughout the discourse is Luther's theology, rather than an even treatment of all the texts in the *Book of Concord*.

This is so for many reasons. For one, the texts and the theological visions contained in the *Book of Concord* have their roots in Luther's teachings, which are explicitly clarified, extrapolated, and debated in the sources included in the collection of the confessional texts. Second, the *Book of Concord* is more historically bound as a whole, and especially so its uses in the beginning decades of the Lutheran movement, particularly in Germany, whereas Luther's voice offers the sustained melody (so to speak), which can speak beyond the geographical, linguistic, and cultural locations of the first Lutherans. Theologically and historically, Luther is the unifying voice for Lutherans, with his reformation calls and freedom theology, the interpretation of which has only multiplied and which lives on in many expressions. That said, the organization of the topics arises from the *Augsburg Confession*, the first shared public exposition of Lutheran theology as a rationale for sweeping church reforms, and the text still used as the most authoritative guide for Lutheran ministries today.

The Word "Lutheran"

Throughout the book the word "Lutheran" is used broadly to speak of a tradition and viewpoints that draw from the legacy of Martin Luther and are associated with faith communities that bear the name Lutheran. The word is employed also when referring to the developments in the Reformation era, even if the term "evangelical" would be most historically accurate, as the sixteenth-century Protestant Christians were identified as evangelicals for their emphasis on the gospel and grace in their proclamation, in distinction from the Catholic teaching of salvation and Christian life. Originally a slandering label from the opponents, the word "Lutheran" was nothing that Luther himself would have welcomed. Apropos, while the term "Lutheran" stuck, the word "evangelical" is used as an adjective in the names of many Lutheran churches around the world. (The word in these cases has a different meaning from, e.g., what it means with the North American faith communities categorized as expressions of evangelical Christianity with a fundamentalist bending.[1])

The word "Lutheran" calls for a rationale in contemporary religious parlance.[2] Why call oneself or a denomination Lutheran, why not Christian or Protestant or evangelical or something else? One reason for these questions is the religious situation of the day. The word "Christian" itself requires explanation, just as different expressions of Christian faith face the challenge to argue for their distinctive contribution amid different world views and in relation to other traditions. Naming is not insignificant in this process.

With the word "Lutheran" the roots go back to the sixteenth-century Europe and to the teachings of Martin Luther (1483–1546), a German ex-monk and a Catholic priest, a biblical scholar, a professor, and a father of six

---

[1] The word "evangelical" in particularly American context is used to refer to those often charismatic groups or fundamentalist movements among Protestant Christians who are oriented with the gospel of salvation by the atoning work of Jesus Christ, the infallible authority of the Scriptures, and personal faith commitment and experiences.

[2] In total, in 2019, about 83 million people were members of Lutheran churches, in over 100 countries, with over 230 church bodies worldwide that identify as Lutheran about 1 percent of the world's population. Also, 75 Lutheran church bodies worldwide were members of the World Council of Churches. The Lutheran World Federation (LWF, since 1947) gathered 75.5 million Lutherans worldwide, in 99 countries, with 148 member churches, 2 associate member churches, 10 recognized churches and congregations, and 2 recognized councils. The International Lutheran Council (ILC, since 1993) had 7.15 million members, with 54 member churches. (United Nations, "Department of Economic and Social Affairs, and Population Division," in *World Population Prospects 2019*.)

children and a husband of Katharina von Bora, a theologian and a reformer. Given that he lived and wrote in a particular cultural, geographic, and linguistic context, what would be the rationale or benefit, or problem, of continuing to use the word "Lutheran"? In testing the relevance of the term, different paths could be taken. First, one could revisit the story of Luther and see what in his experience as a human being and a spiritual seeker resonates with individuals today. Second, one could look at the decisions Luther and his peers had to make with their eyes toward the future, as they set the foundations for (what they understood as) a new expression of the ancient Christian faith. Lutherans today stand on those shoulders, for better and for worse. Third, one could consider Luther's theological vision and assess to what extent it can feed theological imaginations for the future. Fourth, one could begin new conversations with the sources that have historically shaped the Lutheran tradition and take another look in an effort to communicate what is so distinctive and promising about Lutheran religious language and orientation. Last but not least, one needs to address the negative connotations of the word "Lutheran" specifically vis-à-vis the history of anti-Semitism. These possible paths have shaped the decisions made in the creation of this book.

The Plan

In the following, Part One starts with an encounter with Luther via a chronology and a synopsis of his theology from one of his most influential treatises. Part Two offers an orientation to the Lutheran confessional sources and the guiding principles in Lutheran hermeneutics around the central doctrine of justification. Part Three engages the Lutheran confessional sources for critical reflection on the fundamentals of faith and to lay out a current working-grammar for Lutheran theology, mainly employing the *Augsburg Confession* and the *Large Catechism* and the topics they address.

The main sources engaged are the most recent English edition of the *Book of Concord*, by editors Robert Kolb and Timothy J. Wengert (Fortress Press: Minneapolis, 2000) and the revised or retranslated Luther's texts in *The Annotated Luther*, Vols. 1–6, eds. Hans J. Hillerbrand, Kirsi I. Stjerna, and Timothy J. Wengert (Fortress Press: Minneapolis, 2015–17). The latter, with the annotated texts that aim for inclusive translations, is recommended for the *Large Catechism* and *Smalcald Articles*.[3] In light of the intended

---

[3] *The Book of Concord*, eds. Robert Kolb and Timothy J. Wengert et al. (Minneapolis: Fortress Press, 2000) and *The Annotated Luther*, Vols. 1–6, gen. co-eds. Hans J. Hillerbrand, Kirsi I. Stjerna, Timothy J. Wengert (Minneapolis: Fortress Press, 2015–17). For the *Smalcald Articles* and *Large Catechism*, and *Small Catechism*, texts from *The Annotated Luther* are used. Also for other texts, when available, *The Annotated Luther* translations are used. For LC and SA quotes, references to the Kolb and Wengert edition are given in the footnotes for the readers' benefit.

classroom uses of this book, only English sources are referenced and recommended, and quite frugally so. Those aiming for in-depth scholarship on Luther or the confessional texts will naturally consult the texts in their original languages.[4]

In the end, brief conclusions are offered about the promise of Lutheran theology particularly as a freedom theology. The bibliography lists the sources used and those recommended for further reading. Each chapter ends with guiding questions for discussion and review, keywords, and reading suggestions from the sources.

---

[4]The German/Latin edition is the foundation for critical work on the confessions; see *Die Bekenntnisschriften der evangelisch-lutherischen Kirche*, hrsg. Irene Dingel (Göttingen: Vandenhoeck & Ruprecht, 2014). For Luther's works, *Luthers Werke: Kritische Gesamtausgabe*, 65 vols. (Weimar: H. Böhlau, 1883–1993) (abbreviated WA) is the standard source and also the basis for the revised English translations in *The Annotated Luther*, which aims to facilitate access to Luther scholarship for those who operate with other languages.

PART ONE

Partnering with Martin Luther

2

Martin Luther's Voice as the Foundation

Martin Luther's life and works would require their own treatment.[1] Simply for the purposes of orienting the reader to the study of Lutheran theology with the sixteenth-century confessional texts, a brief introduction is offered to Luther as a reformer particularly in terms of his theology.[2] First, the accompanying chronology of Luther's most important life and career events gives the framework for the study of his theology. Second, to dive into the theological world and vocabulary of Luther, his main theological insights are reviewed through one of his most systematic and widespread texts, *The Freedom of a Christian*. The reader is invited to meet Luther as a freedom theologian: First, the reader can observe the significant events and turning

---

[1]Recommended further reading on Luther's life and contributions, see, e.g., Volker Leppin, *Martin Luther: A Late Medieval Life* (Grand Rapids: Baker Academic, 2017); Scott Hendrix, *Martin Luther: Visionary Reformer* (New Haven: Yale University Press, 2015); Alberto Melloni, ed., *Martin Luther: A Christian between Reforms and Modernity (1517–2017)* (Berlin: Walter de Gruyter, 2017); Lyndal Roper, *Martin Luther: Renegade and Prophet* (New York: Random House, 2017). For ample details, see Martin Brecht's three-volume *Martin Luther* (Philadelphia: Fortress, 1985–93); Derek Nelson and Paul Hinlicky, eds., *The Oxford Encyclopedia of Martin Luther* (New York: Oxford University Press, 2017).

[2]Recommended further reading on Luther's theology, see, e.g., Tuomo Mannermaa, *Christ Present in Faith: Luther's View of Justification* (Minneapolis: Fortress Press, 2005); Bernard Lohse, *Martin Luther's Theology: Its Historical and Systematic Development* (Minneapolis: Fortress Press, 1999); Derek Nelson and Paul Hinlicky, *The Oxford Encyclopedia of Martin Luther*; Hans-Martin Barth, *The Theology of Martin Luther: A Critical Assessment* (Minneapolis: Fortress Press, 2013); Christine Helmer, *The Global Luther: A Theologian for Modern Times* (Minneapolis: Fortress Press, 2009); Kirsi Stjerna and Brooks Schramm, eds., *Encounters with Luther*: New Directions for Critical Studies (Louisville, KY: Westminster John Knox, 2016); Else Marie Wiberg Pedersen, *The Alternative Luther: Lutheran Theology from the Subaltern* (Minneapolis: Lexington Books/Fortress Press, 2019).

points in life, career, and relations when Luther faced questions pertaining to freedom, broadly conceived. Second, the reader can contemplate on the undercurrent of freedom themes in Luther's theological vision and spiritual experience, on the basis of the text poignantly titled with the word "freedom." Approaching Luther as a freedom theologian does not set him on a pedestal as a freedom fighter in a modern sense of the word. Rather, the freedom question provides an opportunity for a meaningful and authentic, and critical, encounter with Luther's theology.

Martin Luther in Chronology—Pivotal Freedom Moments

Martin Luther's life could be approached from a variety of angles. The data presented in the following chronology offers a look at his journey from birth to death and notes a fraction of his printed works. His life and career are followed chronologically, from the formative years and the dramatic years of his first reformation calls, to the decades of action, maturation, and debate, and finally the last decades with multiplied responsibilities and tragic events. The reader is invited to peruse the chronology that simply lists known facts, without interpretation (with some contextual information in the footnotes) with one particular word as the focus: freedom. If considering freedom as the first and foremost issue, how does Luther's journey and theological insights look like—as a Christian, as a theologian, as a biblical interpreter, as a preacher, as a leader, as a human being—be it a matter of freedom of conscience, or freedom from authority, or academic freedom to think, speak, and act, or freedom as the ultimate and personal concern and the grounding for human life and teaching of grace?

Luther in Chronology and Context

Early Years 1483–1517[3]

1483, November 10, Martin is born.

Parents Margaretha (Hanna) and Hans Luder; peasant/copper miner/burgher; eight children (?)

---

[3]Contemporary reformers: Andreas Karlstadt (born 1480), Huldrych Zwingli (born 1484). In 1516 *Novum instrumentum*, a Greek edition of the New Testament, published by Erasmus of Rotterdam.

1484–1501, Martin receives education in Mansfeld 1484–96/97, Magdeburg 1497, Eisenach 1498–1501, with matriculation, before moving in 1501 to Erfurt University to study law and then theology.

1505, July 2, Martin's first turning point: caught in thunderstorm, Martin promises his life to God and becomes a monk.

1505, July 17, Martin joins Augustinian Order in Erfurt; ordained. 1507, April 3; Johann von Staupitz as his confessor and mentor.

1511, Monk Martin's trip to Rome, as a delegate of the Augustinian Observants; disillusionment.

1511, Monk Martin transfers to the Wittenberg University (founded in 1502/3 by the Elector of Saxony Fredrick the Wise).

1512, With Doctorate in Theology, Martin becomes Professor of the Bible.

1512–13, Professor Luther's decisive lectures on Psalms 1513–15, Romans 1515–16, Galatians 1516–17, Hebrews 1517, and develops new hermeneutics to the Scriptures (describing it as a "born again" experience).

A turning point, *Turmerlebnis*, tower experience, with Romans 1:17, about justification and being right with God as a gift of faith.

Critical Years 1517–21[4]

1517, September, Luther's *Disputation against Scholastic Theology*.

1517, October 31, Luther writes his *Ninety-five Theses*, in Latin (academic thesis), addressing the selling of the indulgences with false promises and with the false authority of the Pope. (Players in the expanding situation: Johann Tetzel the salesman, Elector Fredrick, Archbishop of Mainz, the Fugger banking house, Pope Leo, and Luther.)

Pausing with the indulgence controversy and the snowballing of events: With his *Ninety-five Theses* Luther publically criticized the extraordinarily ambitious selling of indulgences with false promises and the church unjustly charging money from poor people for forgiveness that was a free gift to begin with. Starting with pastoral concerns, he came to challenge the role, the structures, and the theology of the institutional church of the time, particularly questioning the authority of the Pope and the power to forgive,

---

[4]In 1507 Pope Julius II offers the indulgence for building St. Peter's Basilika. In 1517, Albrecht of Brandenburg, the Archbishop of Magdeburg and (1514) Mainz, indebted to the Fugger banking family, allows selling of indulgences in his territory by Johann Tetzel, the profits going in part to Rome to finance the building of St. Peter's basilica and to pay for the special papal dispensations needed for his episcopal seats.

as well as the entire medieval teaching of salvation and religious life, and also the very rules of theologizing.

Luther's reforming principles concerned both theory and practical matters: insisting on *sola fides* and *sola scriptura*; the authority of Scripture versus tradition or papacy; criticism of the papal institution and scholastics; unfolding the dimensions of justification by faith alone, by grace alone, because of Christ alone; redefining relations between clergy and laity; expanding the idea of the vocation and ministry of all believers; developing (w)holistic perspectives on true Christian living and dismissing unnecessary regulations and unrealistic spiritual aspirations; vehemently teaching anti-celibacy and pro-marriage (also clerical); developing a view of Christian life in two kingdoms and the notion of church as a community of faith with the task to proclaim the gospel and offer the sacraments as ways to communicate grace to people in need of it; reducing the number of sacraments to two and insisting on Christ's real presence conveyed with them, to all; suggesting the most radical teaching on human beings' bondage to sin and the irresistible gift of God's grace; viewing human life as lived *simul iustus et peccator* and therefore deeming it vital that proclamation includes both law and gospel.

In other words, Luther's reformed theology addressed from different angles the basic issue of what Christian life and human-divine relation are all about and resting on, and what structures and teachings in the church are helpful for the benefit of the human being in need of grace, and ultimately, how faith and justification can be experienced and lived out in a life oriented with hope drawing from God. The lens for these discoveries and agendas, for Luther, came from his encounter with Christ via Scripture.

Reactions and Further Developments

1518, Silvester Prierias, Luther's first literary opponent, sets the tone of confrontation.

1518, April, Luther calls for a hearing with the Augustinians in Heidelberg and prepares his *Heidelberg Disputation*.

1518, October 12–14, Luther meets in Augsburg with Cardinal Cajetanus, Pope's delegate; no reconciliation or progress.

1519, June 27–July 16, at Leipzig, Dr. Johann Eck from University of Ingolstadt debates Dr. Andreas Bodenstein von Karlstadt—and Luther (Luther associated with the condemned Bohemian reformer Jan Hus).[5]

1520, Luther publishes his key programmatic reformation writings:

---

[5]In 1519 the Spanish king, Charles V, elected as the emperor, crowned on October 23, 1520; related through marriage to Frederic the Wise. The emperor needed the relatively independent German electors: the four princes of Saxony, Brandenburg, Bohemia, and Count Palatine of Rhine, and the three archbishops of Cologne, Trier, and Mainz.

1. *Address to the Christian Nobility*, in German, in August 1520, calls the leaders for the reforms and attacks the teachings that the Pope was above council, the papal primacy to interpret the Bible, and that clergy was above laity.

2. *Babylonian Captivity of the Church*, October 6, 1520, in Latin, wants to free the gospel from the prison of the institutional church; reforms the teaching of the sacraments; and critiques the doctrine of transubstantiation and the Masses for the dead, among other things.

3. *The Freedom of a Christian*, November 1520, in German, explicates Luther's theology to the masses in a language that could be understood by people in different walks of life, the main teaching being that Christian is freed in faith from everything and bound in love to serve everyone.

In addition, by 1521, Luther had published about eighty other books, eventually about 100 volumes.

Luther Bulled

1520, June 15, Luther is charged with the papal bull *Exsurge Domine*, which lists forty-one errors in Luther's writings.

1520, October 10, Luther receives the bull, with sixty days to recant.

1520, December 10, Wittenberg professors and teachers burn the bull, with the canon law.

1521, January 3, Luther is excommunicated with the bull *Decet Romanum Pontificem*. Luther appeals to the princes and the emperor to be heard in a German council.

Luther Outlawed

1521, March 6, Luther is summoned to the Diet of Worms (German council, started January 27).

1521, April 17/18, Luther is questioned before the emperor; on May 4 he declares his conscience was bound by the Scriptures and he could not retract anything or do otherwise.

1521, May 8, with the Edict of Worms, Luther is outlawed with the imperial ban on Luther and his followers. Luther is kidnapped to the Wartburg Castle.

Bible Work

1521, May–1522, March, Luther is in protected hiding in Wartburg.

1522, September, Luther prepares his (unauthorized) New Testament translation, *Septembertestament*; followed by another in December, *Dezembertestament*. Luther takes freedoms in translation and interpretation for the sake of conveying the proper meaning of the gospel (e.g., with Romans 3:28, he adds the word "alone"—"Word alone"), giving a model for future translations and uses of vernacular.

Teaching and Implementation Years 1521–30[6]

1521, First clergy marries in May 1521, Bartholomew Bernhardi et al.

1521, Andreas Karlstadt writes *On Celibacy*, Luther follows with his *On Monastic Vows*. Protestant theologians develop a new view on priesthood of all believers, divine callings in the varied vocations, and evangelical freedom versus falsely binding vows.[7]

Worship and Church

1521, Christmas Day, new Mass is celebrated by Karlstadt, in lay clothing, offering bread and wine to all.

1521, Luther writes *On the Abolition of Images*.

1521, January 24, the town council endorses changes in worship life; the new Mass.

1521–2, Wittenberg colleagues proceed to implement reforms. Iconoclastic reactions, with riots and chaos.[8]

---

[6]Some of Luther's colleagues: Andreas Bodenstein von Karlstadt (1480–1541), a theologian with a law degree, dean, and archdeacon, with three doctorates; Luther's partner, and later rival. With associations with what later would be known as pietism and lay puritanism, he taught regeneration and inner renewal, employing a mystical term "*Gelassenheit*" about letting oneself be with God, and also used terms "good" and "bad" when describing human beings (unlike Luther who paired the terms "saint" and "sinner"). Philip Melanchthon (1497–1560), a humanist, educator, mediator, and a life-long friend and faithful collaborator of Luther, wrote the *Augsburg Confession* in 1530 and its *Apology* 1531. Called the teacher of Germany, he offered his systematic theology in his *Loci communes rerum theologicarum*, 1521. Of the women reformers, Argula von Grumbach (1492–1554) was an avid supporter of Luther's theology; she was the first Protestant woman writer, applying the *sola scriptura* principle and priesthood of all believers. She corresponded with Reformers, mediated in the Eucharistic controversy, and became known from her published defense of a student accused of holding Lutheran views (1523). Argula met Luther in 1530 and corresponded with him over the years. Both Elizabeth von Brandenburg (1451–1524) and her daughter Elisabeth von Braunschweig (1510–58) were instrumental in supporting the bringing of Lutheran faith to their lands; both were exiled by their Catholic husband(s) and used their power as regents for their underage sons, the heirs, toward legislating the reforms in their territories.
[7]Karlstadt marries on January 19, 1522, causing a sensation. Luther marries later, in 1525.
[8]Zwickau prophets present a different reforming view, preaching against infant baptism and for immediate divine revelations, e.g., Ursula Jost.

1522, March 6, Luther returns to Wittenberg to restore order with *Invocavit* Lenten sermons, cautioning against force in reforms; faith and love being inseparable, reforms take time and Christian freedom necessitates patience and love, also with gospel-induced reforms.

Welfare and Order and Education

1520–1, Wittenberg theologians institutionalize welfare and issue anti-usury regulations.

The common chest from Wittenberg becomes the model for other Lutheran towns. The reforms in theology and worship lead to reforms in legislation and social issues.[9]

Public education is established for both boys and girls; the government's duty is to provide education for its future citizens (humanist influence)—and equip them to read the Bible.

1529, Luther publishes his long-awaited *Small* and *Large Catechisms* to train laity and clergy in the matters of faith.

Lutheran Notion of Vocation

Lutheran idea of the priesthood of all believers and equality in holy vocations develops, as does the idea of Christians living in two kingdoms, each with their own calling. Family life, marriage, and parenthood are recognized as holy vocations God has instituted.

Writings, Meetings, Developments in Church and Family Life after 1522

Theology and Politics

1523, Luther is lecturing again, on Deuteronomy (1524, Prophets) and initiates reforms in education, society, and liturgy, also working on questions pertaining to temporal authority and obedience.

1523, Luther develops the evangelical liturgy, *Formula Missae*; the German Mass prepared in 1526.

1524–5, Luther translates psalms and hymns.

---

[9]Johann Bugenhagen, Dr. Pommer: Priest, Luther's friend and advisor, a gifted organizer, who (1528–42) translated reformation theology into orders pertaining to churches' practices, schools, and arrangements for welfare; for him poor relief was an act of worship.

1523, Edict of the Diet of Nuremberg: Edict of Worms' enforcement postponed.[10]

1524, Philip of Hesse joins Reformation; beginning of the Peasants' riots in southwestern Germany.

1524, October 9, Luther abandons his monastic habit.

1524, Luther writes to the princes against the radicals (e.g., Thomas Müntzer),[11] and for the councilmen urging them to establish Christian schools.

1524, Erasmus of Rotterdam, humanist, writes his treatise on free will, *De libero arbitrio*. Radical reformer Müntzer writes to and against Luther.

1524, Luther and Karlstadt argue over social reform and the notion of Eucharist.

The Year of 1525: Peasants Riots and Marriage Reforms and Debates[12]

1525, Spring, peasants demand their rights with *The Twelve Articles of the Swabian Peasants*.

1525, April, Luther replies to the Twelve Articles; after cautioning against haste and violence from both sides, and holding the rulers accountable, he writes against the "robbing and murdering" peasants; he regrets later his heated words after, in May, in Mühlhausen, thousands of peasants are slaughtered.

1525, June 13, Luther marries Katharina von Bora; June 27, a larger wedding party. Katharina (1499–1552), Luther's wife, an ex-Cistercian nun, escaped from her convent with Luther's assistance with eleven other sisters, manages the Luther household, orchards, and gardens, their finances, and mothers their children (six) as well as several foster children. Luther's theology is concretely influenced by family life and his experience of marital and parental love and relations.

1525, November/December, *De servo arbitrio*, against Erasmus of Rotterdam; the Eucharistic controversy.

1526–34 Luther becomes father; his first son Hans is born on June 7, 1526; Käthe gives birth to six children in total (with at least one miscarriage).

---

[10]July 1, 1523, first Protestant martyrs burnt in Brussels.
[11]Thomas Müntzer (1489–1525), a radical German reformer with "socialist" dreams, who took political action and died with the rebelling peasants.
[12]1525 Charles V defeated; chaos in the war frontier.

Diets, Visitations, Writings

1526, First Diet of Speyer takes place: the reformation is not yet crushed; Luther is getting ill.

1526–30, Luther and colleagues visit in churches and schools in Saxony and see the need for church orders and catechisms.

1527, March/April, Luther writes on Eucharist against the "fanatics." He also writes on whether one could flee from plague.[13]

1528, March, daughter Elizabeth is born.

1528, March, Luther writes *Confession Concerning Christ's Supper*, an important treatise on the sacrament and a summation of his theology.

1528, August, daughter Elizabeth dies.

1529, February 26–April 12, Second Diet of Speyer; a re-affirmation of the condemnation of the 1521 Diet of Worms issued on April 19; the evangelical princes and cities defend themselves by "protesting."

1529, Luther writes about war against the Turks. He also publishes his *Catechisms*, *Small* in March, and *Large* in May; both become central Lutheran confessional texts.

1529, October, Luther attends a religious colloquy with Zwingli in Marburg: no agreement is reached on the matter of Eucharist and how Christ's presence is understood. The chances for a unified front of the German and Swiss Protestants are lost.

1529, Daughter Magdalena is born.

1530, June 20–November 19, the Diet of Augsburg. Luther (as outlawed) stays at Coburg Castle and writes an "exhortation" for all the clergy to attend.

1530, May, Luther's father dies.

Presentation of the *Augsburg Confession*, the central Lutheran confession, by Melanchthon.
The Swiss with Zwingli present their *Confessio Tetrapolitana*.
Both documents are refuted by the Catholic theologians.

Last Years 1530–46[14]

1531, The Smalcald League is founded to protect the Protestant estates, Princes of Saxony and Hesse as its leaders.

---

[13]The emperor sacks Rome on May 6, 1527.
[14]Meanwhile, October 11, 1531, Zwingli is killed on battlefield. The separation of the English church from Rome with the Act of Supremacy of the Church of England, by King Henry VIII. The Reformation takes place in Denmark with King Christian III (a son of Käthe's friend and sponsor).

1531, Luther's mother dies.

1530/31, Melanchthon writes *Apology of the Augsburg Confession*.

1532, Peace of Nuremberg brings temporary peace: Protestants are given freedom to exercise their religion until a general council would meet.

1533, Luther writes about private Mass and ordination.

1533, Son Paul is born.

1534, First complete edition of Luther's German Bible is published.

1534, Daughter Margaretha is born (the mother of still living descendants of Luther).

1534, February–June 25, 1535, the Anabaptist kingdom is established in Munster.

1535, May 12, The Protestant ordination is established.

1535–45, Luther lectures on the Genesis.

1535–46, Luther serves as the dean of the faculty in Wittenberg.

1535, November 7, negotiations take place with the papal nuncio Pietro Paolo Vergerio in Wittenberg about Protestants' participation in future papal council.

1535, Luther presides over doctrinal disputations.

1536, Wittenberg Concord is reached: an agreement between the Wittenberg and Southern German reformers.

1536, January, Luther takes part in disputation on "justification"; in December, Luther publishes his *Smalcald Articles*, his "confession," not accepted at first, but included in the *Book of Concord* of 1580.

1537, Luther is seriously ill with "stones." *Bundestag* in Smalcald: Protestants negotiate about their participation at the upcoming papal council; Smalcaldic league is extended for ten years.

1537–40, Lutherans dispute on the biblical law.

1538, The Catholics' Nuremberg League fights against the Protestants.

1539, Religious truce of Frankfurt promises limited toleration. Luther writes on the councils and churches.

1539–41, Luther revises the Bible translation.

1539, Luther is involved in the antinomian controversies against Johann Agricola.

1540/41, The infamous bigamy of Philip of Hesse, with Luther's discrete approval; the Smalcald league suffers from losing their leading prince.

1540/41, Religious colloquies take place in Hagenau, Worms, Regensburg.

1541, Luther goes on a preaching tour. Luther ordains Nicholas von Amsdorf as bishop of Naumburg.

1542, War between the Smalcaldic league and the Duke Wolfenbuttel.[15]

1542, January 6, Luther writes his will to Käthe as his sole inheritor (Saxon layers later will dispute the will).

1542, September 20, Magdalena, "Lenchen" dies.

1543, January, Luther writes harsh treatises about Jews and their "lies." (See below: On Luther and his writings on the Jews.)

1544, Luther writes his Book of Sermons, *Hauspostille*, and also on the sacrament against Caspar Schwenckfeld.

1545, March 5, Luther writes his autobiographical *Preface* to the Wittenberg edition of his Latin writings.

1545–63, the Council of Trent finally begins, December 13, 1545, and lasts till 1563; no Lutherans present.[16]

1546, February 14, Luther's last sermon, with apocalyptic tones, attacks the Jews and their religion.

1546, February 18, Luther dies in Eisleben, where he had traveled to assist in peace negotiations between two quarreling counts.

1546, February 23, Luther is buried in the Wittenberg Castle Church, Melanchthon and Bugenhagen preach; Melanchthon becomes Käthe's guardian.

After Luther

1546/47, The Smalcald War erupts. In April 24, 1547, Protestants are defeated by the emperors' troops.

1547, May 19, Wittenberg is capitulated.[17]

1555, Diet of Augsburg offers an agreement on the religious compromise *cuius regio, eius religio*.

1580, *Book of Concord*, the "norm and guide" for Lutherans is published, by editors Jacob Andrae and Martin Chemnitz, including the Creeds, *Small* and *Large Catechism*, *Augsburg Confession*, its *Apology*, *Smalcald Articles*, *Treatise on the Power and Primacy of the Papacy*, and *Formula of Concord*.

---

[15]1541–53, Duke Moritz of Saxony switches sides between the Catholic and Protestant leagues. 1542-7, John Fredrick I becomes the new elector.
[16]At the Council of Trento, the Society of Jesus (officially approved on September 27, 1540) serve in key roles; no Lutherans are present at the council.
[17]Elector John Fredrik is forced to give up his lands and electoral dignity to Duke Moritz.

1618–48, Thirty Years' War: in the unhappy aftermath of the Peace of Augsburg, Lutheran and Reformed princes form a military union against the Catholics with the emperor. The devastating war ends in *Peace of Westphalia 1648*: territories (except Austria/Habsburg areas) gain freedom to adopt their religion per the religion of the ruler of the region—only Lutheran, Anglican, and Reformed versions of Protestant faith allowed.

A Topic of Special Concern: Luther's Anti-Jewish Views

Luther's life offers numerous points worthy of pausing for further elaboration. The point here, however, is only to offer a general, initial framework before discussing his theological discoveries. There is one specific topic that merits notation whenever Luther is discussed, one that is not only part of his life story but also involves his theology and its assessment: the question of his writings on the Jews. This topic has been an area of significant scholarly attention and debate, with considerable disagreement on whether there was a change in Luther's views of the Jews and Judaism and in his position on the question of the toleration of Jews in German Protestant lands.

Luther's writings evidence an unchanged conviction: in his view and reading of the Scriptures, the Jewish faith had lost its validity since the arrival of Jesus; the law of Moses was dead; it came to an end after the gospel of Jesus arrived. Toward the end of his life Luther had lost hope for any significant conversions of the Jews, and with vitriolic rhetoric he urged the Protestant princes to expel the Jews and to take measures to end the practice of Jewish faith in German lands. Though he did not call explicitly for physical violence against Jews, his anger against those still practicing a religion he considered dead is evident.

An important point to keep in mind is that Luther spoke of Jews and Judaism primarily in the abstract: with very rare exceptions, he only knew about contemporary Jews from books and from Jewish converts to Christianity. On the other hand, Luther regarded the patriarchs and matriarchs of the Old Testament as being his ancestors in the faith and models for all the faithful; he even esteemed them more highly than he did the traditional saints of the church.

In the articulation of his theology of justification, the word "Jew" plays a complex and yet consistent role. For him, those Jews who continued to practice Judaism after the coming of Christ embodied the law-abiding, "unfree" human being, who stands in opposition to the Christian, who had been freed by Christ and was free from the Mosaic law. Luther's unfortunate and deeply problematic views point to fundamental problems in a Christian theology built on deeply seated anti-Jewish assumptions. Luther, with his visible position and widely distributed publications, stands out in the long line of anti-Jewish Christian theologians, to the extent that the United States Holocaust Memorial Museum in Washington, DC, features Luther in an educational film on the history of anti-Semitism.

While one can appreciate Luther's passion for the truth he personally found in the Scriptures about Christ the Savior who freed him and offered him a new direction in life, that cannot continue to justify hatred of religions that do not teach a similar doctrine. In Judaism, Christ does not have the central place he has in Lutheran Christian faith. Whereas a late medieval man can hardly be expected to emerge as an inter-religiously sophisticated or sensitive person, Lutherans post-Luther have a special moral obligation to be attentive to any speech or action that is built on or trumpets anti-Semitism or anti-Judaism and to cut ties with Luther in those places where his logic would support hatred of the other or suppression of the Jewish religion or any other faith that does not harmonize with certain traditional Lutheran faith convictions.[18] This commitment involves rigorous, open-minded, honest, and informed interpretation of the sacred texts and attention to the ethical implications of our interpretation.

Martin Luther on Freedom and Faith—Freedom Theology

On Christian Freedom—Luther's Theological Synopsis

The year 1520 was in many ways a watershed in Luther's career and in the progress of the reformations he initiated. In the heels of his broadly publicized concerns with this *Ninety-five Theses* of 1517 and in the eve of his banning and excommunication in 1521, Luther aimed his words and call to action to different directions: the authorities, the church, and the people. With three publications he made a gigantic splash with an unprecedented ripple effect. He started by calling the authorities to do their part in protecting the gospel and providing for people (*To the Christian Nobility*). He continued with targeting problems in the church and in its sacramental theology (*The Babylonian Captivity of the Church*). Last, and most ambitiously, he sought to reach the whole world and the entire Christendom with his *The Freedom*

---

[18]Dr. Brook Schramm contributed directly in the writing of this section he called "an appetite wetter." For more, see Brooks Schramm and Kirsi Stjerna, eds., *Martin Luther, the Bible, and the Jewish People* (Minneapolis: Fortress Press, 2010). For more, see Brooks Schramm, "Introduction" to "On the Schem Hamphoras and On the Lineage of Christ" ["On the Ineffable Name"], in *The Annotated Luther*, Vol. 5, ed. Hans J. Hillerbrand, (609) 622–66 (Minneapolis: Fortress Press, 2017). Also, Brooks Schramm, "Like a Sow Entering a Synagogue," in *Encounters with Luther: New Directions for Critical Studies*, eds. Kirsi Stjerna and Brooks Schramm (Louisville, KY: Westminster John Knox Press, 2016), 250–60.

of a Christian, a copy of which he sent to Pope Leo V. The shortest and the most powerful of the three treatises that set the reformation agenda opens a window to Luther's personal theological discoveries already early on in his career; it demonstrates his courage and passion as a reformer. There are obvious reasons why the treatise has continued to inspire readers through centuries. The theological perspectives and the pivotal concepts Luther kneads in this treatise provide a foundation for the study of other sources in Lutheran theology that one way or the other position themselves in relation to Luther's fundamental arguments.

Freedom in Faith, Service in Love

"I am sending you this little treatise dedicated to you as a token of peace and good hope," Luther wrote in his accompanying letter to Pope Leo X.[19] "It is a small book if you regard its size. Unless I am mistaken, however, it contains the whole of Christian life in a brief form, provided you grasp its meaning. I am a poor man and have no other gift to offer, and you do not need to be enriched by any other but a spiritual gift" (LW 31:343).

The gist of the book, dedicated to his friend Mühlphordt, Mayor of Zwickau, is found in his statement: "One thing, and only one thing, is necessary for Christian life, righteousness, and freedom. The one thing is the most holy Word of God, the gospel of Christ" (LW 31:345). He offered in its pages a masterful exposition of the Christian life through the lens of the gospel and faith, addressing such themes as human nature, the law and gospel in Christian life, the change caused by the Word, justification by faith and the indwelling of Christ, the work of the Holy Spirit and works of love, and the nature of Christian faith-based freedom, both in the scope of eternity and in this life.

The key statement in the text characterizes the two-fold reality of Christian life: freedom in faith and the bondage with the Spirit for love. "A Christian is a perfectly free lord of all, subject to none. A Christian is a perfectly dutiful servant of all, subject to all" (LW 31:344).[20] This duality

---

[19]With the publisher T&T Clark's permission, this text is a partial (pages 340–7) and mildly revised reproduction of the chapter 3.2 "Freedom of a Christian (1520). Martin Luther (1483–1546)," in *Reading Christian Theology in the Protestant Tradition,* eds. Kelly M. Kapic and Hans Madueme (London, Oxford, New York, New Delhi, Sydney: T&T Clark, 2018), 335–50, with endnotes adjusted into footnotes. The citations with the English translation of the *Von der Freiheit eines Christenmenschen* (in German WA 7:20–38, in Latin WA 7, 49–73) come from LW 31:333–77 (*Luther's Works—American Edition,* eds. Jaroslav Pelikan and Helmut T. Lehman, 55 vols. [Philadelphia: Fortress Press, 1957]). The newer translation by Timothy Wengert can be found in *The Annotated Luther,* Vol. 1 (Minneapolis: Fortress Press, 2015) and is referred to with selected quotations, in footnotes.

[20]"The Christian individual is a completely free lord of all, subject to none. The Christian individual is a completely dutiful servant of all, subject to all." Wengert translation, in *The Annotated Luther,* Vol. 1, 2015, 488.

describes how men and women relate to God and to their neighbors in this world. At its foundation, the treatise is Luther's teaching on justification and Christian life: when Christ becomes the subject of our being, life from then on is shaped by the experience of liberation and the resulting compassionate responsibility for justice.

The Dimensions of Human Life: Two Natures, Two Realms

Much like his medieval contemporaries, Luther believed that human beings live in two dimensions, a spiritual dimension with regard to their souls (their inner persons) and a fleshly dimension with regard to their bodies (their outer persons) (LW 31:344–5). Christians must find conformity between the inner and outer persons in order to experience freedom and to exemplify conduct shaped by neighborly love. The inner person becomes righteous and free through God's Word and keeps the outer person under control through "reasonable discipline" of the body and subjecting it to the Spirit (LW 31:358, 369). While he recognizes the many temptations that beset our physical senses, Luther does not simplistically equate flesh and sin with bodiliness. Writing that "only ungodliness and unbelief of heart, and no outer work, make him [her] a guilty and damnable servant of sin" (LW 31:347),[21] Luther points out that the "flesh" is most detrimental in its spiritual manifestation when involving the soul, the central agent in human life. In Luther's explanation of the mystery of salvation, faith that saves belongs to the realm of the soul, and saving faith that manifests in bodily existence also depends on the soul.

Luther typically casts human existence into two fundamental realms. He uses the expression *coram deo* (before God) for all matters pertaining to salvation and our relationship to God, and he uses *coram hominibus* (before humans) for our temporal relations with other creatures. *Coram hominibus* we experience incompleteness, failures, and progress, whereas *coram deo* we are either the beneficiary of Christ's perfect holiness or completely doomed because of sin. Christians deal with this duality in their daily lives through the work of the Word, which both reveals what is missing and gives what is needed for the soul to receive the gift of grace.

Faith Alone, Word Alone: Dynamics of Law and Gospel

Luther paints a bleak picture of original sin and our inability to resist sin, but in the process he underscores the vital work of God's Word. He argues, "One thing, and only one thing, is necessary for Christian life, righteousness, and

---

[21]In Wengert translation, *The Annotated Luther*, Vol. 1, 493: "the inner person becomes guilty and a condemned slave of sin only by ungodliness and unbelief of the heart and not by any external sin or work."

freedom. That one thing is the most holy Word of God, the gospel of Christ" (LW 31:345). The "Word" has many nuances for Luther, but typically when he writes of the Word he means "the gospel of God concerning his Son, who was made flesh, suffered, rose from the dead, and was glorified through the Spirit who sanctifies." In short, the Word is Christ. The Word also creates the faith that brings human beings into personal communion with God: "faith alone is the saving and efficacious use of the Word of God" (see Romans 10:9) (LW 31:346).

Reflecting the basic duality within human experience, the Word also has two dimensions: In commandments and promises the Word speaks to the alternating experience of despair and hope. The law works first to humble and to bring human beings to recognize the nothingness in themselves; the gospel then arrives bringing hope. The law is necessary; because of sin, human beings are unable to obey even God's basic command to "believe." The law makes human beings realize their sin of unbelief as the most terrible disobedience against God, provoking them to repent, receiving the promise of God's Word in saving faith. Luther writes about this dynamic:

> We must bring forth the voice of the law that men [human beings] may be made to fear and come to a knowledge of their sins and so be converted to repentance and a better life. But we must not stop with that ... we must also preach the word of grace and the promise of forgiveness by which faith is taught and aroused. (LW 31:364)[22]

Ultimately, as Luther puts it, "To preach Christ means to feed the soul, make it righteous, set it free, and save it" (LW 31:346).

Salvation by Faith: Oneness with God

Faith is a divine gift. It returns to God what is God's (LW 31:351). "Therefore true faith in Christ is a treasure beyond comparison," urged Luther, a treasure "which brings with it complete salvation" (LW 31:347). This is the message Luther underscores. "No other work makes a Christian" (LW 31:347). He writes, "Therefore it is clear that, as the soul needs only the Word of God for its life and righteousness, so it is justified by faith alone and not any works" (LW 31:346). The man or woman who has faith has everything and will be glorified by God (LW 31:351). Like his experience with the Word, Luther's notion of faith is quite mystical, just as his experience of the Word is.

---

[22]In Wengert translation, *The Annotated Luther*, Vol. 1, 518: "For we must preach not only one word of God but both, 'bringing forth new and old from the treasure'—both the voice of the law and the word of grace. The voice of the law ought to be 'brought forth' so that people may be terrified and led to a knowledge of their sins and thereby directed towards repentance and a better basis for life. But the word must not stop here. ... Therefore, the word of grace and promised forgiveness ought also to be preached in order to instruct and awaken faith."

Luther points to the dynamic of faith and Word when explaining the mystery of reconciliation, our justification before God. Faith acts in three ways. First, faith draws human beings to God with the "most tender spiritual touch," the Word. Faith, then, gives God what God wants, namely, righteousness. Finally, faith unites the soul with Christ (LW 31:348). Faith shields Christians from sin, death, damnation, and then—in a glorious exchange—it enables them instead to receive grace, life, salvation (LW 31:351). In Luther's soteriology, faith is exclusively the engine—"a Christian has all that he [or she] needs in faith and needs no works to justify him [or her]" (LW 31:349), and it is always so with the Word that brings things home. God is the doer, the one who makes human beings holy, and he [God] accomplishes this wonder through his [God's] own Word.[23]

Human works can never unite us to God. Such a miracle requires the mystical work of the Word. "Just as the heated iron glows like fire because of the union of fire with it," Luther explains, "so the Word imparts its qualities to the soul." The power is in the Word. "If a touch of Christ healed, how much more will this most tender spiritual touch, this absorbing of the Word, communicate to the soul all things that belong to God. This, then, is how through faith alone without works the soul is justified by the Word of God, sanctified, made true, peaceful, and free, filled with every blessing" (LW 31:349). Luther is a Word-mystic and his notion of justification is utterly mystical.

Justification as Forgiveness and Transformation

Luther is famous for his doctrine of justification by faith. The word "justification" in his usage refers to sinners made right with God, forgiven and restored to a personal relationship with God. One aspect of justification is the forgiveness of sins, known in Lutheran language as "forensic" justification. It is the reality of being "declared not guilty" and free from

---

[23]In Wengert's inclusive translation, in *The Annotated Luther*, Vol. 1, 496–7: "no good work can cling to the word of God or even exist in the soul. Instead, faith alone and the word rule in it. For the word is of such a nature that the soul is formed by it. Just as heated iron glows like fire because of its union with fire, so it is clear that Christian needs faith for everything and will have no need of works to be justified. ... So this is the Christian freedom referred to above, namely, our faith, which does not cause us to be lazy and lead evil lives but instead makes the law and works unnecessary for the righteousness and salvation of the Christian" (ibid., 496–7). And furthermore, because of God's holy and true promises, referring to John 1:12, Luther writes, "The soul that adheres to them with a firm faith is not simply united with them but fully swallowed up by them, so that it not only shares in them but also is saturated and intoxicated by their every power. For if Christ's touch healed, how much more will this tender touch in the spirit—or, better, this ingestion by the word—communicate to the soul all things that belong to the word. Therefore, by this means, through faith alone without works, the word of God justifies the soul and makes it holy, true, peaceful, and free, filled with every blessing and truly made a child of God" (ibid., 496).

the punishments of original sin. The other aspect of justification is a special oneness with God and with that holiness of the Spirit, known as "effective" justification. The sinner is mystically transformed as Christ enters her life; Christ brings along all of his goodness and removes all of her sins. In the words of Luther: the "happy exchange"!

Justified life, however, does not imply a problem-free (i.e., sin-free) life. Justification does not render some human beings "better" than their neighbors. Rather, forgiven persons remain in this life vulnerable, faltering, and lacking free will to choose right; they must discipline themselves and work at their human relations (the *coram hominibus* reality). At the same time, a person justified is fully transformed, internally, with holiness and righteousness originating from Christ (the *coram deo* reality) (LW 31:358–9). The justified are thus appropriately named after Christ who dwells in them—Christians are like Christ (LW 31:368).

The fundamental tension in Christian life can be expressed with Luther's foundational insights that human beings are simultaneously righteous and sinners, *simul iustus et peccator*. On their own, everyone is a sinner, while in Christ everyone is a saint. Righteousness has two dimensions. Righteousness is grounded in the passive, "alien" righteousness of Christ. In their own "proper" righteousness, human beings can make progress in baby steps. Proper righteousness implies a need for action and an experience of incompleteness, whereas alien righteousness is mystical and complete, effected by the Word alone regardless of human works or desire. Luther portrays the Christian life as rooted in God's free gift of grace, while simultaneously calling for active participation in God's work in this world, for the benefit of others: mostly because God's Spirit cannot be idle!

On Good Works in the Christian Life: Not to Be Rejected!

The question of the role of good works in the Christian life was heavily debated among Protestants in Luther's time and beyond. Luther's point was clear: "We do not, therefore, reject good works; on the contrary, we cherish and teach them as much as possible" (LW 31:363). Good works belong to the Christian life but they do not save anybody or make anybody better or holier (just as evil works do not make a person actually wicked). Rather, good works are expected as a natural outcome of the gift of righteousness, and one "must do such works freely only to please God" (LW 31:360).

Because of faith, the soul can be expected to love God (LW 31:359). Faith gives the right attitude so that "our hearts will be filled by the Holy Spirit with the love which makes us free, joyful, almighty workers and conquerors over all tribulations, servants of our neighbors, and yet lords of all" (LW 31:367). Good works prompted by faith are pleasing to God. Christ is the real subject in these works; from him comes the faith that justifies, makes holy, and effects the kind of response God desires (LW

31:361). The good works that God wants, then, are inspired by love, after the model of Christ (LW 31:369).

Conformity with Christ, Dwelling in Christ

Having unraveled all the theological complexities in this treatise, Luther returns to basic spiritual teaching. Christian life is about Jesus. Ordinary men and women, Luther promises, can expect to be mystically confirmed to Christ; they will serve others as Christ did because they are in union with that same Christ, on the one hand, and of the Christ-foundation for human beings' call to love one another, on the other: "Surely we are named after Christ, not because he is absent from us, but because he dwells in us, that is, because we believe in him and are Christs one to another and do to our neighbors as Christ does to us." Because of Christ, his followers are to live not in themselves but in Christ and their neighbor (LW 31:368). "Otherwise he [or she] is not a Christian. He [she] lives in Christ through faith, in his [her] neighbor through love. By faith he [she] is caught up beyond himself [herself] into God. By love he [she] descends beneath himself [herself] into his [her] neighbor. Yet he [she] always remains in God and in his [God's] love" (LW 31:371).[24]

Luther drills home the gift-nature of holiness and salvation, the indispensable role of faith, and the mystical outcome of the process that gives the human being a "form of God": "So a Christian like Christ his [her] head, is filled and made rich by faith and should be content with this form of God which he [she] has obtained by faith." This faith is one's life, righteousness, and salvation, making one acceptable to God, and so one "should increase this faith until it is made perfect" (LW 31:366). These realities cannot be rationally explained but are a matter of divine truth and belief. Luther advises his readers to pray that God would make them *theodidacti*, taught by God (as in John 6:45). Being taught by God makes people humble and inspires them to live not in themselves but in Christ through faith and in their neighbors through love (LW 31:376–7).

How Christians live out this tension between freedom and responsibility in their daily lives is a challenge for which they need the constant guidance from the Spirit. *The Freedom of a Christian* underscores the agency of God's Word and the Holy Spirit while stressing the importance of active faith and love. Freedom is the fertile ground for such extroverted spirituality.

---

[24]In Wengert translation, *The Annotated Luther*, Vol. 1, 530, Luther writes (referring to John 1:51): "Therefore, we conclude that Christian individuals do not live in themselves but in Christ and their neighbor, or else they are not Christian. They live in Christ through faith and in the neighbor through love. Through faith they are caught up beyond themselves into God; likewise through love they fall down beneath themselves into the neighbor—remaining nevertheless always in God and in God's love."

Radical Bondage: Passivity of the Will, Activity of God

Luther's understanding of justification and the Christian life involves a radical view of the human will and its bondage to sin. Luther agreed with Augustine that human nature is fatally compromised since the fall so that people are always inclined to want the wrong things. On this opinion he never wavered. This perspective lies at the root of every statement Luther made about the God-human relationship, and thus about sin and grace. Luther articulated this view especially in *The Freedom of a Christian* first and later, in 1525, *On the Bondage of the Will*, which is a heated response to Erasmus of Rotterdam who strongly defended human freedom in response to Luther's 1520 work. Luther considered both works as his most important ones, and both have made an enormous impact not just in scholarly debates on the vexing topic of free will versus grace but also in the lives of Christians trying to find a balance between receiving and giving.

Conclusion

The Freedom of a Christian offers a theological vision for Christian living. The treatise continues arguments made earlier in the *Ninety-five Theses* about God's grace as the basis for salvation and forgiveness. It also spells out why this vision matters: those existentially and spiritually liberated by God's Word and made holy by God's own act are thus humbly bound to one another socially and relationally. The universal need for forgiveness and liberation should guarantee solidarity among God's people who stand together equally in need of God's grace. Luther writes, "Just as our neighbor is in need and lacks that in which we abound, so we were in need before God and lacked [God's] mercy." Just as Christ came to our help, we should hurry to freely help our neighbors (LW 31:367). True freedom, a divine gift, is underserved and comes from our consciences liberated. In Luther's prescription, this kind of liberation does not lead to anarchy—even if it should be used "constantly and consistently in the sight of and despite the tyrants"—but to profound love, compassion, and commitment to the neighbor's benefit. Freedom feeds justice (LW 31:374, 367).

This beloved text gives a profound sense of who Luther was as a theologian, what he believed as a Christian, and what drove his Reformation vision. In the shadow of Luther's most outrageous argument about the absolute bondage of will, his most far-reaching vision may actually concern justice arising from Christian freedom. If the later Lutheran tradition sometimes overemphasizes passivity of faith in salvation, it does so at the expense of the active vision Luther had for a Christian life. Those "passively" justified by faith in Christ are expected to be "actively" working toward justice in the world with the same love that has liberated them in the first place. Furthermore, Luther offers individuals and communities a compelling recipe for emotional, social, spiritual, and political well-being based on the experience of freedom. He casts a vision of Christian life, redemption, holiness, and justice—all of these powerfully rooted in love that is divine and fertile with a freedom beyond words. *The Freedom of a Christian* demonstrates how happiness and freedom, love and equality, compassion and justice are all interrelated, and it makes a theological argument for the deep correspondence between inner freedom and outer responsibilities. The seeds that Luther sowed were revolutionary in his day, but no less for our time as they can still set the world on fire.

I. Central Topics and Learning Goals

1. A basis for understanding Martin Luther and his contributions as a reformer in context and in light of his chronology.
2. A basic vocabulary with Luther's theology, with introductions to one of his key texts.
3. A beginning comprehension of Luther's central theological insights and reformation calls.
4. Stimulus to interpret Luther from the perspective of freedom, as a freedom theologian.

II. Questions for Review, Discussion, and Further Reflection

1. What was Luther's context and stimulus for his reformation theology and what were Luther's major theological insights and arguments?
2. What language and terminology does Luther employ to articulate his faith and theological convictions?
3. How does Luther's life and contribution as a reformer look like if considering him from the perspective of freedom issues? What were his freedom moments and freedom questions and how did they shape his theology?
4. What contemporary questions arise with Luther's *The Freedom of a Christian*?

III. Keywords

Martin Luther, *coram deo–coram hominibus*, faith, forgiveness, freedom, grace, justification, *sola scriptura*, salvation, will/bondage of the will.

IV. Readings with the Chapter

Luther, *The Freedom of a Christian*.
Luther, *Large Catechism*.

Lutheran Confessions—A Road Map

PART TWO

3

Orientation to the Texts in the *Book of Concord* and the Lutheran Hermeneutics

The Texts in the *Book of Concord*

Lutherans today are united with three written sources: (1) the Scriptures, the primary sources for all Lutheran communities of faith, (2) the ecumenical Creeds that provide the doctrinal foundation that unites Lutherans with other main Christian traditions, and (3) the historical confessions written particularly for Lutheran communities of faith.[1] Based on how these three sources guide Lutheran communities' lives today and how the sources' intersections and mutual hierarchy are understood in theory and applied in practice, significant differences can be observed among Lutherans worldwide.[2]

---

[1]Readings on the history and meaning of the Lutheran confessions; see, e.g., Günther Gasmann and Scott Hendrix, *The Fortress Introduction to the Lutheran Confessions* (Minneapolis: Fortress Press, 1999); Martin J. Lohrmann, *The Book of Harmony: Spirit and Service in the Lutheran Confessions* (Minneapolis: Fortress Press, 2016); Carl E. Braaten, *Principles of Lutheran Theology*, 2nd ed. (Minneapolis: Fortress Press, 2007). Also Charles P. Arand, Robert Kolb, and James A. Nestingen, *The Lutheran Confessions: History and Theology of the Book of Concord* (Minneapolis: Fortress Press, 2012). Also, Leif Grane, *The Augsburg Confession: A Commentary* (Minneapolis: Augsburg Publishing House, 1987); Scott Hendrix, *Recultivating the Vineyard: The Reformation Agendas of Christianization* (Louisville: Westminster John Knox, 2004).

[2]A helpful overview on the history from Luther to global Lutheranism, with an introduction to topics and sources in Lutheran confessional discourse; see Eric W. Gritsch, *Fortress Introduction to Lutheranism* (Minneapolis: Fortress Press, 1994), particularly chapters 1–6. Also, Martin J. Lohrmann, *Stories from Global Lutheranism: A Historical Timeline* (Minneapolis: Fortress Press, 2021).

Generally speaking, the confessional texts are formally accepted by global Lutheran communities as the foundational sources that both explain the past decisions and Lutherans' path to, what is called, concord and that manage to hold together the globally and theologically diverse Lutheran constituencies around the world and across the centuries. The key texts are collected in a book titled *Book of Concord* from 1580. The name implies the rationale and the uses of the collection.

Lutherans have struggled to agree with one another and have needed to explain their agreement and disagreement with neighboring faith communities. They have labored to find a concord amid ongoing disagreements, starting from the use of the Scriptures and the ecumenical Creeds as sources of authority and particularly vis-à-vis the later, distinctively Lutheran sources. Even in their employment of these foundational texts, Lutherans have differences of emphasis, and an internal hierarchy can be noted between the sources.

The sources contained in the *Book of Concord* are the ecumenical Creeds of the early church, the *Augsburg Confession* and its *Apology* (1530, 1531), Luther's *Small Catechism* and *Large Catechism* (1529), Luther's *Smalcald Articles* (1537) and Philip Melanchthon's *Treatise on the Power and Primacy of the Papacy* (1537), and the *Formula of Concord*, which consists of two parts, the *Epitome* and the *Solid Declaration* (1577). Together the sources constitute the 1580 edition of the *Book of Concord*, signed by nearly two thousand Lutheran theologians, pastors, and rulers and city councils.[3]

The sources each have a distinctive character. The *Augsburg Confession* could be characterized as a document for public faith, as a relatively short summation of the main teachings of those identified as Lutherans, presented primarily in comparison to the teachings of the medieval Catholic church and the early church, the latter serving as the sounding board.[4] This text has been typically cited in negotiations on the parameters of Lutheran faith and its expression in faith communities and in explaining the particularly

---

[3]Of the modern English editions available, this is recommended; Robert Kolb and Timothy J. Wengert, eds., *The Book of Concord* (Minneapolis: Fortress Press, 2000). Three of the texts are included in *The Annotated Luther*, Vols. 1–6 (Minneapolis: Fortress Press, 2015–17), with new introductions and aim toward inclusive English language; Vol. 2 includes the *Smalcald Articles* and the *Large Catechism*; Vol. 4 includes the *Small Catechism*. The German/Latin edition is the foundation for critical work on the confessions; see *Die Bekenntnisschriften der evangelisch-lutherischen Kirche*, hrsg. Irene Dingel (Göttingen: Vandenhoeck & Ruprecht, 2014).

[4]On the European Reformations and their context, see Carter Lindberg, *The European Reformations* (Chichester, UK: Wiley-Blackwell, 2010); Hans J. Hillerbrand, ed., *The Protestant Reformation. Revised edition* (New York: HarperCollins, 2009); Euan Cameron, *The European Reformation* (Oxford: Oxford University Press, 2012); Carlos Eire, *Reformations: The Early Modern World, 1450–1650* (New Haven: Yale University Press, 2016); Christopher Ocker, *Luther, Conflict, and Christendom: Reformation Europe and Christianity in the West* (Cambridge: Cambridge University Press, 2018); and Kirsi Stjerna, *Women and the Reformation* (Malden, MA: Wiley-Blackwell, 2009).

Lutheran identity as a denomination. The *Catechisms* are more of an internal source: they have served as vital resources for teaching the faith, for laity and the clergy, organized from teaching the law and the confessions of faith to how to pray and use the sacraments. The *Catechisms* offer a specifically Lutheran interpretation of the Christian faith on the foundation of the ecumenical Creeds, and they have guided the expressions of this faith in both individual and congregational levels.

Another text from Luther is his *Smalcald Articles*, a feisty confession of evangelical, gospel-oriented faith with ample criticism of the late medieval Catholic practices in need of reforms and written in preparation for Lutherans needing to defend themselves, even with arms. Melanchthon's *Treatise on the Power and Primacy of the Papacy* focuses, as the title reveals, on papacy and reads as a lengthy addendum to the *Augsburg Confession* on a topic that had been left out but that required elaboration: the Lutherans' position on the office and authority of the Pope and, with that, on the episcopal office. The *Apology of the Augsburg Confession* from the same author is a lengthy defense and clarification of the shorter arguments made earlier. The *Formula of Concord* extrapolates further from the basic statements of the *Augsburg Confession*: a new set of articles reflects where the intra-Lutheran conflicts had continued and they take a stab at topics that had emerged in relation to other reforming movements of the time.

The texts are written in different styles, in different situations, and for distinct purposes; they are not all of equal value or have an even or normative weight in their reception and uses. Only some are employed formally by most Lutheran churches: *the Augsburg Confession*, Luther's *Catechisms*, and the ecumenical Creeds. The rest carry a varying degree of weight in the lives of the Lutherans and in the intra-Lutheran discourses. As a matter of fact, most Lutherans are hardly aware of even them existing, not to mention them having importance in their expression of faith or spirituality.

As said above, the *Augsburg Confession* and the *Large Catechism* inform the reflections in this book. For an orientation, however, all the texts are herewith introduced with a just few words on their historical context and distinctive contribution.[5]

The Ecumenical Creeds

The word "Creed" comes from the Latin verb *credere*. *Credo* in Latin means "I believe." The word Creed springs from this root and has become the ecumenical way to express what Christians together believe or hold true or confess as their shared faith. It was extremely important for the reformers to

---

[5]On the Creeds, see online sources: http://www.creeds.net/creed.htm and http://www.ccel.org/ccel/schaff/creeds1.iv.ii.html (accessed March 1, 2020).

be absolutely clear about this: that they shared the ancient faith of the early Christians as stipulated by the ecumenical councils of the first centuries.

The Creeds are the universal foundation for Lutherans, who have insisted since the Reformation that nothing doctrinally new was being introduced to the centuries-old Christian faith but rather purging with a renewed focus on the gospel of Christ. The oldest texts in the *Book of Concord*, the Creeds unite Lutherans liturgically to the rest of Christendom and to the earliest of Christian sources and traditions. As one of the Reformers'—and the humanists'—call was to return to the most ancient and original Christian teachings, *ad fontes*, the Creeds became the obvious stepping stone.

The history of the Creeds takes the reader to the exciting first centuries of the Christian faith in formation. It is important to note that the context for the formation of the Creeds was religious and political: (1) the baptismal practice of early Christians, where the creedal wording comes from, (2) the persecutions under the Romans when Christians' faith was tested and when confessing was as a life-and-death issue, and (3) and the political fragmentation in the Roman Empire and the councils being called together by the emperor to restore unity. Following the debates leading to the actual wording of the confessions of faith illuminates the importance of language in communicating convictions and how language can effectively both unite and divide. The history of the Creeds also reveals the courageous passion of the first Christian leaders, who were willing to confess their faith first of all with their lives and their bodies—that is, being willing to confess their faith in Christ and die by the sword or in an arena—and, second, who were committed to protect and explicate the central faith with the best wording possible and with a language that resonated with the other languages and worldviews of the time. Modern users of the Creeds do well in reckoning how difficult this task was and the fact that the wordings are still used centuries later, as nothing better or more unifying has been formed since.

Briefly said, the Scriptures give snippets of the first confessions.[6] One of the earliest is the simple statement "Jesus is the Lord." Already during the persecutions, such confession developed into formulas (with local variances) used in baptism. Creedal formulas were used in the Christian practice of welcoming new members and teaching them the basics of faith and baptizing them into the community believing accordingly.[7] In the fourth

---

[6]Early creedal statements can be found in the Bible, e.g., Deut. 6:4, 1 King 18:39, Matt. 16:16, Matt. 28:19, John 1:49, John 6:68–69, John 20:28, Acts 8:36–37, Acts 16:31, 1 Cor. 8:6, 1 Cor. 12:3, 1 Cor. 15:3–7, Phil. 2:6–11, 1 Tim. 3:16, Hebr. 6:1–2, 1 John 4:2. See http://www.ccel.org/ccel/schaff/creeds1.iv.ii.html (accessed March 1, 2020).
[7]The predecessors of the Creeds are the Rule of Faith from Irenaeus of Lyons (second century) and the Hippolytus account of the formula used in baptism (215). The Apostles' Creed (second-ninth century) originates from a Roman baptismal formula (140), with text variations: a Greek text from Marcellus of Ancyra (341) and a Latin text from Rufinus (390). See http://www.ccel.org/ccel/schaff/creeds1.iv.ii.html (accessed March 1, 2020).

century the Creeds became the tool for unity among Christian groups and for, by then, the Christian emperor, to unify his empire. The alternative would have been an eventual irredeemable fragmentation to the point of no coherence or shared narratives or tenets of faith for the multiplying Christian communities. The writers of the Creeds, mainly bishops, many of them who had suffered persecution at the time when Christians in the Roman Empire were vulnerable and outlawed, fought for the survival of the Christian message. The Creeds express that theological commitment, just as they facilitate coming together of different parties who negotiated on the language and the content of the Creeds at the councils. The Creeds used even today come from the politically charged Council of Nicaea (325) and the Council of Constantinople (381).[8]

None of the doctrines expressed in the Creeds are disputed or modified in the Lutheran tradition, generally speaking. In Lutheran communities of faith, the Creeds are frequently used in liturgy as a form of confession of faith and in catechesis for teaching the faith. They give the ecumenically agreed-upon foundation for the language about the Triune One God of the Scriptures. They outline the parameters for what Lutherans believe about God, Christ, the Spirit; about creation, redemption, and sustenance of all that is; about the church and its message; and about the hopes for life hereafter. Sharing these general tenets of belief with other Christians, while differences of emphasis and interpretation are to be expected, Lutherans have their distinct dialect of faith that explicitly centers on the teachings about Christ, the second article in the Creeds.[9]

The intent with the rest of the texts in the *Book of Concord* is to shine light on the central theology presented in the Creeds, to illuminate the divine promise presented in them, and to equip people with effective teaching to live their lives in accordance with this faith that was proclaimed as the saving kind.

---

[8]The Nicene [-Constantinopolitan] Creed is based on the baptismal formula used at the first ecumenical Council of Nicaea 325 and was revised at the following Council of Constantinopolis, 381. Later the Council of Ephesos, 431, named Mary *theotokos*, and the Council of Chalcedon, 451, offered a definition on Christ's two natures as united but not mixed, distinct but not separate. The Athanasian Creed (*Quicumque*) from fifth century, with a detailed wording on the nature of Trinity, presents believing the Creed with the church as necessary for salvation. See http://www.creeds.net/creed.htm and http://www.ccel.org/ccel/schaff/creeds1.iv.ii.html (accessed March 1, 2020).

[9]The Apostles' Creed: "I believe in God the Father, Almighty, Maker of heaven and earth, and in Jesus Christ, his only begotten Son, our Lord, who was conceived by the Holy Ghost, born of the Virgin Mary, suffered under Pontius Pilate, was crucified, died, and buried; He descended into hell. The third day he rose again from the dead. He ascended into heaven and sits at the right hand of God the Father. He will come to judge the living and the dead. I believe in the Holy Spirit. I believe in the holy Catholic church, the communion of saints, the forgiveness of sins, the resurrection of the body, and the life everlasting. Amen." Not originating from the Apostles, this formulation comes from the seventh century and is the most commonly used of the Creeds.

Catechisms from Luther, 1529[10]

Catechisms are manuals and doctrinal expositions used to summarize the faith and assist in memorization, and they typically use question and answer format. Luther wrote two such manuals, but Lutherans did not invent *Catechisms*. The history goes back to the early church and even beyond to the world of the ancient Greeks: the art of teaching with questions and memorization is an ancient one. In the Middle Ages, where the word "catechism" comes from, the manuals served as memorization and instructional tools on the Creed, the Lord's Prayer, and the sacraments. Protestants employed this method to communicate their Christian theology to the laity, as well as to teach the clergy on the reformed theology.

Martin Luther's *Small* and *Large Catechism* come from the pivotal year 1529. The same year the Diet of Speyer reissued the original excommunication degree of the 1521 Diet of Worms against Luther and the like-minded, a moment that led the evangelicals gathered to protest—thus came the label "Protestants." Luther had been asked to write a Catechism for quite a while by then, and other authors, some of them Luther's colleagues, had taken up the challenge already. People were hungry for information and instruction on how and what to believe, how to pray, and what to expect with the sacraments now that they found themselves outside the familiar practices of the Catholic church. Upon visiting the new evangelical communities, Luther and his colleagues were shocked to witness the lack of knowledge and proper preparation of the pastors, not to mention the people of the church. For that reason, and for not being impressed with the other alternatives published at the time, Luther finally put other work aside to craft his catechism, on the basis of his series of sermons with which he had been instructing people from the pulpit. Employing the previous form, with some additional parts, Luther wrote his *Catechisms* to teach about the Law with the Decalogue, about the Christian theology and convictions about Christ with the Creeds, and about Christian life and spirituality with the Lord's Prayer. He added instruction on the (now only) two sacraments, Baptism and the Lord's Supper and, as related, on the practice of Confessions. He also included instructions on the matter of marriage.

The *Catechisms* of Luther come in two versions, Small and Large, both written in the language of the people, in German; the Small is meant for a general lay audience, the Large, also translated into Latin, for the clergy and teachers and more advanced in faith. Together they have served as the lay Bible, especially in the aftermath of the Reformations when it was still

---

[10]In addition to Kolb and Wengert, *Book of Concord*, a revised English translation, with an introduction and annotations, is available in *The Annotated Luther*, Vol. 2, ed. Kirsi Stjerna, 2015; it is also published as a separate study edition (2016). Similarly the *Small Catechism, The Annotated Luther*, Vol. 4, ed. Mary Jane Haemig, 2016.

relatively uncommon for every household or individual to actually own a Bible of their own. Likewise, it would take a while before it could be expected for everyone to be able to read and study the Bible by themselves. Thus the *Catechisms* served an extremely valuable role in teaching and, importantly, feeding the faith. Not only a pedagogical tool used in, e.g., with the teaching of the youth and new members, Catechism has fed individuals and communities as a book of faith as a spiritual resource. Today its uses as a handbook on Lutheran spirituality are multiplied, facilitated so with the translations of the text in different languages.

It is not a surprise that of the Lutheran confessional texts, Catechism is the most widely known and used, locally and globally. Via translations it has spread around the world like no other Lutheran document. A precious factoid: the very first text the European settlers in North America decided to translate into a tribal language was Luther's *Small Catechism*. A less positive factoid is the evidence of Lutherans in the nineteenth century using the same book to justify slavery and forms of oppression. This is to say that learning from its origins and its different uses is illuminating for contemporary Lutherans who can learn from the past and be critically attentive to how and what to teach with the *Catechisms* today, with what authority and expectations, and how to honor their original intent: to invite and equip each person, on their own, to explore and embrace the matters of faith. Such uses of the teaching tools promise change, not a status quo.

The Augsburg Confession by Philip Melanchthon, 1530, and Its *Apology*, 1531[11]

In comparison to the *Large Catechism*, the *Augsburg Confession* is different. It is short—just twenty-eight articles—and it is political. In a somewhat diplomatic tone, the articles make a case that Lutherans had the right interpretation of the Scriptures and had the right to worship, teach, and confess accordingly, and that they were not teaching anything against or apart from the true Catholic faith.

The *Augsburg Confession* was written by Luther's close associate and colleague and a fellow reformer, Philip Melanchthon.[12] It is his words and tone, while the work builds on the teamwork of Lutheran theologians, including Luther himself, who had prepared for an occasion to present

---

[11]See Grane, *The Augsburg Confession* (1981; transl. John H. Rasmussen), for a helpful study of the content.
[12]Philip Melanchthon (1497–1560), Luther's closest long-term colleague, a humanist, on Wittenberg University faculty, contributed fundamentally as a systematic theologian, organizer, and communicator of Luther's theology with different constituencies.

the Lutherans' case in front of the emperor at the Diet. Diets were, namely, the forums where matters of importance like that would be judicated. For the Lutherans to exist and practice their faith legally, that is, without breaking the laws of the Holy Roman Empire, they would need the approval of the emperor—unless the entire Catholic church would embrace the reform calls and the Pope join the reformation.

The context of the text is important for understanding it. Since the 1521 outlawing of Luther at the Diet of Worms, Lutherans had operated without a protection, as convicted heretics and thus transgressors in the eyes of the law as well; heresy was a crime and could lead to a punishment by death. The recent Diet of Speyer 1529 had reenforced the efforts to extinguish Protestant faith. This threat did not stop the Lutherans by any means from continuing to teach Christian faith with a Lutheran perspective and organizing faith communities accordingly. It was understood, though, that sooner or later, an official case had to be made and the right to exist legally to be secured. Should there be an opportunity to speak in public of the validity of the Lutherans' teachings, there might be a chance to convince those in power to secure the legitimacy of the Lutherans. That said, the original albeit waning hope of Lutherans was still that there would be no need for a Lutheran tradition but a reformed Catholic tradition where they would be happy to stay in.

When the call for the Diet of Augsburg came—from an emperor who needed the support of the German princes in his impending war against the Turks—Lutheran troops prepared a document for Melanchthon to bring in. This was an opportunity for the Wittenberg theologians to explain as if to the whole world what Luther and Lutherans were teaching; it also gave a chance to distinguish Lutherans from other reforming groups. Also, the Lutheran princes and rulers, just as the theologians publicly speaking for the Lutheran faith, needed a unifying manifesto-type of a document to gather around. The Diet gave an invitation to present one.

Lutheran theologians had been already laboring on such a statement for quite some time, with preliminary documents already prepared.[13] As Melanchthon arrived at the scene, he encountered feisty printed and verbal propaganda against the Protestants (including the Swiss) and realized that a succinct written document was vital for the Diet. Thus he proceeded to

---

[13]The preceding documents were the *Schwabach Articles*, written in 1529 by Wittenberg theologians (also Luther) keeping the military league of Lutherans in mind; Luther's 1528 confession *Concerning Christ's Supper*; the *Marburg Articles* from the 1529 (failed) colloquy of Wittenberg and Swiss theologians; the 1530 *Torgau Articles* (on human ordinances, clergy marriage, Eucharist, Mass, confession, ordination, vows, invocation of saints, jurisdiction/church, vernacular worship).

craft one, just in time to have its twenty-eight articles read at the Diet, on July 12, 1530.[14] This was a momentous occasion, a watershed. The text was read in German—a language the emperor did not understand—and it was also presented in Latin in writing. The rejection, *Confutation*, came swiftly; after the July 2 draft, it was read on August 3. The Lutherans and their points were refuted, dismissed, rejected.[15]

It would not be until 1555, after another Diet in Augsburg, that the so-called Augsburg Peace formally accepted—only—the Lutherans' *Augsburg Confession* and legalized its practice. For the other Protestant groups, it would take several more decades before getting to a similar place of acceptance. While many factors contributed, it warrants to acknowledge the singular importance and effectiveness of the *Augsburg Confession,* as the stepping stone to new era where Christianity is practiced in multiplying different forms. It was a step toward ensuring religious freedom and diversity.

Going back to the scene in 1530, Melanchthon being in the forefront for the Wittenberg evangelicals and slapped in the face, so to speak, with the *Confutation*, did not know what to expect. He most certainly did not foresee the Augsburg Peace and the future establishment of Lutheran tradition standing on his words. Still hoping to make the case for the Wittenberg theologians' desire for unity and to walk with and within the Catholic church, as long as necessary reforms took place, he proceeded to write more to explain the articles he had presented. He did so in light of the Catholic side's criticism he had heard (but without a written text of the Confutation at the time) with his *Apology of the Augsburg Confession.* This much lengthier treatise, published in 1531, is written in Melanchthon's own voice and it stands in a different category of importance in relation to the original document. The text had no impact vis-à-vis the imperial decision at the council, but it has served as an important elaboration on the issues quite briefly addressed in the *Augsburg Confession*. It demonstrates, with its lengthier treatment, particularly on the most contested issues (such as justification, original sin, and confession), how many questions were left

---

[14]"Never before, however, had a confession of faith delivered in a public forum by lay people acquired ecclesiastical or theological authority. Not since the Council of Nicaea had a confession created in such a forum become a standard of dogma, a secondary authority for teaching the faith, and a key interpretation of Scripture. Not since Nicaea had such a confession become a fundamental definition of what Christians believe and teach .... It became their agenda as they proclaimed, taught and lived out the Christian life." Robert Kolb, *Confessing the Faith: Reformers Define the Church, 1530–1580* (St. Louis: Concordia Pub. House, 1991), 14–15.

[15]Writers of the Catholic Confutation were Johann Eck, Bishop Johannes Fabri, Johannes Cochlaeus, Konrad Wimpina, Johann Dietenberger, and Julius Pflug; Cardinal Lorenzo Campeggio assisted.

open or unresolved at this point of time. Those questions would need returning to in later documents.[16]

From its first presentation at the Diet of Augsburg to make the case for Lutherans' legitimacy, the *Augsburg Confession* has been instrumental in shaping and guiding and organizing Lutheran teaching and preaching over the centuries. It has been explicitly used as a tool to measure how Lutheran a church or an individual or a doctrine is. It is still the document Lutheran pastors are expected to adhere to in their teaching and proclamation. A nimble document, it allows freedoms and negotiations on local levels and has by its very nature nurtured diversity and flexibility in Lutheran communities of faith. Nothing of equal importance has been written since. Lutheran social statements can be considered as modern clarifications, adjustments, and developments but they do not have the global standing and acceptance.[17]

The topics included in the document reflect the time and situation of crafting the confession, while they also mark the main Lutheran highway, doctrinally speaking. The first twenty-one are doctrinally oriented; the last seven address reforms with practices; of course, theology and practice are intertwined throughout. The first four (AC 1–4) give the foundation for Lutheran notion of God, humanity, and their relation restored. The articles begin with a statement on the Triune one God, followed by an article on the original sin. Article on the Christ leads to the brief statement on justification. The next nine (AC 5–13) address the matters of church and sacraments, baptism and the Lord's Supper. The third part (AC 14–21) consists of miscellaneous articles on order and regulations, the cause of sin, office, and saints. The last seven articles, longer than the earlier articles, address varied issues of contention and reform urgencies, such as the right to marry, the futility of monastic vows and celibacy, the importance of serving communion in both kinds to all (i.e., bread and wine to all), the parameters for the office of episcopacy, and the rationales for repentance.[18]

Looking at the length of the corresponding articles in the *Apology*, it is easy to see where the major tensions percolated; the more contested the issue, the longer Melanchthon would write about it, e.g., sin, freedom, communion practice, teaching of repentance, and the key teaching of justification. In

---

[16]After the fifteen months it took for Melanchthon to finish the text after the Diet of Augsburg, without a written text of the *Confutation* at first but just notes from stenographers, he first published a "quarto" edition in April/May 1531 and later in September the "octavo" edition, which he was more pleased with and which was signed by the Smalcald League in 1537 and was translated into German by Justus Jonas.

[17]For example, on ELCA social statements on a variety of contemporary issues calling for a theological attention, see https://www.elca.org/socialstatements (accessed March 1, 2020).

[18]The articles address the following questions: God, sin, Christ, justification, church, new obedience, sacraments, human order and regulations, confession, free will, Mass and saints, matters of Christian perfection/spirituality, sacramental practice, clergy marriage, celibacy and vows, repentance, and episcopal office. These will be addressed in the following pages.

other words, the most salient reformation points were met with friction, as was to be expected, and seemed to require more elaboration. However, writing on the contested points more would not change the bottom line that the major reform calls of the reformers were rejected. Catholic religion in its teaching and practice would not change as a result of these texts; Lutherans themselves had perhaps more clarity about their beliefs—and of the ambiguities and disagreement among themselves. Looking at the topics of the articles, several gaps appear as well: the confession does not include a separate article on the Scriptures (*sola scriptura*), predestination, Holy Spirit, papacy; Mary; or faith or grace. These topics needed revisiting later.

Looking at the whole, a contemporary reader can learn where the tensions were and what the reformers were most fired up and passionate about. This is helpful information in terms of the past and in comprehending the ongoing diversity among Lutherans globally around a variety of things. At the same time, for a contemporary reader, the topics shaping the confession are not binding or limiting. New issues, unimagined to the sixteenth-century writers, would require similarly serious attention today, just as some of their issues hardly need to excite readers today.

Last but not least, a mentioning is needed of the text known as the *Altered Augsburg Confession* from the 1540s. In his eagerness to foster a pan-Protestant coalition and unity among reformers, and while negotiating on such partnership with the Genevan reformer Jean Calvin, Philip Melanchthon in 1540s tweaked the wording of the confession in certain decisive places. Namely, one of the topics of contention between the Swiss, Genevan, and Lutheran reformers was their different understanding of the Lord's Supper and how Christ's presence there should be understood: as a real or symbolic presence, or as something to remember. In preparation for Colloquies in Worms (1540) and Regensburg (1541), Melanchthon altered the wording on the matter in the confession, producing thus the *Altered Augsburg Confession (Variata)*. While Calvin was pleased, Melanchthon's outraged Wittenberg colleagues rejected the document. In the *Book of Concord*, the statement is made repeatedly that only the *Unaltered Augsburg Confession* is considered as the proper interpretation of the Scriptures and Luther's theology.[19]

---

[19]In Weimar 1557, at a Catholic-Lutheran meeting, Gnesio-Lutherans disagree with Philippists about the *Variata*, worrying about the blurring of the Lutheran identity. In 1561 Naumburg, Elector Fredrick III of Palatine proposes *Variata* as a legitimate interpretation of the 1530 document, wishing to win Calvin over and sanction Calvin's teachings in Germany. Calvin himself approved the *Variata* at the 1540 and 1541 Colloquies. However, the *Variata* is rejected by Lutherans, even if Fredrick approved it anyway, making the Palatinate a Calvinist territory, later adopting the Heidelberg Catechism in 1563.

The Smalcald Articles, Luther, 1537

Perhaps the most intriguing text in the collection is Luther's attempt for a single-volume confession in his *Smalcald Articles* of 1537.[20] The situation of its writing explains the tone, to a degree: the Wittenberg troops were preparing to fight for their confession in arms, against the Catholic opponent. The Pope announced (June 1536) an upcoming Council in Mantua, 1537— a council that the Lutherans had been waiting for in order to make their case in front of the Pope, but this council actually never met. Instead, by the time the Council of Trent commenced in 1545, lasting till 1563, no Lutherans participated. Before that, to prepare and bolster the Lutheran front, Luther was requested (December 11, 1536) by the Elector of Saxony, John Fredrick, to write a manifesto, both to support the Lutheran constituency and also to clarify their positions of agreement and disagreements and possible areas of compromise. Luther gathered a team of theologians for discourse, Melanchthon, Nicholas von Amsdorf, Johan Agricola, George Spalatin, Justus Jonas, Caspar Cruciger Sr., and Johan Bugenhagen, to work on a Lutheran statement.

The articles, written in German originally, but soon translated into Latin, were presented to the Smalcald League (February 8, 1537); Luther was not present. A colorful and polemical summary of Luther's theology includes his rendition of the necessary reforms that had taken or should be taking place. He concludes: "These are the articles on which I must stand and on which I intend to stand, God willing, until my death. I can neither change nor concede anything in them. If anyone desires to do so, it is on that person's conscience" (SA Part III art. 15).[21]

The tone is polemical, breathless, lacking the diplomatic tone of the *Augsburg Confession* or the pastoral sensitivity of the *Catechisms*. The articles were not immediately accepted by all or officially (signers included Melanchthon,[22] and Luther's close colleagues Justus Jonas, Johann Bugenhagen, Johann Agricola, Andreas Osiander, and several pastors and theologians). The work was published in 1538, with Luther's added Preface explicating the reform program and some revisions and additions, and was early on paired with another text from the same year, Philip Melanchthon's

---

[20]In addition to Kolb and Wenger, *Book of Concord*, a revised translation with new introduction and annotations, by Kurt Hendel, is available in *The Annotated Luther*, Vol. 2, ed. Kirsi Stjerna, 2015.

[21]Quotations from SA from *The Annotated Luther*, Vol. 2, ed. Stjerna. See also Kolb and Wengert, *The Book of Concord*, SA Part III art. 15.

[22]Melanchthon signed with a reservation regarding the topic of invocation of saints and papacy: "concerning the pope I maintain that if he would allow the gospel, we, too may (for the sake of peace and general unity among those Christians who are now under him and might be in the future, grant to him his superiority over the bishops which he has 'by human right'" (SA, Subscriptions, 466).

Treatise on Power and Primacy of the Papacy. In the 1550s, the articles were included in the church orders that were crafted to assist evangelical congregations organize their teaching, proclamation, and religious life around the Lutheran principles of faith.

With a feisty tone and wording, Luther provides an energetic document with a personal voice. While Luther never really managed to write a single summa of his theology, this one could be considered a very big step to that direction. In it, the reader encounters Luther at his most passionate, spirited mood and a theologian writing with his unique style. The text offers quite a comprehensive take on the evangelical theology and principles of faith à la Luther. Luther articulates with gusto the major points of faith for the evangelicals and points out where they differ from the Catholic teaching. He also gives a rationale for the reforms and reflects on the practical issues with the religion that Lutherans would have a different take on. The work is divided into three parts: The first affirms the creedal teaching of the divine majesty and Trinity and Christ's two natures. Part II focuses on Christ's office and work for human beings' redemption, articulating the core teaching of justification by faith alone. On these, Luther is adamant; there is no room to negotiate. Part III addresses a variety of reformation issues, from the Mass and vows to saints and sacraments and human regulations. Imagining the situation, Luther expecting fully the destruction of Wittenberg, the demolition of the Lutheran armed forces, and the world slowly coming to an end—at least for him—helps the reader to engage the text with proper distance as well as appreciation. His bottom line is his Christological discovery: all Christian hope depends on Christ and what Christ gives to humanity. On this principle rests Luther's faith and with him Lutheran theology. When he says "Nothing in this article can be considered of given up," he really means that.

The *Treatise on Power and Primacy of the Papacy*, Melanchthon, 1537

It is interesting to note that the Lutheran princes, warriors, and clergy gathered for the bolstering of their spirit to defend Lutherans with arms did not resonate at first with Luther's feisty text but, instead, adopted another work: Philip Melanchthon had written a focused *Treatise on the Power and Primacy of the Papacy,* as if the long, missing article for the *Augsburg Confession.* The two texts are not really with equal weight or in comparison, in terms of their coverage and argument. This shows in the ongoing reception of the texts; while Melanchthon's work is included in the collection, it is quite unknown to the larger public and not the commonly used source for the reformation agenda and principles. The text is, however, important in Lutherans' ongoing deliberation on the foundations and value of office and ordained clergy in the church and on the office of papacy. It also has value in ecumenical work where Lutherans with other Christians consider the value of the papal office and related episcopal structures.

The main reason for Melanchthon to write the text was to fill the gap left in the *Augsburg Confession*. Also, the Lutheran princes who wished to reject the upcoming Pope-convened council needed a theologian to address the issue of papacy. They requested the document on Monday, February 1537, and Melanchthon's Latin text was ready by Saturday, February 1537; a German translation was provided.

The content is focused and Melanchthon at his most animate as he addresses the issue of ecclesiastical power and office of bishops and papacy. He considers the possibility for the Lutherans to grant the Roman bishop the superior status, established so by human right—not divine—and this was feasible as long as the Pope in office adhered to the gospel. A historical review is given to support the argument: Ordination by bishops is explained from the history, tracking the succession of bishops to the commission Jesus gave to Peter and a tradition in which priests and bishops have been ordained and sent ever since. However, such an office or tradition is no longer absolutely necessary for the church, especially in light of the inadequate handling of their offices by the current bishops. It was more urgent to get rid of the bad bishops and appoint new ones. Namely, Melanchthon observes, the reason for schism is in bad bishops—not in people or in teachers like Luther.

To sum up with Melanchthon and the Lutheran sixteenth-century position on papacy: First, the Roman bishop is not superior among other bishops by divine right. Second, there is no superiority among apostles. Third, just as Paul was not ordained by Peter, authority in ministry of any person depends on the Word of God. Fourth, in this, on the basis of the Word calling people to ministry, all ministers are equals in the church that is superior to its ministries (TPPP 7–8). Last, Melanchthon phrases the conclusion pertinent in their century's vulnerable situation where the Lutherans stood in an apparent opposition to the most powerful office in the church and world: "even if the Roman bishop did possess primacy by divine right, obedience is still not owed him when he defends ungodly worship and teaching contrary to the gospel. Indeed, it is necessary to oppose him as the Antichrist. The errors of the Pope are blatant, and they are not trivial" (TPPP 57).

The text was signed by the Lutheran leaders at the meeting in Smalcald, from which Luther was absent due to illness. It was published in Strasbourg in 1540 in a larger book, with no signatories, and with a German translation in 1541 in Nuremberg. The connection to the *Augsburg Confession* was forgotten for a period of time, as was the priority of Latin text, until the *Book of Concord*'s 1584 printing.

The Formula of Concord, 1577

Last but not least, the *Book of Concord* includes texts called the *Formula of Concord*, from 1577.

It has two parts, two different but interrelated texts, *the Epitome* and the *Solid Declaration*. The order and the topics of the articles are identical, but the treatment is more extended in the latter. Whereas the *Augsburg Confession* was crafted with the Catholic conversation partners in mind, this document has neighboring Protestant confessors in the horizon. It also aims to fill in the gaps left with the earlier confession. Most importantly, in retrospect, it provided a voice of unity for Lutherans who were at risk of disappearing in their internal debates and without a cohesiveness needed to stand in front of the Catholic emperor and the papal authority.

The concrete stimulus for the text was the ongoing, disruptive intra-Lutheran controversies that threatened to splinter the Lutheran front for good.[23] Endless debates, in the 1540s in particular, and the increasing unclarity about where Lutherans stood in relation to other Protestant groups, particularly the Swiss and the Genevan Christians, did not help in an already fragile situation. After Luther died in 1546, a moment of disorientation followed in terms of no single strong leader emerging but more leaders and them in different configurations. Plague threatened the lives of many in its unpredictable arrivals to villages and towns and killed indiscriminately. War was in the air—in the Eastern border with the approaching Turks and closer to home in the armed conflicts between Catholic and Protestant troops. The defeat of the Smalcald League and losing Wittenberg in 1547 to the imperial army seemed like the end of the evangelicals' story in German-speaking lands. And yet evangelical preaching had reached significant enough numbers that it proved impossible to imminently uproot all of that or force people to return to Catholic faith.

Compromises—and survival—were sought in the form of interims. There were territorial agreements where certain, if not most, Catholic practices would be returned in exchange of ending the violence. The Interim of Augsburg and Interim of Leipzig were notable for such proposals, with slight differences. Both interims shared two concessions to the Protestants: their clergy could marry—or at least stay married—and laity could receive

---

[23]Controversies and corresponding FC articles: Antinomian controversy, 1520s–1546, FC V, VI; Adiaphoristic controversy, 1548–52, FC X; Majoristic controversy, 1551–8, FC I; Osiandrian controversy, 1550s, FC III; Crypto-Calvinist controversy, 1558–73, FC VII, VIII; Synergistic controversy, FC I, II.

the communion as proposed by the Protestants, in bread and wine both.[24] For some this seemed satisfactory; besides, for many it had proven painful to let go of many of the familiar expressions of religion in the Protestants' pruning process.

It would have seemed reasonable to accept this compromise and thereby save the major fragmentation from becoming a permanent one. But Lutheran front was divided in this matter and in terms of what was considered as nonnegotiable issues and what were the limits of negotiations. Nicknamed after the always-negotiating Philip Melanchthon, the Philippists had a broader tolerance for gray areas and compromises. The Gnesio-Lutherans were a different breed of cat: their list of necessities was far longer and they considered no ceremony or practice as harmless if it was presented as something necessary.

This dispute led to a controversy concerning the *adiaphora* (indifferent matters) in 1548–52 (treated in FC X): what compromises were acceptable and what not. This tension has hardly disappeared but can be witnessed in the different moods of different Lutheran communities and confessional schools of thought. Whereas today such disputes hardly disturb the life in the commonwealth, back then these questions led to the chambers of power. There matters not only presented headaches for theologians but involved political leaders from the highest of seats.

The text can be fairly described as political, or at least politically pertinent, while its attention at the core is theological. The topics that needed attention circled around the fundamental Lutheran teaching of grace—the justification doctrine. The most radical arguments from *Augsburg Confession*, as well as the contested but omitted topics, sparked serious discourse and back and forth. In the order in which they appear, they can be briefly characterized as follows.[25]

The articles start with sin (FC I), particularly how Lutheran views differ from Catholic teaching on sin. The contents of this article pertain to the rest of them. The question of free will and good works (FC II, V) led to a

---

[24]The emperor issued Augsburg Interim as a temporary religious solution in Augsburg to last from September 1, 1547, to June 30, 1548, aiming to return Catholic practices. In twenty-six articles it reinstated Catholic bishops with jurisdiction, seven sacraments, Mass, festivals, and fasting/religious customs and regulations. Only two compromises were made: Protestants could receive communion in both kinds and their clergy could marry. In Leipzig interim, some Catholic practices were allowed to return as a matter of adiaphora, as matters not contradicting Scripture or jeopardizing salvation (such as the Catholic celebration of Mass, extreme unction, confirmation and ordination by bishops, Corpus Christi celebration, fasting on Fridays and Saturdays). On the other hand, prayers to the saints, private masses, and the canon of the Mass were not adiaphora issues. Both interims were lifted in the Treaty of Passau 1552 and then in the Peace of Augsburg of 1555 when the Lutheran confession became legal.

[25]FC articles I–II parallel AC 2, 18, 19; FC articles III–VI parallel AC 4 and 6, 22; FC article VII parallels AC 10; FC articles VIII and IX parallel AC 3, 17; FC article X parallels AC 14–15; FC article XI parallels AC 17, 18, 19.

so-called Synergistic controversy: can human being in any way participate, collaborate with (*synergo*), or even respond to God in the justification, or can they (only) resist grace? The issue of synergism, debated since the Augustine-Pelagius or Luther-Erasmus confrontations, was well and alive, touching the heart of Lutheran teaching of salvation and holiness.[26] The controversy relates to other disputes, one dealing with the function of law in Christian life and the other with the possibility of Christian obedience producing good fruit. The former is known as Majoristic controversy, from 1530–40s (FC IV, named after a major proponent of good works, Georg Major). The latter, Antinomian controversy, from 1520s–1546 (FC V–VI) involved already Luther and Melanchthon and their colleague Johann Agricola, the question being how both law and gospel were needed for Christian life. Also, addressing the dialectic of law and gospel, which has been employed to express fundamental Lutheran principles vis-à-vis the Word and its proclamation, importantly filled a gap left by the *Augsburg Confession*.

The article on the person and indwelling of Christ (FC III) brings attention to the mysteries of justification, clarifying Lutherans' Chalcedonian position on Christ's two natures and thus full presence in the believer. Behind the article lie two controversies, one on justification and the other on the sacrament of the Lord's Supper and Christ's presence there. The so-called Osiandrian controversy, from 1550s (FC III), involved both Gnesio-Lutherans and Philippists opposing their colleague Andreas Osiander's explanation of justification meaning God's indwelling in the believer, the unclarity concerning whether the transforming inner justification effected the indwelling of only the divine nature of Christ or of the whole of Christ.

Relatedly, Lutherans disputed over the question of Christ's presence in the Lord's Supper in particular; this Crypto-Calvinist controversy, 1558–73 (FC VII, VIII), employed the teaching of ubiquity to find a solution to a question that, till today, distinguishes the Protestant groups. Last but not least, the article on predestination (FC XI) clearly arises from conversations with the Calvinist colleagues. Calvin paid more attention to the question of predestination than Luther had but, in line with Lutheran teaching of the debilitating sin on the one hand and the irresistible grace of God on the other, the article on predestination is a logical one. Basically, doctrinally speaking, the articles offer fine-tuning on the relation between grace and human response/lack of response and lay out the parameters within which Lutherans understand the issue and what articulations would be rejected as not-Lutheran.

---

[26]Already in the fifth century, Augustine and Pelagius had presented mutually opposing views on the matter of human freedom vis-à-vis grace; the medieval church since then had taken a middle road, allowing will, to a degree, to collaborate with grace; similarly, Luther's response to Erasmus's optimism drew from Augustine's experience of the bondage of will.

It is hardly a surprise that the movement toward unity started with passionate sermons and earnest individuals committed to unity and with powerful-enough political support. This resembles the beginnings of the Lutheran reformation with Luther. Unity-oriented sermons and articles led eventually to a written and signed Formula of Concord. As the title reveals, the mission was to achieve a formula for Lutherans to stand together in concord with one another and with a clearer identity in relation to others, while agreeing to live in tension with unresolved theological questions and gray areas with assorted religious practices.

Jacob Andrae, from the South, and Martin Chemnitz, from the North, deserve the credit for instigating this.[27] Both were supported by their respective dukes, similarly committed to finding unity between different Lutheran fronts. It was Andrae's Five Articles 1568 and Six Sermons 1573 that provided the starting point.[28] In a team effort,[29] these texts were developed into the Swabian Concord in 1574, which in turn served as the basis for Chemnitz and the Saxon-Swabian Concord in 1575. Yet another consensus between North and South was reached in Maulbronn Formula in 1576 (Chemnitz and Chytraues). With Andrae, the Swabian-Saxon Concord was worked into the Torgau Book in 1576; Andrae's summary of the Torgau Book is included as the *Epitome* of Formula of Concord. After receiving reactions to that document, a longer text, the Bergen Book, was completed in 1577 and is included in the *Formula* as the *Solid Declaration*.

---

[27]The key voices were Swabian theologian Jacob Andrae (1528–90), doctor of theology, from South/Württemberg, pastor superintendent of Göppingen, and Braunschweig superintendent Martin Chemnitz (1522–86), doctor of theology, from North/Braunschweig, a humanist, schoolmaster, ducal librarian. Also, Leipzig professor of theology Nicholas Selnecker (1528–92); David Chytraeus (1531–1600), professor in Rostock; Christopher Korner (1518–94) and Andreas Musculus (1514–94), professors at Frankfurt/Oder.

[28]Prince cousins Duke Christoph of Württemberg, Southwestern Germany (Swabia), and Duke Julius of Braunschwcig-Wolfenbüttel, North, were both committed to unity. Duke Christoph's chief theologian Andrae was initially sent to the North to negotiate with the evangelical governments there; eventually the two teamed up with Duke Julius and his theologians, Martin Chemnitz and Nicholas Selnecker (from Saxony). In the end, Duke Julius and Chemnitz had a fall-out and Duke did actually not endorse the final formula.

[29]Andreas Osiander (1498–1552), reformer from Nuremberg, to Prussia; controversy over justification and indwelling of Christ; Nicholas von Amsdorf (1483–1565), a friend of Melanchthon and Luther, reformer of Magdeburg, opponent of the Philippists; George Major (1502–74), Melanchthon's ally, a player in intra-Lutheran disputes on good works; Matthias Flacius Illyricus (1520–75), a leader of Gnesio-Lutherans, attentive to hermeneutics and church history works; Johan Agricola (1492–1566), a student of Luther, opponent in the issue of law; Johannes Aurifaber (1519–75), an editor of Luther's works; Johannes Wigand (1523–87), a pastor in Magderburg; Caspar Schwenkfeld (1490–1561), a mystic and radical opponent of Lutheran sacramental and Christological views; Johann Saliger (*c.* 1500–77), a preacher from Lübeck/Rostock, involved with the issue of the Lord's Supper; Viktorin Strigel (1524–69), a professor in Jena, Leipzig, Heidelberg, Melanchthon's student; Caspar Cruciger, Sr. (1504–48), a student of Melanchthon, professor; and his son Caspar Cruciger Jr. (1525–97), also a professor and Crypto-Philippist.

It took about two years, 1578–80, and several rounds of reading and feedback before the Preface met everyone's satisfaction to sign.

In sum, a few poignant confessional points are made about the Lutheran sources and the source of authority. For example, the Solid Declaration explains its "binding summary":

> Fundamental, enduring unity in the church requires above all else a clear and binding summary and form in which a general summary of teaching is drawn from God's Word, to which the churches that hold the true Christian religion confess their adherence. ... we have made this mutual declaration with hearts and mouths that we intend to create or accept no special or new confession of our faith. Rather, we confess our adherence to the publicly recognized writings that have been regarded and used as creeds and common confessions in all the churches of the *Augsburg Confession* at all times. (FC SD, p. 526)

The status of the *Augsburg Confession* is unambiguously underscored in the Solid Declaration's beginning statements (FC SD, 524–5): "Once again we wholeheartedly confess our adherence to this same Christian *Augsburg Confession*, solidly based as it is in God's Word, and we remain faithful to its simple, clear, unequivocal meaning, which its words intend." The early Christian roots similarly are highlighted from the start, to express the Catholicity of Lutherans' faith. "We regard this confession as a pure, Christian creed, which (after the Word of God) should guide true Christians in this time, just as in earlier times Christian creeds and confessions were formulated in God's church when major controversies broke out .... We do not intend to deviate in the least from this Confession". (ibid., 525)

The Lutheran sources and their order of importance are articulated for the reader in the beginning statements on the "binding summary" in Epitome (FC Ep., pp. 486–7):

> [W]e regard as the unanimous consensus and explanation of our Christian faith and confession, especially against the papacy and its false worship, idolatry, and superstition ... the first, unaltered Augsburg Confession ... along with the Apology of this Confession and the articles that were presented at Smalcald in 1537 ... And because these matters also concern the laity and the salvation of their souls, we pledge ourselves also to the Small and Large Catechisms of Dr Luther ... as a Bible of the Laity, in which everything is summarized that is treated in detail in Holy Scripture and that is necessary for a Christian to know for salvation.

In sum, that *Formula of Concord* was a success is shown in its reception: it was accepted in eighty-six territories and cities and was signed by 8,188 theologians, pastors, and teachers. For later generations, the texts give a precious view to the intra-Lutheran discourse and theological controversies during and post-Luther's lifetime. They demonstrate the resiliency and commitment of the Lutherans to hold different groups together and secure effective and faithful proclamation and teaching of the Christian faith, in accordance with the spirit of Luther and the *Augsburg Confession*. While the Formula has less clout among global Lutheran communities, it is a valuable piece of Lutheran confessional history and provides materials for ongoing theological discourse on matters that continue to excite Lutherans and their neighbors.

Freedom and Ambiguity with the Texts and the *Sola Scriptura* Principle

These texts introduced above form the *Book of Concord*. Together the texts give a distinctive foundation for the Lutheran tradition. They serve as a record of Lutherans' path to concord from difficult circumstances, and they serve as a testimony to the early Lutherans' success in rescuing the movement. That said, the individual texts do not hold a similarly and uniformly weighty position among all Lutheran. There are historical reasons to that as well as theological and cultural.

For instance, in the Scandinavia, most of the documents in the *Book of Concord* were considered as German documents, not pertinent to their context. The *Catechisms* and the *Augsburg Confession* were adopted earlier. There are also theological reasons: beyond the *Augsburg Confession's* sparse presentation of the Lutheran views, some of the texts express more detailed and complex debate on matters that Lutherans have not (still, yet) seen eye to eye on and that have given birth to known controversies, some of which led to the writing of the *Formula of Concord* and presenting the *Book of Concord* as a stool for at least rudimentary agreement and harmony rather than facing Lutherans disintegration due to their internal battles. It seems that the shorter the wording, the more shelf-life the text has and the more applications have been possible in new contexts; the wordier and more detailed the argument, the chances for disagreements and non-concord seem to increase by the word.

The *Augsburg Confession* and the *Catechisms* are different as relatively brief texts and with their constructive orientation with an explicit aim to unity and harmony. The former is politically savvy, the latter spiritually and pastorally designed. Both continue to serve as (potentially) unifying texts, leaving room for interpretation and even disagreement. Reading them together or side by side with the other texts opens a window to the Lutheran past and tensions within the Lutheran circles and in conflicts with others. Looking at the whole, for the future uses of the text, rather than repeating the past conflicts or limiting concerns to those that energized the sixteenth-century Lutherans, perhaps the most valuable contribution of the texts is their adamant and consistent underscoring of the primacy of the Scriptures and the *sola scriptura* principle. In the beginning statement of the Epitome (FC Ep., 486), they write:

> We believe, teach, and confess that the only rule and guiding principle according to which all teachings and teachers are to be evaluated and judged are the prophetic and apostolic writings of the Old and New Testaments alone ... Other writings of ancient or contemporary teachers ... shall not be regarded as equal to Holy Scripture, but all of them together shall be subjected to it. ... the early church prepared symbola ... which were regarded as the unanimous, universal, Christian creed and confession of the orthodox and true church of Christ ... We pledge ourselves to these and thereby reject all heresies ....

The *sola scriptura* principle is the golden thread of Lutheran tradition as well as the battle call for the Protestant reformers in general. In its simplicity it is enormously complex and leaves ample room for interpretation. Luther famously referred to his conscience and the Scriptures at the Diet of Worms 1521 before his condemnation. That confessing moment with Luther's brave statement explicates a decisive hermeneutical move and refines the foundations of authority for Lutherans. Moving from the Catholic position of Scripture-plus-Tradition—meaning the Scriptures are to be interpreted within the tradition and by proper authorized channels and guided by the papally sanctioned teaching—Luther and his peers restated the Scriptures as the utmost and ultimate authority, as the living Word that could and would speak beyond the parameters set by human beings.

The move was necessary for Luther initially to defend himself and to argue his case against some of the teachings of the church under the papal authority. He found himself standing against some of the teachings and practices of his church and needed authorization to stand against the tradition; he found it in the Scriptures. This "conscience move" liberated the Scriptures, for him, from the binds of the existing rules of interpretation. At the same time, it created a vacuum: because the Scriptures always require interpretation, the question arose, whose interpretation was right and would matter the most? What would be the rules and channels for the interpretation from henceforth, as the Catholic parameters of authority were being dismissed or, if not, then at least seriously challenged?

Of the Christian movements originating from the sixteenth-century reforms, Lutherans have taken a middle road in this regard, standing between the so-called Radicals and the Catholic position, in terms of the dynamics between the biblical authority and the ecclesial power. Radical reformers[30] were more extreme in their application of the *sola scriptura* principles: initially lay leadership and role in the interpretation was much more prominent in these groups than among Lutherans. In the other end of the spectrum stands the Catholic church, where the vocation of the clergy in the task of interpretation was and has been affirmed and where the Scriptures were and are read in light of the official teachings of the church.

It is to be noted that women's activity in the interpretation of the Christian vision was more prominent in the radical groups at first, whereas in the Catholic tradition this path was open for women mystics but not other female teachers. Lutherans stood in the middle in this regard: not officially opening the task of biblical interpretation for women as teachers and preachers, while equipping women from young age on to read the Scriptures, for themselves, and for teaching them in their households to their children and dependents. Luther's own wife, Katharina von Bora (1499–1552), seems to have been satisfied with this. Some other women, e.g., Argula von Grumbach (1492–1554/68) from Bavaria, claimed for themselves more freedoms and responsibilities in this regard. Whereas in the Middle Ages the few women who had felt empowered to break the rules and publish their theological views had done so typically on the basis of their empowering spiritual experiences that had compelled them to do so, the Reformation women would have a different form of authorization: their knowledge of the Scriptures and its content.[31]

Another factor would be motherhood and how women understood it: never before had theologians and preachers publicly praised and validated motherhood as a holy calling. For women so inclined, such preaching gave women theological rationales to develop their own interpretation of that calling's realm to include public theologizing and leadership. For example, Katharina Schütz Zell (*c*. 1497–1562) in Strasbourg considered motherhood as a theologically based calling that invited women outside of their private homes to the public realm to take care of things as needed, even exercising leadership and, in her case, occasionally preaching at funerals. The theoretical

---

[30]"Radical" is used as a term for those reforming voices and movements who were willing to go further in terms of what was pruned out of the religious practices and institutional ways of religion. The believers' baptism rather than infant baptism is often noted as a distinctive mark of radical Protestantism, as is the question of authority: Spirit-led communities resisted established channels of power and sought to separate themselves from the world, e.g., by not serving in certain offices and not giving an oath or carrying weapons. Some of the early leaders were Thomas Müntzer (*c*. 1489–1525), Andreas Bodenstein von Karlstadt (1486–1541), Felix Manz (1498–1527)—the first martyr of the radical reformers—the Zwickau Prophets, and Menno Simons. The Hutterites and Mennonites and the Brethren are just some of the descendants of these heavily persecuted Protestants.

[31]Stjerna, *Women and the Reformations*, esp. chapters 1, 3, 4, 5, 6. Also Stjerna, "Reformation Revisited: Women's Voices in the Reformation" in *The Ecumenical Review*, Vol. 69, no. 2 (July 2017) and "Women Writers of the 16th Century" in Kapic and Madueme, eds., *Reading Christian Theology in the Protestant Tradition*.

seed for women's emancipation and full inclusivity in ministry and teaching has been maturing ever since, on these foundations of equipping women to go to the sources by themselves.[32] The reformation foremothers' reading their Bibles foreshadowed the future when women would become ordained in Lutheran tradition and enter the teaching profession. In the meantime, Lutherans have been singing a hymn written by Elizabeth Creutziger (Cruciger) (*c.* 1500–35), who wrote the first Lutheran hymn ever published.

In addition to the question of who has the capacity and the invitation to interpret the Scriptures, Lutherans also have a distinct take on how to interpret and with what tools. For Lutherans, the Bible is the primary authority; it is, however, not understood to stand alone as such but as a living source that needs to be interpreted for the benefit of individuals and faith communities, to be read afresh in new contexts and with the aid of the confessional texts. In other words, Lutherans in the end saw the value of some principal guidance from the tradition, mainly with the confessions expressing a particularly Lutheran perspective. Underscoring scriptural authority does not imply biblical literalism; no simplistic answers are to be expected to current situations from these ancient texts. Rather, a Lutheran position holds that the texts are God's revelation, written in human hands, and containing divine wisdom that is to be explored and discerned and listened to, with openness to new insights. The confessional texts were meant to guide people's reading and point to the gospel promise embedded in the texts, to be interpreted anew for new situations. Most explicitly, the

---

[32]On November 22, 1970, Elizabeth Platz became the first woman of European descent ordained in a Lutheran church body in North America. She was ordained in the Lutheran Church in America (LCA), which later merged with the American Lutheran Church (ALC) and the Association of Evangelical Lutheran Churches (AELC) to form the Evangelical Lutheran Church in America (ELCA) in 1988. It was not until nearly ten years later that the first women of color were ordained in a Lutheran church body in the United States: Lydia Rivera Kalb, ordained in the LCA on March 4, 1979, was the first Latina woman ordained in a Lutheran church body in the United States and Earlean Miller, ordained in the LCA on August 26, 1979, the first woman of African descent (Evangelical Lutheran Church in America, "We Are Church, We Are Called," 2019, accessed February 29, 2020, https://www. elca.org/50yearsofordainedwomen). Lutheran church bodies around the globe have formed an important part of the legacy of reformation-era church mothers, like Katharina Schütz Zell, in their ordination of women, however delayed. As of 2016, more than 80 percent of Lutheran World Federation (LWF) member churches ordain women. The Estonian Evangelical Lutheran Church, for example, has been ordaining women since 1967. The Evangelical Lutheran Church of Finland has ordained women since 1988, the Evangelical Lutheran Church in Tanzania since 1991, and the Mexican Lutheran Church since 2009. More recently the Evangelical Lutheran Church in Mozambique ordained the first woman in its church in 2013, and just in 2018, the Evangelical Lutheran Church in Thailand ordained the first woman to its church. Despite continued controversy, women-identified faith leaders around the globe make up an important voice in the global Lutheran church, thanks in part to the faithful witness of women reformers of the sixteenth century. ("Affirming Women's Ordination as Our Shared Goal," *The Lutheran World Federation*, last modified June 6, 2016, accessed February 29, 2020, https:// www.lutheranworld.org/news/affirming-womens-ordination-our-shared-goal.)

Augsburg Confession and the *Catechisms* have been presented as the guides, with the ecumenical Creeds as the first and ancient expression of the central scriptural truths.

In other words, a Lutheran approach to biblical interpretation leaves room for ambiguity and disagreement. It does not endorse biblical literalism, while it fosters authentic exploration of the biblical texts for divine wisdom that pertains to the human situation in endless variations. In a Lutheran position, biblical scholarship assists in faithful reading of the texts. Given Luther's own expertise as a biblical scholar and the model he gave for seeking the plain or the core meaning of the sacred texts via critical reading, Lutheran biblical hermeneutics distinctly endorse and draw from exegetical scholarship. Critical reading of the sacred texts is encouraged, to unclutter the written words so as to hear the divine Word communicated through them, with many surprises to be expected. The model for this comes from Luther, a biblical scholar, who valued critical study of the Scriptures and who in his time and place promoted historical and critical exegetical reading of the sacred texts.

This approach is liberating and appealing to modern readers, as it assumes a critical stance and welcomes conversation with other academic disciplines. At the same time, the application and its parameters remain a dividing issue among diverse Lutheran groups, who actually disagree on this neuralgic question. For example, the member churches of the Lutheran World Federation witness to the great variety of hermeneutics in this regard.[33] Where this dissonance manifests itself especially is in how the Bible is read vis-à-vis current social issues and the ongoing disagreements on the status of women in the church and matters of human sexuality and orientation. With these currently debated issues, the roads lead back to the principles of reading the Scriptures, with the fundamental questions: whose interpretation matters and how biblical words can—or cannot—be applied today.

Just as Lutheran communities around the world have a different take on the meaning and application of the *sola scriptura* principle, similarly there is a difference between faith communities regarding which is held in higher regard, Luther or the confessional texts, as the final authority. The word "Lutheran" may mean a variety of things, without straight lines to Luther, and yet it is in Luther that contemporary Lutheran discourse can find a more flexible and open-ended source than in the confessions that are written more distinctly to particular historical situations. Furthermore, readers of the *Book of Concord* are repeatedly reminded of Luther's theology that is being

---

[33]An example of Lutheran biblical scholarship on a highly divisive matter; see Martti Nissinen, *Homoeroticism in the Biblical World*, transl. Kirsi Stjerna (from the 1998 Finnish original) (Minneapolis: Fortress Press, 2004).

interpreted and debated—the confessional texts themselves thus setting a hierarchy in terms of the priority of the sources.

Luther's Voice and the Confessions

It may be surprising to consider that the entire Lutheran book of confessions was not written by Martin Luther, the principal reformer, with only three of his central works included. While Luther wrote an incredible volume of texts, he did not leave just one opus that would have sufficed for those continuing the Lutheran tradition and steering direction in the sixteenth century when the foundations for Lutheran faith tradition were laid. One of the reasons for Luther not being the single steering voice for Lutherans, confessionally speaking, is in the context and the demand. One single work from one person would have hardly sufficed in the complex and volatile Reformation situation, with a rising number of Lutheran communities, and as the Reformation very quickly ceased to be a one-man show but rather has been led by a diversity of voices and visions that erupted with different options for religious life being offered. No single work, not even from Luther, would have been able to rise to the occasion to meet the multiple demands to unite the constantly debating Lutherans; a team effort was needed to produce a work that intentionally and consciously aimed to interpret the Scriptures with Luther authentically. The texts in the *Book of Concord* give a lively testimony to this decisive collaborative process.

Another reason why Luther did not write the single, definitive opus that would have been a portable summation or a handbook for Lutheran faith is that while he wrote an amazing volume of texts, his life situation was never ripe for him to sit down and write a summa with ample time to contemplate and systematize. Rather, he worked tirelessly in a context of debate and danger, responded to requests to attend to a broad variety of issues, and carried the burden of pioneering in the new ministry, while constantly teaching and preaching.

Looking at the big picture, and in retrospect: Luther's mission was not to sit down to write a text for the purposes of a unifying confessional text. He was intentional with kindling the Reformation with his deliberate written calls for reforms and changes with his 1517 and 1520 texts; there is a reason why those texts were enthusiastically received and energized people near and far. From there onward, it was rocky times and endless situations demanding his attention and his production is voluminous, with distinctive contributions from the German Bible and the *Catechisms* that reached a huge audience to smaller treatises and, importantly, his tireless correspondence.

All this considered, the three texts included in the *Book of Concord* could—with some caveats—be used as "stand alone" texts from which to glean the essentials of Lutheran teaching, with Luther's unique voice. Particularly the

Catechisms significantly present the central Lutheran theology defended in the *Book of Concord* and in a language that anyone can understand—as they were written for people, not for any particular situation. Masterfully written as such, the *Catechisms* have the power to hold together widely different Lutheran constituencies, due to the nature and the premise of the texts and their purpose as a book of faith that aims to equip the spiritual life of the individuals and communities.

The fact that the *Book of Concord* includes three texts from Luther, all influential in their own right and independently of the collection, and that his name is evoked throughout the *Book of Concord*, indicates Luther's key role in steering what it means to be theologically speaking Lutheran. At the same time, that other authors are included—and the persons who provided the collection in the *Book of Concord* were not Luther but his associates— and that the Lutheran reformation from the start was teamwork, even if with the charismatic stimulus and original theological visions coming from Luther, reveals another aspect of Lutheran hermeneutics: it has historically speaking been considered a group effort, a dialogical process, where concord and discord are possible and tolerated. This reality conveys fundamentally important principles on what it means being theologically Lutheran: one engages Luther's original reformation principles and also the conversation on the meaning and weight and application of those principles in new situations and this entails collaborative exchange and debate, careful deliberations, disagreements, and always remembering the roots, but not granting any source or author the last word, not even Luther.

On the Meaning of Confessing

To conclude on the sources called confessions, it is helpful to pause with that very word: confessing. Basically, what it meant in the early church to confess—*credo*—that is also the fundamental reformation meaning for the word, and for the act, too. Confession expresses basic, vital, non negotiable beliefs for which one is willing to stand, come what may. The words imply both a personal faith statement and a communal faith statement. As such, they give a theological position and foundation to one's situation in the world, which requires a variety of daily negotiations and decision-makings. The confession with the Creeds expresses a personal conviction rooted in the faith of the community; it is a private and intimate commitment in the Christian continuum of faith, while it is a public joining of individuals who hold true and draw strength and hope from the articles of faith that have united Christians over centuries.

In addition, it needs to be noted that for the reformers, the word had clearly both religious and political meaning. This is particularly clear when comparing the context for the *Augsburg Confession* and the

Large Catechism with their different audiences and rationales, both texts giving a voice for confessing the Lutheran Christian faith, but in different frameworks and with distinct agendas and modes. The former needed to be politically attuned and nuanced as it was given in a politically charged situation; the latter could focus on matters of the spirituality and flesh out the faith for a broad audience to understand; the latter also was a text meant for application of the faith, whereas the former's aim was to win approval for such teaching and practice.

With these core texts, Lutherans continue to confess their particularly Lutheran Christian faith in terms of the content of what they believe in with the Creeds and with the positions Lutherans have historically taken a stand on. With both, continuing in this trajectory, confessing is never just a private, spiritual matter but requires standing in public, willing to face the opposing powers and challenge authorities, even at cost, and being willing to say "No" with a "Here we stand" position, in light of the Lutheran theological convictions, as needed. The internal understanding of what it means to confess as Lutheran was first written in the *Book of Concord*. The quotes highlighted above explicate the foundation and the parameters, in terms of sources. This does not imply an end to the deliberation of the content of this faith being confessed or the limits of action that it can inspire. Quite the contrary. Each generation adhering to the confessions faces the challenge to move onward with their interpretation and sense of call for the "Here I stand" opportunities.

For Lutherans, the act of confessing is not just a private act or an internal act but a statement to others and to the world of one's fundamental convictions. The very word "Protestant" (originating from the resisting moment at the Diet of Speyer 1529) implies courage to "stand up," not only in doctrinal issues but also in facing the uses of force and in promoting freedoms of all Christians—to confess and express their faith.[34] For contemporary Christians the word "confessing" may be provocative and cause a pause. With the many wrongs in our world, with much room for improvement, a fair question to ask is, what are Lutherans willing to live with and tolerate, and what are they not? What do Lutherans want to protest for, and what do Lutherans want to protest against? After all, such a faith-inspired activity is at the heart of being a confessing Lutheran.

Basically with the confessions, be it in the sixteenth-century climate or today, the question is what are Christians confessing for and with, and who cares? It would be one thing if it was just a private matter of faith—but it never is: religion is never just a private matter but a force in the world. Lutherans have historically always negotiated this, the division of power,

---

[34]On Lutherans addressing contemporary urgencies and social issues with Luther, see Carter Lindberg and Paul Wee, eds., *Forgotten Luther I* (Augsburg Press, 2016) and Ryan Cummings, ed., *Forgotten Luther II* (Minneapolis: Fortress Press, 2019).

and standing in the middle of things, with the faith that is worth defending. The Lutheran ancestors were willing to die for their confession. Continuing on that trajectory, the question for this generation, again, is, what are the religious and existential matters and human rights issues Lutherans can stand for and are willing to take significant risks for? Considering freedom as a central issue, how might that shape Lutherans' theological standing, and action, today?

Namely, for Lutheran confessional theology, this remains the golden principle: freedom—not only freedom to believe and practice one's faith, but freedom as a human being with all that it entails. The ultra-Lutheran term "justification" renders itself meaningful in a new way when understood in light of freedom as the basic human right and need. Justification speaks to this issue of justice, and then some. If not—then, what would be more important for the purposes of confessing?[35]

Concluding Reflections: Confessing in the Company of Others

The Scriptures do not belong to Lutherans alone, neither do the Creeds. Neither were the Lutherans the only ones to write their confessions of faith as a result of the sixteenth-century turmoil. Nor are the issues causing tension among Lutherans unique to them.

The Scriptures both hold together widely different Christian communities and divide them. The same is true not only within the Lutheran circles but also in relation to other Protestant traditions, built on the same *sola scriptura* principle. Each tradition has had to explicate, for themselves and others, how they interpret the Scriptures to speak to pertinent theological issues and apply them in their own operations and visions. Like Lutherans, all the first Protestant groups faced great dangers, and risked death, and needed manifestos to state what exactly they wanted to live by or die for. In other words, confessions of faith were needed. Today different Protestant denominations have their own equivalent sources. Their birthing has similar histories: new Christian groups that diverted away from the Catholic Christian church enough so that it was impossible to continue under the

---

[35] A powerful example of peaceful confessing comes from 1989 Leipzig, former East Germany: a Lutheran church had hosted discussions on prayer and politics over a decade, and one evening, on October 9, 1989, nearly 8,000 people who had filled the church began a candle-lit walk through the city of Leipzig to resist the tyranny of communism, facing the Stasi (police who chose not to shoot, confessing for peace in their own way). The march led to the taking down of the Berlin Wall. Similar stories come from, e.g., Norway where Bishop Eivind Josef Berggrav led the resistance of Norwegian Lutherans against the Nazis. See Kirsi Stjerna, "Lutheran Faith: Rebellion and Responsibility," in *Forgotten Luther II*, ed. Ryan Cummings (Minneapolis: Fortress Press, 2019).

same umbrella to articulate—for themselves first and for the rest of the world second—what they believed in and how they understood the Christian faith could be best expressed and with what structures.

Some of the central questions were and are: how do people understand the Christian church and the channels of authority and decision-making in that; what are the central teachings to proclaim and live by and express in church and in society; and, very importantly, how are the means of grace, aka sacraments, understood and celebrated; and, last but not least, how is the gospel to be interpreted, by whom, with what sources, and with what principles? The resulting confessions from the sixteenth century have served both as internal documents to hold the group together enough to survive but also as political documents as they have been used to explain to the world, and authorities, what the movement was about. How well these confessional books managed to communicate the core of the group's ideology and intention in the most nonthreatening and clear ways was decisive for the longevity and survival of the movement.[36]

I. Central Topics and Learning Goals

1. The rationales for *confessing* with the sixteenth-century texts.
2. Overview of the history, context, and significance of the different Lutheran confessional texts.
3. Approach the texts with historically enlightened perspectives and in light of Luther's theological commitments.
4. The complexities of the *Scripture alone* principle.

II. Questions for Review, Discussion, and Further Reflection

1. What were the processes and the stimuli for the writing of the Lutheran confessions?
2. What is behind the *Scripture alone* principle? What is protected with that? What are its challenges?

---

[36]Examples of other Protestant confessions: The *Schleitheim Articles* (1527), by Michael Sattler, served as the confessional document for Anabaptists. The Church of England is united with the *Book of Common Prayer* (1549 and different editions) and *the Thirty-nine Articles*. Reformed churches' confessional documents include, e.g., the *Belgic Confession*, the *Heidelberg Catechism* (1563), the *Canons of Dort* (1619), the *Westminster Standards*, consisting of the *Westminster Confession of Faith* (1646), *Westminster Shorter Catechism* (1649), the *Westminster Larger Catechism* (1649), and the *Scots Confession* (1650).

3. How does the Lutheran history of confessing resonate with Luther's freedom theology insights and his commitments as a reformer and freedom theologian?

4. If a *Book of Concord* was written today, what issues do you imagine would be included and which issues would require extensive treatment?

III. Keywords

Apology of the Augsburg Confession, Augsburg Confession, Book of Concord, Catechisms, confessing, confessions, controversies, Creeds, ecumenical, *Formula of Concord,* Protestant, *Smalcald Articles, Small Catechism, Large Catechism, sola scriptura, Treatise on the Power and Primacy of the Papacy.*

IV. Readings with the Chapter

Introduction to the *Book of Concord.*
Introductions to the texts in the *Book of Concord.*

4

Lutheran Faith Grammar—
Justification and Freedom
Perspectives

About the Key Terms and the Vision

For life's big questions, religions offer different orientations. Religions offer a grounding and values. Religions spur doctrines or sets of beliefs and identify sources for individuals and communities to draw from in setting parameters for their lives, individually and collectively. Religions offer rituals and facilitate experiences that accompany systems of beliefs that give a sense of belonging, codes for right and wrong, rationales for hope and accountability, and, fundamentally, an explanation for the existence and purpose of a human being in the face of all that there is to life as we know it. Religions shape values and equip one with a language to address a wide gamut of issues and experiences in human life. Each religion gives a particular language to name realities both human and divine and their intersections.

Lutheran faith is a form of Christian religion and offers its own distinctive grammar for religious speech. It is founded on the historic Christian sources: the Scriptures and the first centuries' ecumenical Creeds. Since the times of Luther, Lutherans have stood on the shared grounding of a Christian faith, from the start not suggesting a new church. And yet, with the excommunication of Luther (1521), the tradition named after Luther (who

---

Read AC 1. (Skim Ap. 1.) SC, Creed, third article; SA Part II art. 1, Part III art. 13, 4. Recommended FC III, IV. Read AC 6, 16, 20. (Skim Ap. 6, 16, 20.). SA Part III art. 13. Recommended FC III–IV (V–VI). Recommended SC/LC Ten Commandments.

preferred the word "Christian" rather than "Lutheran") had to develop outside the Catholic church, and toward distinguishing its own direction, to bearing its own name, building its own structures, and forming its unique identity among other emerging Christian groups, in the aftermath of the reformations.

Several principles and emphases defended by Lutherans have become the hallmark of the Lutheran language of faith. They each either support, spring from, or illuminate the doctrine of justification, which is the distinctively Lutheran approach to the central Christian teaching of salvation.[1] These words are not exclusively Lutheran but their interpretation and the emphasis expressed with them are so. All these words lead to Christology, that is, what is believed about the impact and role of Christ in human life. The Lutheran emphases stress the meaning of Christ and his life, death, resurrection, and ongoing presence for all that there is in human existence.

Theologically speaking, the Lutheran reformation was an effort to underscore the ancient Christian statement of faith expressed in the second article of the Creed, about the meaning of Christ for the human existence. The Lutheran rationale for the proclamation of the gospel, the purpose of the church and the sacraments, as well as Lutheran understanding of Christians' responsibilities in their communities—religious and political— fundamentally draw from the ecumenically held Christological beliefs. The strong Lutheran emphasis is that of the ongoing and real presence of Christ in all the aspects of life, and death, and that the gospel of Christ conveys transforming and sustaining hope to individuals and communities. These faith convictions are expressed from different angles in a particular Lutheran grammar that utilizes several key concepts.

In a Nutshell

Sola scriptura or Scripture alone, justified by faith through grace, *simul iustus et peccator* or simultaneously a saint and a sinner, law and gospel have been used as fundamental expressions of Lutheran theological principles. They emerged in the sixteenth-century religious scene, where the evangelicals (as then identified) needed to clarify where their theologies differed from that of the mainstream Catholic teaching. These terms indicate a shift in argumentation or direction, then, and have stuck as paradigms and benchmarks for theology that would be recognized as Lutheran specifically.

---

[1]In this book, the word "salvation" is used without a detailed elaboration on the different uses and meanings of the term in the Christian past and without assuming that salvation language is necessarily a given or without problems in contemporary parlance. The word is used in its traditional meaning of deliverance and liberation from the effects of sin or danger.

Today they may seem odd or at least require explaining and, in some cases, could be replaced with new words to convey their meaning more effectively.

That said, the words continue to be used to describe the theological discovery of Luther on the realities and hopes of human beings in light of Christian faith about God. Each of the words has a place in the Lutheran grammar that seeks to explain what happens in God-human relationship and thus in human condition and status in light of the biblical wisdom. The key terms used to express the Lutheran interpretation of Christ's impact in human life have already been briefly addressed with Luther's *The Freedom of a Christian* treatise (see On Christian Freedom—Luther's Theological Synopsis in Chapter 2). Before reviewing the Lutheran articulations with the *Augsburg Confession*, the following is offered as a synopsis of Luther's theological vision and emphasis.

Luther's major insight was that justification is a grace event where one is gifted freedom and forgiveness, solely by the act of Christ, who has made the reconciliation between God and human possible. This is a matter of faith. In the Lutheran reading of the Holy Scriptures—the main source, above any other source—human life is viewed in two overlapping dimensions: one that is lived with God in full holiness even if life in human time is experienced in its brokenness. Faith in this view is a gift and not a matter of right doctrinal belief. It is about trust, and it is ultimately in the category of its own, a mystery. Faith signals the fundamental switch in human beings' orientation toward God and God-grounded life where faith holds one in the position of hope and trust.

Faith is not, however, a miracle cure and a fixer of all problems. A Christian cannot expect to be more than human or attain perfection but will continue to falter in this life, even after being made holy by God. Regardless of the reality of sin, since Christ has taken on full humanity, on that basis human beings can expect to be received into a union with God via Christ, who in his divinity is able to make this possible. Lutheran expression of *simul iustus et peccator* crystallizes this new paradoxical existence. On the one hand, in the godly realm, in relation to God, one is already holy and righteous—a saint, to use the *simul* language. On the other hand, in the human condition and relations experienced in human space and time, one is not free from sin or sinning or the impact of all that it entails. The holiness that justifies is complete as a gift coming from a source that knows no sin, outside one's own being, and is thus appropriately named as *alien* righteousness. How it unfolds in one's life is a work in progress and what Luther calls *proper* or human beings' *own* righteousness. This tension is the starting point to comprehend, e.g., Lutheran spirituality and practice of sacraments.

The idea of justification by faith is the basis for the Lutheran orientation in interpreting the Scriptures, practice of the sacraments, and proclamation: because of the *simul* existence, Christians need to hear a daily dose of law and gospel/gospel and law and thereby be met by Christ in their current situation. The church's function is to deliver this proclamation and to offer sacraments as a tangible symbol of the new beginnings for each day, regardless, because of Christ. So nurtured, Christians are called to live Christ-like in their situations, with multiple implications for responsibility in society and varied relations. This view is profoundly egalitarian and inclusive in the sense that each individual is considered similar in this regard, both in their fallibility and vulnerability and in their sanctity and worth.

The rock for the inclusive vision and premise is in the first step Luther and his peers took: to start with the Scriptures and highlighting the revelation of grace and promised freedom there. At the heart of Luther's reforms was his observation that the message of freedom and God's love embedded in the Scriptures had been forgotten or had become unnecessarily complicated in the delivery modes of the church of his time. Taking the authority for himself to suggest a Christ-centric view of human life, Luther employed as his key concepts *sola scriptura*, justification by faith, simultaneously a saint and a sinner/*simul iustus et peccator*, and law and gospel. With these convictions, Lutheran faith language offers a grace-centered and God-grounded approach to reality and a theological foundation for life where freedom is of utmost value.

These ideas, expressed here in a condensed form, are fundamental ingredients in the Lutheran grammar that is engaged in the following pages, starting with a few more words on the enigmatic expression of justification by faith.

Justified by Faith, by Grace, by Christ[2]

The doctrine of justification offers a particular lens to human reality. Lutheran approach to the question of justification is philosophical and mystical and suggests a faith language about the human existence, addressing theologically the different aspects of human life and hopes in this life and beyond.[3] In Lutheran grammar, the keys to understand human experience and the sources of hope are described with a theological terminology that draws attention back to Christ and what Christ does for human beings: that Christ *justifies* and sets one free. Luther's teaching of grace and holiness, forgiveness and freedom are all encompassed with the term "justification," which is the heart of Lutheran theology. Luther or Lutherans did not, however, invent the word.

---

[2]Readings; see footnote 1.

[3]On doctrine of justification, see Veli-Matti Kärkkäinen, *One with God: Salvation as Deification and Justification* (Collegeville, MN: Liturgical Press, 2004); Tuomo Mannermaa, *Christ Present in Faith: Luther's View of Justification*, transl. Kirsi Stjerna (Minneapolis: Fortress Press, 2005); Alister E. McGrath, *Iustitia Dei: A History of the Christian Doctrine of Justification*, 3rd ed. (Cambridge: Cambridge University Press, 2005).

The word "justification" in English sounds like the word "justice"; they come from the same root. In German, *die Rechtfertigung* and in Latin, *iustitia* similarly enough generate an image of a court room, law, and judging. Whereas in a religious sense the word strikes alien and requires explaining, in everyday use it is more easily understood, as a word referring to right-ness or entitlement or permission to do something. In religious discourse, behind the use of such a term is a long history of theological phrasing about the status of human-God relationship and the processes through which human beings have a chance to be redeemed or restored in their condition vis-à-vis their God and thereby be saved.[4] Since the days of church father Augustine of Hippo, Christian theology has assumed and taught that human being had to be made right in this relationship. The relationship itself had to be *made right*, restored, to use the traditional Christian terminology.

Given what is known of Luther's *Anfechtung* and feeling of not meeting the expectations of God and failing miserably in his hopes to attain even satisfactory holiness, it is logical that he would employ the word "justification." Based on how he understood the just and merciful God of the Bible, something had to take place to justify one's return to the kind of status and relationship with God that God had intended. A justification act was needed to override what was separating human being from God—that is, be free from or overcome those factors that would separate one from God, which would mean the end of all ends and a status or condition of hopelessness, with no hope beyond death. Ultimately salvation language, which justification language is, sets hopes for life after death and eternal union with God the source of life. Behind justification language, thus, is a theological assumption that there is a problem in God—human relationship and, in all human relations and the human existence in general, a distortion that needs correcting. A related assumption is that something must take place to override this dissonance and to restore the human being to a fresh relationship with God. In thusly corrected relationship, God is encountered merciful and not wrathful.

This was Luther's transforming, life-changing insight, finding the merciful loving God, revealed to him in the Scriptures. The word "justification" worked for Luther in his efforts to explain this experience and the theological rationales and hopes for that. The word "justification" became his word to explain the impact of Christ's person and life on human beings' condition and fate; Christology is the framework for his arguments. Thus, regardless of how awkward the word is in today's language, theologically it is an unmovable fixture in Lutheran theology. It only works, though, when paired with another powerful word for Luther, namely, "faith."

---

[4]The rich and multilayered term "justification" in theology has typically referred to the act or process of one being made right, acceptable, and reconciled with God.

In Lutheran faith language, justification by faith is an umbrella statement as well as the specific core for every other theological statement in Lutheran grammar. Given such weight, it is stated strikingly succinctly in the *Augsburg Confession* article four:

> Likewise, they teach that human beings cannot be justified before God [*non possint iustificari coram Deo*] by their own powers, merits, or works. But they are justified as a gift on account of Christ through faith when they believe that they are received into grace and that their sins are forgiven on account of Christ [*gratis iustificentur propter Christum per fidem*], who by his death made satisfaction [*satisfecit*] for our sins. God reckons [*imputat*] this faith as righteousness [*iustitia*]. (Rom. 3[:21–26] and 4[:5] (AC 4:1–3)[5]

The emphasis in the article is two-fold: first, that forgiveness is the specific personal impact of what happens in justification, and second, that human beings as a result of this restoration are received into a restored communion with God—in grace—without their own earning or demonstrated worth and achievement; the communion has been justified, healed, and made possible, by Christ. The article thus speaks of a gift, from God, to the human being. Christ is the hinge and the rationale, the justifier. The article assumes that Christ's contribution is necessary, explicating the centuries earlier established Christian belief about atonement[6]—that is, that a reconciliation was indeed necessary, because of the reality of sin and because of who and how God is as God of justice and mercy.

The placing of this article in the *Augsburg Confession* is important. It comes after the statements of faith in God (AC 1) and concerning Christ (AC 3), and the original sin (AC 2); they set the foundation for why justification can and needs to happen: because of who God is and what sin does. What follows is an article on ministry (AC 5), which is explained to exist for the purpose of "obtaining" the kind of faith that justifies, and after that an article on "new obedience" (AC 6) that the justifying faith naturally produces. This article needs to be read side by side with the justification article; together they underscore faith as the central agent, stimulus, and

---

[5]From the German text, a slightly different wording of the article: "Furthermore, it is taught that we receive forgiveness of sin and become righteous before God out of grace that we cannot obtain forgiveness of sin and righteousness before God through our merit, work, or satisfactions, but we receive forgiveness of sin and become righteous before God out of grace for Christ's sake through faith when we believe that Christ has suffered for us and that for his sake our sin is forgiven and righteousness and eternal life are given to us. For God will regard and reckon this faith as righteousness in his sight, as St. Paul says in Romans 3[:21-26] and 4[:5]" (AC 4:1–3).

[6]Atonement theories refer to theological rationales for the reasons and means of reconciliation between God and human beings, whose sin, disobedience, is atoned via Christ's redeeming work and obedience (e.g., Anselm of Canterbury).

fruit. Faith justifies, makes one right with God, and the same faith then results in "good fruits" in human life. "Likewise, they teach that this faith is bound to yield good fruits and that it ought to do good works commanded by God on account of Gods' will and not so that we may trust in these works to merit justification before God. For forgiveness of sins and justification are taken hold of by faith" (AC 6:1–2). To avoid any misunderstanding here, referring to the Scriptures and ancient authors, such as Ambrose of Milan, the article repeats the underlying conviction that God has designed it so that via faith alone human beings receive the gift of forgiveness (AC 6:3).

In their emphasis on the gift nature of justification, Lutherans in the past have employed article four at the expense of article six. In their defending the gift nature and underscoring the human passivity in receiving grace, Lutherans have downplayed the teaching of the natural consequence of good works or good fruit. There is a reason for this, already imbedded in the confession itself. Article twenty-two (20:1–2) responds to the false accusations that Lutherans would in any way prohibit good works. The lengthy article explains: "In former times, consciences were vexed by the doctrine of works, they did not hear the consolation from the gospel" (AC 20:19–20). The human conscience was the main concern. "Consequently, it was essential to pass on and restore this teaching about faith in Christ so that anxious consciences should not be deprived of consolation but know that grace and forgiveness of sins are apprehended by faith in Christ" (AC 20:22).

Luther's stimulus for his calls for reforms had been exactly his concern for the teachings of the church that had burdened human consciences, an untenable situation that could be remedied with proper teaching of the gospel and proclamation of the gift of God's grace. This did not, however, mean that Christians were expected to remain passive hence. Quite the contrary, the gift of righteousness would most certainly, naturally and logically, yield good fruit, just not as a mechanism to earn anything, a different status or worth, spiritually speaking. That said, any suggestion or inclination to consider that anything else was needed but Christ's doing for the justification of a human being would, in a sense, mean defaming exactly that—what Christ had done. That would be utterly scandalous in Christian imagination.

The debate over the "necessity" or expectation of "good works" later evolved into the so-called Majoristic controversy where Lutherans took different sides on the matter, the controversy proving the difficulty of teaching passivity in receiving grace and activity in conveying it to others, the core message of Luther's *The Freedom of a Christian*: in faith and with faith matters human beings are free; with love and in love they are bound to serve.[7]

---

[7] On Majoristic controversy, see *The Formula of Concord*, 1577 in Chapter 3.

In his *Smalcald Articles* Luther writes of the "chief article" (with Paul's words in Romans 3:26): "For we hold that a person is justified by faith apart from works prescribed by law" (SA 429). And this faith is a matter of faith and, as such, a life-and-death issue. "Nothing in this article can be conceded or given up" (ibid.). "On this article stands all that we teach and practice against the pope, the devil, and the world. Therefore we must be quite certain and have no doubt about it. Otherwise everything is lost" (ibid.).[8] Luther being quite dramatic here, his Christological argument is clear.

It is perhaps a surprise but disagreements continued also among Lutherans themselves about the very Christological argument. A controversy erupted particularly on the specifics of justification as a Christ event: different parties taught differently on what it would mean that Christ justified human beings, whether it implied a deeper communion or even oneness with the said Christ and if so, on what basis and with what results. A later document in the confessions, the *Formula of Concord*, attends to these complexities with the justification doctrine by returning to the Christological basis; for example, it is stated in the Epitome (FC Ep. 3:1) that Lutherans teach "unanimously" that righteousness, justification, and thus salvation happen by faith alone, as "Christ alone is our righteousness." Christ being true God and true human makes this vicarious saving work possible; removing Christ from the equation would pull the rug from under the entire doctrine. Justification is all about Christ or nothing.

Just as the debate on Christ's two natures vexed the early theologians who formulated creedal theology on this pivotal issue, Lutherans in the sixteenth century found themselves standing on slightly different positions on this when getting deeper into the meaning of Christ's justifying work. Would that imply his indwelling in the human being, in his full humanity and divinity, or something less? A controversy around this erupted, named after Luther's colleague Andreas Osiander, who was judged to teach that only the divine Christ would dwell in the justified. (It is quite probable that behind the controversy is a misunderstanding Osiander's point about the fullness of union. See earlier discussion in *The Formula of Concord*, 1577 in Chapter 3.) Affirming the Chalcedonian teaching of Christ's two natures and their unbreakable unity,[9] Christ was believed to unite himself, in faith, with the human being in the gift of justification.

After naming the dangers of splitting Christ, that is, speculating on Christ's presence being different or distinguishable in his human and divine being, the article draws attention to the fullness of Christ's work for the humanity in justification: "Our righteousness consists in this, that God forgives us our sins by sheer grace, without any works, merit or worthiness of our own" (FC

---

[8]See also Kolb and Wengert, *Book of Concord*, SA 301, 4, 5.
[9]The Council of Chalcedon, 451, added important wording to the creedal decisions about the nature of Trinity by clarifying Christ's human and divine natures being both equal, united but not fused, distinguishable but not separate.

Ep. 3:4). Forgiveness is thus underscored, and the gift nature of this merit of Christ is regarded to benefit humanity. Faith is specified as the instrument: "We believe ... that faith alone is the means and instrument through which we lay hold of Christ" (FC Ep. 3:5). *Formula of Concord* also specifies what is meant with this faith:

> We believe ...that this faith is not a mere knowledge of the stories of Christ. It is instead a gift of God, through which in the Word of the gospel we recognize Christ truly as our redeemer and trust in him, so that solely because of his obedience, by grace, we have the forgiveness of sins, are regarded as godly and righteous by God the Father, and have eternal life. (FC Ep. 3:6)

The bottom line is that the word "justify" means "to absolve" (FC Ep. 3:7). This point is made clear. Also, the *Formula of Concord* article does clarify the ultra-Lutheran position of unmerited gift of grace and names faith as the uniting agent. However, it leaves untreated the question of the depth of God's indwelling in human being via Christ. Formula's clarification had an impact in the future generation's understanding of the dimensions of justification. The emphasis has generally speaking remained on the wording "regarded" righteous with little attention been given to the meaning of "made" righteous. The common words[10] in Lutheran discourse to describe these two dimensions of justification are "forensic" and "effective," paired with other clarifying terms, "alien" and "proper" righteousness. How Luther uses these terms manifests most succinctly in his 1519 sermon-treatise *Two Kinds of Righteousness*.[11]

In short, forensic language illustrates the absolution aspect of justification, the meaning of Christ as a favor for human beings, his merits and sacrifice being considered for the benefit of the human being. The term brings to mind a courtroom and the judgment about freedom or guilt. The term "effective" targets the inner impact of justification in the human beings' existence when Christ enters as a gift. As the word "effective" implies, the question is how the justification transforms the human existence once Christ becomes the subject. Luther uses an expression *happy exchange* to describe this transformative, new, and intimate relationship: Christ takes on all of the burdens and guilt of the human beings who in turn receive all of Christ and thus his holiness. The holiness of Christ gives the human being what Luther names as alien righteousness; forensically speaking, this external grace is

---

[10]Some of the key terms are forensic and effective righteousness, Christ as a favor and a gift, happy exchange, alien and proper righteousness, and *coram deo—coram hominibus*.

[11]See the revised English translation with an introduction and annotations by Else Marie Wiberg Pedersen, in *The Annotated Luther*, Vol. 2, ed. Kirsi Stjerna (Minneapolis: Fortress Press, 2015). This translation is the most inclusive in terms of gender and pronouns, on the basis of the Latin original.

regarded by God to human being's benefit. Effective language reckons the reality of this event and the real presence of Christ and his holiness in the human being whose own, proper righteousness is then percolating. Luther's own words phrase this the best: "The first is alien and infused from outside of oneself. This is the righteousness by which Christ is righteous and by which he justifies others through faith." This alien righteousness, infused, is what justifies and is the reason "a human being can with confidence boast in Christ and say: 'Mine are Christ's living, doing, and speaking, his suffering and dying, mine as much as if I had lived, done, spoken, suffered, and died as he did'" (*Two Kinds of Righteousness*, 13; see also 14, 15).[12]

Yet another perspective from Luther needs to be added to the mix: the *coram deo, coram hominibus* distinction in viewing human existence theologically. Without this, Lutheran view of the dimensions of justification would be quite difficult to comprehend. What is meant with these words is a dual view of human existence: *coram hominibus* pertains to human life in relation to other creatures, and *coram deo* to the divine realm of God and human being's relation to God. In the latter, human beings' alien righteousness effects complete holiness in God's eyes and relation to God. In the former, the human being is a work in progress as holiness is experienced in part and as human being wrestles with one's *own* righteousness. (These terms were discussed in Chapter 2)

To conclude at this point, for the Lutheran justification language to work, one needs to assume an approach to human reality lived in two overlapping dimensions: life as it is experienced here and now and life as it is not yet visible in full to human beings in this lifetime but is equally real. Human daily existence in body and spirit right here and now with the many human and creaturely relations overlaps and coincides with the life

---

[12]See Tuomo Mannermaa's exposition and drawing attention to the reality of Christ's indwelling in the human being through faith, in *Christ Present in Faith* (2005) and *Two Kinds of Love: Martin Luther's Religious World* (Minneapolis: Fortress Press, 2010), both translations from the original Finnish works (see Bibliography). The late Tuomo Mannermaa spearheaded what has become known as the Finnish Luther School that had its start in already existing strong roots in Finnish and Scandinavian research. When Mannermaa participated in 1970s in an ecumenical dialogue between Luther scholars and Russian Orthodox theologians to find connecting points, upon reading Luther's interpretation of Paul's letter to the Galatians, it became evident that Luther's understanding of the reality-changing effect of justification when Christ becomes ontically present in the human being importantly resonates with what is meant with *theosis*, divinization, in Eastern Orthodox—and Patristic—thought. Mannermaa guided several dissertations that continued to elaborate, and critique, these findings. The above-cited works list the first substantial rounds of these publications that have attracted ongoing global interest and debate. For an early example on the conversations, see Carl E. Braaten and Robert W. Jenson, eds., *Union with Christ: The New Finnish Interpretation of Luther (Paperback)* (Grand Rapids, MI: Wm. B. Eerdman, 1998). The perspectives gained from Mannermaa's fresh reading of Luther have opened new avenues for ecumenical conversation and study of Lutheran spirituality, not to mention reconsideration of Luther's core theology.

in the realm of God, the everlasting kind. In these two interwoven realities, human beings know themselves differently; they get a glimpse of how to see themselves through God's eyes. This is where the language of faith, a theological grammar, is needed.

In the former, human beings feel their finitude and know their imperfections; they probably feel more the sinner part than the holy part of their existence. In the latter, as a matter of faith, human beings are assured that they are whole and holy, 100 percent; this reality and this faith rely on the promise of God. The latter trumps the former, takes precedence, in the eyes of God, which is what matters the most: being accepted, beloved, considered worthy and authentic by God the source of life is the foundation for a life that can be characterized with the word "freedom." It is the foundation for life that allows one to wake up to each day with no regrets and freedom to hope beyond what seems humanly impossible. It is the foundation for a life that is not satisfied with one's own security but seeks to ensure freedom for others as well, and this includes all creatures and living beings. Freedom from attempts to prove one's worth, freedom from the damaging sense of condemnation, most of which is precipitated by one's own fear or experience of failures. Freedom to be beloved and to love—freedom like this that starts from faith, another word for which is "trust."

The reality check for Lutheran justification talk comes from the individual experience, which gives proofs for how well this language speaks to the human condition. Even with archaic words that per se or from the first look may have little or no obvious meaning to contemporary people, what is meant to say with them is not outdated. This becomes clearer when considering the word "freedom" in place of or as attached to the word "justification." Freedom—a desire for freedom or lack of freedom—is a ubiquitous human experience, which immediately opens relevant conversations with Luther, to whom freedom was the ultimate concern and really the heart of his justification doctrine.

Lutheran Teaching of Forgiveness, Grace, and Freedom

Given the importance of the topic of justification, and underscoring its roots in Luther's personal experience, even at the risk of repeating, a few more moments will be spent here with Luther and his theological insights, this time explicitly from the perspective of freedom.

Martin Luther's lasting contribution to Christian theology and spirituality was his discovery of the freedom that comes from forgiveness. His life was transformed with the realization that he was free, regardless of how he felt, existentially speaking; internally free (which empowered him to take on some freedoms but did not make him free to act or free from danger politically speaking). Freedom from damning guilt, freedom to forgive himself, freedom to love others—this for him was the fundamental experience that changed his outlook on life, his career, and his faith. The other way to say it: Luther's starting point for his discoveries was his feeling of guilt and bondage to burdens he could not shake off, burdens of emotional and spiritual nature. These experiences could be also identified as depression, anxiety, hopelessness, if wanting to diagnose. Resonating with the journey of Augustine of Hippo[13] centuries ago, Luther left a written record of his *Angst*, pain, and restlessness and his feelings of self-doubt and being surrounded by negative forces in life that led him to a place of hopelessness. He thus experienced hell, spiritually speaking, in that feeling of abyss and existential loneliness, fearing the possibility of being separated from God in this life and beyond. This anxiety manifested physically as well, with various ailments, including migraines and other somatic symptoms and perhaps even panic attacks.[14] Luther's experiences are relatable, even if the words used today to name such suffering would draw more from psychology than theology. The same is true considering the remedies possible.

In his own words, the Word of God was the source of consolation and hope for Luther. Reading critically the Scriptures, taking freedoms from his tradition for his own interpretation, and reading the words of Paul, and the Psalms, in light of his own experience, while scrutinizing the words in the original languages, he had a transformative liberating experience. In his 1545 *Preface to Luther's Latin Works*, he writes: "At this point I felt that I had been completely born again and had entered paradise itself through wide open doors. There a completely different face of the entire Scriptures appeared to me." (Preface, 502).[15] This was a theological discovery with therapeutic implications.

His profound discovery could be rephrased like this: "I have been fooled. I am not doomed. God is not God of wrath but God of love. I am saved without my own doing and regardless of my finitude and failure to meet my standards. I am free. There is hope after all!" And yet there is no promise for Luther or from Luther that all the dark feelings and fears would be gone; no, they remain, but so do hope and the light that are stronger. *Simul iustus et peccator*, that is the mode of human existence, in Luther's experience of grace.

---

[13]Augustine of Hippo, *Confessions*—a theological autobiography that tells one man's story of seeking for a theological grounding for peace.

[14]See Denis R. Janz, "To Hell (and Back) with Luther: The Dialectic of Anfechtung and Faith" in *Encounters with Luther: New Directions for Critical Studies*, eds. Kirsi Stjerna and Brooks Schramm (Louisville, KY: Westminster John Knox, 2016).

[15]*Preface to Luther's Latin Works*, 1545, in *The Annotated Luther*, Vol. 4, ed. Haemig, 2016. See Peter S. D. Krey, "Luther's In-depth Theology and Theological Therapy: Using Self Psychology and a Little Jung" in *Encounters with Luther: New Directions for Critical Studies*, eds. Kirsi Stjerna and Brooks Schramm (Louisville, KY: Westminster John Knox, 2016), for suggestions on Luther's theological insights as "divine therapy."

Luther made sense of his experience with the language that was part of his inherited religion. He named his experience, which most apparently was cognitive before it was about feeling, as that of grace. For Luther, it was a word to describe an external force, impact that had a reality-altering power. Grace is not of human origin but from God who has the power to change the reality of human being, personally and existentially. Grace, for Luther, was what the Scriptures communicate about God, mostly through the story of Christ. Also, grace was for Luther about naming and experiencing the reality change that occurs when human being is connected ontologically with God.

The experience of grace for Luther resulted in a reorientation with his ultimate concerns. It made Luther reconsider who he was as a human being and, before that, who God was and what the nature and premise of the relationship between the two was. Using traditional language of Christian faith, he posed the question as that of salvation. How are human beings saved? Luther did not divert outside the Christian imagination of God wanting human beings' salvation and human beings needing that because of sin. He did, however, offer new ways to think of the impact of sin and how the salvation would take place, under which conditions and with what kind of premises; here he proposed new ways of thinking.[16]

While the Lutheran notion of sin is returned to later, at this point it is simply noted that Lutheran theology assumes the experience of sin for all human beings and in such a devastating way that no human being would be free from it, on their own. With the words "original sin," in continuity with the Catholic teaching, Lutheran position holds that this condition and disposition that makes one a sinner is inherited and unavoidable. Ultimately sin is understood as unfaith, not having a God or not believing in God and therewith looking for love and meaning from all the wrong places, while it manifests in different deeds and desires and dispositions. Luther's thinking clearly resonates with that of Augustine, who associated sin with a wrongly directed love and all the hurt that follows. Salvation language then attends to how the human being can be freed from the fearful existence of feeling condemned and hopeless and detached from God. Lutheran theology draws the solution from Christ and his love for the humanity. With the wording "happy exchange" Luther described what Christ does for the sinner: he takes their sin (and with that fears and despair) and gives them back holiness (and with that hope and confidence). This is what words "grace" and "salvation" communicate: a change that occurs in the human beings' ontological status and existence, and in their

---

[16]On this topic, Dr. Risto Saarinen, a Finnish theologian, has authored an important book on hope, in Finnish, *Oppi toivosta* (Helsinki: Gaudeamus, 2019), offering a philosophically grounded horizon of hope at the time of multiplying crises and negativity. He names fear as the opposite of hope. Theology can address such fears, as well as give substance for reasons to hope.

new orientation with hope, while their "I/me" remains the same. *Simul iustus et peccator* is the idiosyncratic Lutheran characterization of this existence.

Language of grace is a language to describe this complexity: that a human being is loved as one is, even and particularly as a sinner. Today the more fitting words may be hope and sense of worth and human integrity. With all the "false" and distorted messages of oneself that human beings receive from the moment of their birth and that make them doubt their own holiness and worth, grace language offers a different reality check, moving attention to the source of life, God. Grace language counters human reasoning and logic about worth, merit, and causality. Grace speaks of the reality of divine love that sustains and the source of which is *extra nos*, in God's doing and, most specifically, in Christ's doing for the sake of human beings. Grace sets the stage for the most powerful experience in human life, freedom, just as an individual's experience of grace is the utmost experience of freedom. At the center of this grace language and freedom idea in Lutheran grammar is Christ.

As already underscored above, Luther's and thus Lutheran language of freedom, forgiveness, holiness, and grace circle all around the person and meaning of Jesus Christ. The syntax of grace is built around the fundamental truth Luther experienced to be true for him: that Jesus Christ has died for him, lives on, and has given all God's goodness and holiness to the human being who is thus beloved beyond words. Without Jesus, Luther would not see a way for human beings to experience holiness, or wholeness, and, to begin with, forgiveness. His view of God as just and merciful entailed that a retribution was needed for human beings to be all right in relation to God. Employing the centuries-old Christian salvation language, with a Christ-centered twist, Luther explained how God becomes present in human life, even in oneness with the human being, because of Christ's person and work. Faith is the language to express this oneness or union.

In Christ's living, doing, dying, and resurrecting, human being participates in the holiest of the holy: in the life of God through faith. Luther's theology of grace and salvation, holiness and freedom is thus fundamentally Christ-centric with a particular emphasis. Luther's underscoring of Christ's impact goes hand in hand with his consistent arguments against any other ways that could lead one to God and into a restored relationship with God, in other words, against any idea of humans on their own volition to merit their worth as human beings. This has become the distinctive and a definite Lutheran emphasis. At the bottom of these convictions is the basic Christian belief of God's omnipresence and that there is no life apart from God. Any disillusionment of the opposite would qualify as a "lie" and a distortion of reality; Christ came to correct this distortion of reality. For Luther, Christian proclamation of Jesus is the ongoing communication of this correction, the point being the worth and holiness of every human being.

Law—Gospel Hermeneutics and the *Scripture Alone* Principles

Lutheran hermeneutics and convictions regarding the sources and authority in proclaiming the message of Christ can be identified as follows: First, that the Scriptures speak to human beings with two voices, as that of the law and that of the gospel, and both are needed throughout one's life. Second, the insistence that the primary and ultimate authority in faith matters draws from the *sola scriptura* principle.

The law-gospel perspective sets the stage and extends an invitation for individuals to engage the Scriptures in their daily lives.[17] As the human beings live with the impact of sin even when justified and freed, these sinner-saints need a constant flow of divine communication to maintain the grace-God-grounded orientation with hope. One is never free from the need to hear the admonishment and the guidance of what is called the law. Especially in the realm of one's so-called proper righteousness, this feeding with the Word's counsel is instrumental. At the same time, because of the burdens of sin and human beings' chronic failure to heed to the divine guidance, a constant dose of gospel is needed even more.

Lutheran theology distinctly honors the tension and necessity to uphold both aspects of the Word and the law-gospel dialectic, because of the overlapping existence of human being as a sinner and as a saint. This distinction is important for the sake of effective proclamation of the Word. In his *How Christians Should Consider Moses* (1525)[18] Luther names a conflict between the two "sermons" God had delivered the people:

> The first sermon and doctrine is the law of God; the second is the gospel. The two do not agree. Therefore one must have a good understanding of them, such that one knows how to distinguish between the two and knows what law is and what the gospel is. The law commands and demands of us what we are to do. (*Moses*, 133, also 134)

Luther's point is clear that it is pivotal to distinguish between the word of the law and the word of the gospel, namely, to remember that there are "two kinds of doctrines and two kinds of works: those of God and those of human beings." There is a great relief in putting these two communications in perspective and starting with the proper foundation, the gospel of Jesus, "For the gospel teaches solely what has been given to us by God, and not—as in the case of the law—what we are to do and give to God" (*Moses*, 134).

---

[17]See Stjerna, "Law and Gospel," in *Martin Luther in Context*, ed. David Whitford (Cambridge: Cambridge University Press, 2018).
[18]*How Christians Should Regard Moses*, ed. Brooks Schramm, in *The Annotated Luther*, Vol. 2, ed. Kirsi Stjerna (Minneapolis: Fortress Press, 2015).

In Luther's own words (particularly in his 1522 *What to Look for in the Gospels*, 1522):[19] the one and only gospel is about the meaning of Jesus Christ for the humankind (*Gospels*, 28). "Thus the gospel is and should be nothing else than a chronicle, a story, a narrative about Christ, telling who he is, what he did, said, and suffered". Luther continues, "For at its briefest, the gospel is a discourse about Christ, that he is the Son of God and became a human being for us, that he died and was raised, that he has been established as a lord over all things" (*Gospels*, 28–9). Here Luther identifies the "right foundation" for reading the Scriptures (ibid., 30). For a "proper grasp of the gospel, that is, of the overwhelming goodness of God," one needs to embrace the chief article of faith: "The chief article and foundation of the gospel is that before you take Christ as an example, you accept and recognize him as a gift, as a present that God has given you and that is your own" (ibid., 30). When one then lives with this foundation, and when one proclaims the gospel, it is all about Christ and his full and real presence for the human life. "For the preaching of the gospel is nothing else than Christ coming to us, or we being brought to him" (ibid., 32). The Gospel is about justification and freedom.

The other side of the coin, due to human beings' *simul-simul* condition, as well as the expectations for the results of the justifying work of the gospel to realize in life, is that a regular dose of law is needed. This is crucial for nurturing the so-called proper or human being's own righteousness, which, Luther clarifies, works not alone but "with that first and alien righteousness. This is that manner of life spent profitably in good works" (*Two Kinds of Righteousness*, 16). The second righteousness results from the first and follows the example of Christ in whose image human beings are made to conform and to "set the same example for our neighbors" (ibid., 16–17). That is the ideal and the impossible. The law reminds of this reality.

In conclusion, on the basis of how Luther understood the human condition as a saint-sinner and how he saw Christ at the center for human hope, he deemed it crucial to hold gospel and law both as relevant truths human being needed from the Word, which, in his experience and conviction, spoke to the realities of human life with an affirmation of hope that came from the Christ story. The spiritual insights with the law-gospel dialectic are endless, as the framework allows tension and surprises in the reading of the Scriptures in the midst of personal lives and with the trust that God's interest and involvement in human life is all-encompassing. Importantly, this reading activity belongs to all.

In this regard, the most famous reformation slogan, *sola scriptura*, was not about theory or meant just for school theologians' speculations. Rather it radically called everyone to the task of grabbling with the Scriptures. Freeing the interpretation thus from the mechanisms that had kept the Scriptures

---

[19] *A Brief Instruction on What to Look for and Expect in the Gospels*, ed. Wanda Deifelt, in *The Annotated Luther*, Vol. 2, ed. Kirsi Stjerna, 2015.

from the hands of the people, laity (in itself a problematic word expressing hierarchy and privilege), the reformation principles invited a whole spectrum of human experiences and voices to illuminate the meaning of the Word.

The topic of *sola scriptura*, already introduced earlier (Chapters 3 and 2), merits a few more reflections at this point. Luther's bold insistence that the authoritative source in faith matters is the Scriptures was radical in his context. In the Catholic tradition, the Scriptures were and are interpreted within and by the tradition, by those duly trained and authorized, and all this under the teaching authority and auspices of the highest bishop—the pope. One of the radical departures from the tradition with the reformation was exactly that: to relativize tradition and place it under the authority of the Scriptures that was believed to contain the immutable and living Word of God.

This could be understood from different angles. First, the Word of God is alive and to be found by readers of the Scriptures, all and any of them. Second, the Word of God can be heard by any reader, not just those with an authority within the tradition. Third, the Word of God deserves revisiting, careful critical reading, and listening, in order for God's Word to speak anew to new situations. Tradition is the movement and the bodies engaged in this rereading and reinterpretation. Tradition has only the authority human beings choose to afford it, and this authority is not immutable; it fluctuates. Tradition, which includes doctrines of faith, rules for practice of faith, and regulations about "who does what" and where the authority lies in all of this – is a human endeavor and never in the same category as the living Word of God.

For Luther, a renegade monk proposing new ways of reading the Scriptures and challenging the church's core teachings, drew his authority from this conclusion: the ultimate authority in faith matters belongs to God and God's Word. Standing against his tradition, in many ways, Luther radically proclaimed that his right to critique his tradition and to propose new ways of thinking about faith matters arose exactly from the source, the Word of God, that seeks to speak to people, again and again, and in new ways.

The primacy of the Scriptures over any other source or authority does not render human tradition irrelevant. The main argument is this: tradition, for Luther and for Lutheran theology, can never have the status of infallibility. Tradition is about people interpreting and expressing faith that leads back to the Scriptures but is not equivalent to them; it is about human decisions and constructions. Whereas the Word of God is immutable in its divine origin, tradition changes with people as its carriers and communicators. No human tradition as a human construction can be deemed as infallible or universally and timelessly normative. Traditions change through times and with human beings who create and determine the parameters of the traditions. In theological world, tradition means the ways in which the faith has been interpreted and exercised and with what guidelines and structures, all of which can and should change over time if the tradition is to serve people in new times.

Because the Lutheran tradition does not have the papal office or a similarly authoritative teaching office, or the reverence of the historical teachings and structures as a binding tradition, the Scriptures are at the center of attention. With the emphasis on the living God working and speaking through the living Word, Lutheran hermeneutics do not in any way condone biblical literalism. There is no assumption of the Word unambiguously and inerrantly speaking straightforward unchanging truths to a reader, regardless of time, place, and situation. Instead, critical wrestling is to be expected. The Scriptures contain the Word of God for the reader but it needs to be searched, through critical unpeeling and deliberation.

How would this principle of *sola scriptura* function today, or does it? One way would be to consider it a reminder of the fallibility and limitations and expiration dates of human conventions, while stating a hope-filled belief and trust that God has indeed revealed and keeps revealing divine truths to human beings through the human words and stories recorded in the Scriptures that are held dear by religious communities who find them life-giving. Another consideration is the emancipating power of inviting every human being to read the Scriptures, with the recognition that no person on this earth possesses or holds all the divine knowledge that is embedded in the Scriptures and that they are meant for all to read and engage with. The *sola scriptura* principle is thus a useful statement of the importance of inclusion of all those interested in the mysteries of God and that each person has the same amount of authority and access with the divine truths, the living Word speaking to a person directly.[20]

The idea that the Scriptures belong to all was one of the original reformation calls. Martin Luther and his peers were frustrated that people did not have access to or did not know the Bible. How could one be a Christian without reading and loving the Bible? They proclaimed from the pulpit and classrooms about the equal nature and needs of all Christians and took active measures to equip all Christians to read the Bible. Toward this goal, the reformers proceeded to translate the Bible into vernacular languages, as well as launching public education systems to equip people to read, clergy and laity, men and women.[21] For women, as mentioned above, it took some time to have full access to the Scriptures and, definitely, to

---

[20]See, e.g., Surekha Nelavala, "Martin Luther's Concept of Sola Scriptura and Its Impact on the Masses: A Dalit Model for Praxis-Nexus," in *Encounters with Luther*, eds. Kirsi Stjerna and Brooks Schramm, 2016.

[21]The example of Finland is worth mentioning: as the Wittenberg-influenced reforms were brought to Finland by students, most notably Mikael Agricola, the first steps included formalizing a written native language before translating the Bible into Finnish and teaching people to read with ABC books. The reformation theology became legislated and steered the vision and practical steps to provide welfare and education across the board. Today Finland is known for its egalitarian legislation, women's strong involvement in political leadership, publically funded stellar higher education, and tax-funded health care; the roots go back to the reformation principles.

the task of interpretation and proclamation. Taking a global look at the situation of women today in this regard, it is evident that Lutherans have much to do to abolish the many still existing gender barriers. The original inclusive and emancipating Lutheran vision is still fermenting, with much potential for the contemporary world where equality in many ways is still a work in progress. In theory and in its spirit, the *sola scriptura* idea has had legs and continues to energize people to engage the Scriptures first hand.

I. Central Topics and Learning Goals

1. Lutheran perspectives on justification and the rationale and framework for the doctrine of justification.
2. The meaning of being *made* and *regarded* righteous.
3. Justification as language of salvation and freedom.
4. Keywords of the Lutheran faith grammar.

II. Questions for Review, Discussion, and Further Reflection

1. How does justification speak of forgiveness and holiness?
2. How can Luther's teaching of freedom be employed internally, in personal life? How about externally, in human relations and in the world?
3. Are there other ways to speak of what happens in justification without atonement language?
4. How do Scripture-alone principle and law-gospel dialectic serve as a starting point for inclusive and "just" or justice-oriented theologies?

III. Keywords

Alien and proper righteousness; *Christus solus*—Christ alone; *coram deo—coram hominibus*; *extra nos*—outside of us; faith; forensic and effective righteousness; forgiveness; freedom from and freedom to; happy exchange; holiness; justification and justice; justification by faith, by grace, by Christ; law and gospel; *sola fides*—faith alone; *sola gracia*—grace alone.

IV. Readings with the Chapter

AC 4. (Skim Ap. 4.) AC 6, 16, 20. (Skim Ap. 6, 16, 20.)
LC, Creed's third article. LC, Ten Commandments, 4–10.
Also FC III, IV. FC IV–VI. SA Part II art. 1, Part III art. 13, 4.

PART THREE

Lutheran Faith Language—An Orientation

5

God-talk—Ecumenically with the Creeds and with Contemporary Questions

One God

The Ecumenical Foundation

The fundamental Christian belief is that God exists and that there is only one God. Christian religion is zealously monotheistic. The oneness of God has been defended and extrapolated with a Trinitarian doctrine, which has given the tone for Christian liturgical speech on the divinity. The grammar for God-talk has been set in the ecumenical Creeds of the early church. Lutherans root their discourse on God with these Creeds that call to confess, "'I believe in God the Father, who created me; I believe in God the Son, who has redeemed me; I believe in the Holy Spirit, who makes me holy.' One

In the following, central Lutheran arguments are articulated on the basis of what was considered important in the *Augsburg Confession*, without attending to all the topics considered energizing at the time of writing the document. Occasionally new questions are introduced to consider with the confessions in their contemporary uses. Unless otherwise stated, the translation from the Latin text of the *Augsburg Confession* is used from Kolb and Wengert, eds., *Book of Concord*. For the *Large Catechism* and for the *Smalcald Articles* references, *The Annotated Luther* (TAL), Vol. 2 is used.
Read AC 1. (Skim Ap. 1.); LC, Explanation of the Creed in full. Recommended: LC, 1–3 Commandments; LC, Lord's Prayer, 1–3 petitions; SA Part I. The Ecumenical Creeds.

God and one faith, but three persons, and therefore also three articles or confessions." (LC 353).[1,2]

Since the sixteenth-century turmoil, Lutherans have confessed their basic belief in God in formal unison with the Trinitarian monotheism articulated in the Creeds: belief in one God, known by human beings in three distinct persons, and Christ at the center of this knowing, as the revelation to the humanity about who God is in relation to human beings and what all God does for the humanity.

The *Augsburg Confession* starts with an affirmation of the faith in the Trinity: that God has been revealed to humanity and is known in one divine essence and three equal persons (AC 1:1–3). Herewith it makes the decisive stance for Lutherans'—or evangelicals', as they were known at the time of writing the document—position within the Christendom:

> The churches among us teach with complete unanimity that the decree of the Council of Nicea concerning the unity of the divine essence and concerning the three persons is true and is to be believed without any doubt. That is to say, there is one divine essence which is called God and is God: eternal, incorporeal, indivisible, of immeasurable power, wisdom, and goodness, the creator and preserver of all things, visible and invisible. Yet, there are three persons, coeternal and of the same essence and power: the Father, the Son, and the Holy Spirit. And the term "person" is used for that meaning which the church's authors used in this case: to signify not a part or a quality in another but that which subsists in itself. (AC 1:1–4)

It is not a coincidence that the *Augsburg Confession* starts with the article about one and Triune God, given the rationale for the confession to prove the evangelicals' Catholicity on matters that pertained to orthodoxy versus heresy. It was a matter of survival too. In the Middle Ages, not believing in the Trinity or worshipping more than one God could have led to a capital punishment. The doctrine of Trinity was a litmus test for orthodoxy.

In the *Augsburg Confession*'s first article, Lutherans make an explicit break with the groups whom they consider wrong and either jeopardizing the principle of oneness within God and the unity and equality of the three persons, or compromising the divinity of Christ and the Holy Spirit. In other words, Lutherans reject any forms of anti-Trinitarianism as erroneous and also any attempts to overly humanize Christ and thereby denying his full divinity, or vice versa (AC 1:5–6). To amplify their affirmation of faith in one God who is omnipotent and in Christ's full humanity as well as divinity, several other orientations are rejected (such as Manicheans, Valentinians,

---

[1]The wording "Father" is mostly retained when quoting the Creeds and the reformation texts, aknowledging the problems pertaining to the traditional exclusive Father-language or He-language about God.

[2]See also Kolb and Wengert, eds., *The Book of Concord*, LC 432:7–8.

Arians, Eunomians, Mohemmedans, Samosatenians).[3] With this standing, early Lutherans revisited the early church's Christological debates that led to the writing of the ecumenical Creeds initially.

Some observations could be made with the first statement in the *Augsburg Confession* being about God and particularly about the oneness of God and the Trinitarian doctrine. It reminds the reader of the reality that the notion of one God in three persons is not a particularly Lutheran doctrine and that Lutherans do not have a distinctively Lutheran interpretation of it. Just as in the reformation century, this is the fundamental orientation that rather unites with than separates from other Christians who affirm the same creedal teachings. In terms of other religions, whereas with their monotheism Lutheran Christians line up with the Jews and Muslims who also believe in one God only, the Trinitarian doctrine sets Christians and thus Lutherans apart; so does the heart of this doctrine, the beliefs about the second person of the Trinity, Jesus Christ. This reality of the differences in the ways the divinity is understood and spoken about can be taken as an entry point to appreciate different orientations in faith, such as Lutheran, one among many, rather than as ways to prove one's own orthodoxy and the other's heresy, as was the motivation in the sixteenth century.

The Nonnegotiables and Contemporary Questions

The reformers concluded that the Trinitarian language of God has been already settled and there would be no need to discuss that foundation. This shows, for instance, in the minimal space devoted to the topic in the *Augsburg Confession*. The article one (AC 1) with its two paragraphs is followed first by an article on sin (AC 2) before returning to the God-issue with article three "Concerning the Son of God" (AC 3:1–6), also stunningly short given the amount of Christological debate leading up to the Creeds. Similarly curious is the absence of a separate article on the Holy Spirit, the work of whom is addressed only briefly in junction with the work of Christ in article three and intermittently. More on the Holy Spirit is found in Luther's *Catechisms* (later more).

Luther gives a synopsis statement of the unshakeable fundamental stance of Lutherans in harmony with that of the Catholic and the Eastern Orthodox Christians and the mainstream fellow Protestants. In the first article of Part I in *Smalcald Articles*, Luther outlines the "lofty articles of the divine Majesty" and the foundation on which Christian proclamation about Christ stands:

---

[3]For definitions of these terms and movements, see Kolb and Wengert, *Book of Concord*, 36, footnotes 30–6.

That Father, Son, and Holy Spirit, three distinct persons in one divine essence and nature, is one God, who created heaven and earth, etc. That the Father was begotten by no one, the Son was begotten by the Father, and the Holy Spirit proceeds from the Father and the Son. That neither the Father nor the Holy Spirit, but the Son, became a human being. That the Son became a human being in this way: he was conceived by the Holy Spirit without male participation and was born of the pure, holy Virgin Mary. After that, he suffered, died, was buried, descended into hell, rose from the dead, ascended into heaven, is seated at the right hand of God. In the future he will come to judge the living and the dead, etc., as the Apostles' and the Athanasian Creeds and the common children's catechism teach.

Luther reiterates that "[t]hese articles are not matters of dispute or conflict, for both sides [Catholic and Protestant] confess them. Therefore it is not necessary to deal with them at greater length now" (SA 4278).[4]

As Luther underscores it, these were nonnegotiables for the Lutherans of this time. The same is not necessarily the case for contemporary Lutherans, though, who live in a world where the Creeds do no hold such an authority and where orthodoxy is not a matter of life and death and where people are needing to reconsider the language they use about God or their belief in God. Especially in interfaith company and expanding conversations between different faith orientations, the Trinitarian language if rigidly conceived, and especially when presenting a predominantly male-image of the divine, can hardly be taken as the end of conversation and imagination. It is helpful to note that the philosophical and linguistic arguments for the essence-talk of the three-in-one may have made better sense in the fourth-century Greek discussions, from where the terminology with the Trinity is inherited and then fixed with the Creeds and consequently (with better or worse success) translated into other languages. Bringing the ancient philosophically rooted terms to serve contemporary religious language requires revisiting the original rationales and deliberating on how the arguments and language can function today. And last, most obviously, the traditional Father-language and He-pronouns used in the ancient Trinitarian formulations and their translations present a fruitful challenge to, first, recognize the power of naming and language in human imaginations of God, and second, open the door to new human words and vistas about the Divine who, ultimately, escapes human constructions.

Considering the history behind the wording of the Trinitarian doctrine is helpful. Emphasis on the personal relating of God to the humanity, as a Father, and the interpersonal relations within the Trinity—named as Father and the Son and the Spirit—was distinctive of Christian faith in the ancient world

---

[4]See also Kolb and Wengert, *The Book of Concord*, SA Part I art. 1.

where deities were not perceived in such a way. The personal language holds together the otherwise superbly abstract view of the transcendent divine who is, through the persons of Trinity, believed to be also tangibly present in human life. The Father-Son language has underscored this, particularly functioning as a liturgical language and a way of communicating about God that invites a more personal relation than if God was addressed as a higher power, deity, or with other impersonal terms. That said, the way Father-Son language about God has developed and has been used in the Christian church in tandem with male-centric ideologies and practices, presents a reforming challenge today: how to honor the personal language about God and draw from the ancient vision and faith expressed in the Creeds, but at the same time be free to imagine and experience God in other ways and with other words? How to avoid mis-association of a gendered God and, with that, of a hierarchy between human experiences, or further yet, how to free the imagination of God from such binary vistas?

Against eloquent dismissals of such concerns, even a child could attest to this: consistently calling God with male pronouns and labels can imprint in one's heart an image of a male God. The ramifications of that can be understood already at the young age. Experimenting with the language of mother, sister, friend, or lover—as proposed by many a feminist theologian—can in powerful ways invigorate God-talk and keep it relevant.[5] Also less personal names for God may be yearned for, especially when the words "mother" and "father" are associated with hurtful experiences with mothers and fathers after whom one might not want to imagine God. In today's religious discourse, there is an invitation to imagine more broadly and to listen to the varied human experiences, while mirroring that with the wisdom of the Scriptures, with an ongoing reinterpretation.

To conclude here, for Lutheran theological language, the Creeds continue to be relevant as the foundation and a sparkle for theological imaginations about God. Honoring the fact that the Creeds have traveled with Christians over the centuries while reckoning with the fact that they do come from another era, perhaps the best way to deal with the gaps experienced with their expression of God and contemporary experience and language is to keep in mind the Creeds' primary contribution, understood in their context. It cannot be underscored enough the eloquence, and success, with which the Creeds have defended and facilitated Christians' belief in the reality of one God, and not just any God but one who cares about humanity personally and intimately, to the point of uniting with the humanity in flesh. In the context of the formative years when Christians' God was considered

---

[5]See, e.g., Sally McFague, *Models of God. Theology for an Ecological, Nuclear Age* (Minneapolis: Fortress Press, 1987); and Elizabeth A. Johnson, *She Who Is. The Mystery of God in Feminist Theological Discourse* (Chestnut Ridge, NY: Crossroads Publishing, 2002).

just one among many, convincing philosophically geared reality talk was needed about the depth and parameters of existence, human and divine, in a specifically Christian language fed by and interpreting the Christian sources. Uniquely, Christians' creedal language about the divinity points to an essence and existence beyond human experience, while also pointing to the personal nature of this God who relates to human beings in person and via Word.

Speaking of existence beyond humans, in light of the current ecological crisis and the vulnerable status of the creation, it is vital to deliberately discern and name God's presence and action and will vis-à-vis the larger picture of creation. In light of the new evidence pertaining to the reality of beings that exist, a variety of ways to name and address God can emerge, not to replace the creedal personal language but to enhance and expand it.[6] God's omnipresence is communally experienced in the life of faith communities, the church, where the Creeds continue to liturgically spur believers' imagination about who God is for them and how to best call this God that, in Lutheran conviction, is personally and intimately present in human life. The labels "Father" and "Creator" and "the Spirit", when freed from gender-dividing conventions, and perhaps best when approached with a trans perspective (nonbinary, not male, not female), could lead to further revelations about the Divinity and how the Divinity can be known by human beings. At the center of this seeking stands the Christian teaching about Jesus.

Christian communities were built on the basis of the Jesus tradition: the early Christians' experience and witness of the Jesus of Nazareth. Whereas the historicity of Jesus of Nazareth was clear, with sources religious and secular to prove it, the early church experienced serious division in the religious opinions about who this Jesus was—human or divine, or both? Relatedly, the pivotal question for the Christians was the meaning of Jesus Christ: what was his point, what was the purpose of his life and death, what did Jesus tell humanity about God, first, and second, about the fate of human beings in the larger scheme of things?[7]

The doctrine of Trinity evolved as a result of debates around this kind of questions. God's oneness and Triune nature became articulated as a consequence of questions about Jesus. Jesus was the watershed; the birth of Christianity can be timed in his birth. Already during his lifetime but

---

[6]The Creeds express a belief in the fundamental involvement of the divine in the life forms on earth and in the cosmos, as well as in human beings' life. Most recently, the Scandinavian theologians have returned attention to creation theology from multiple perspectives. See, e.g., Elisabeth Gerle and Michael Schelde, eds., *American Perspectives Meet Scandinavian Creation Theology* (Aarhus: Church of Sweden Research Department, The Grundtvig Study Center, Aarhus University, 2019).
[7]See Paula Fredriksen, *From Jesus to Christ: The Origins of the New Testament Images of Christ*, 2nd ed. (Yale: Yale University Press, 2000).

definitely after his crucifixion and the reports of his resurrection, coined with his promise of return and a cosmic change of things, a new view of God emerged: of God who wants to be intimately involved in human affairs to the extent of becoming human, living as human, and dying as human, and foreshadowing a resurrection from death to also human beings after him. The Creeds express the culmination of these deliberations and the beginning of what is called Christology—and, relatedly, Soteriology.[8]

Christ at the Center

Fundamentals on Jesus—Scriptural Evidence

Lutheran confessions and theology rest on what the early church theologians collectively concluded about Jesus. The articles pertaining specifically to Jesus are sparse and thin in the Lutheran sources that explicitly apply the grammar of the ecumenical Creeds. Contemporary readers can benefit from modern research and discoveries about the historical Jesus.

On the basis of the written sources of the earliest Christians, the following general narrative portrait of Jesus emerges:[9] he was born into the Jewish family of Mary and Joseph in Bethlehem, near Jerusalem, and he was subsequently raised in the Galilean village of Nazareth. After he was baptized by John the Baptist (the son of his mother's cousin, Elizabeth), he gathered twelve men as his closest disciplines. Primarily around the Sea of Galilee, he began teaching, healing, working miracles, attracting crowds, and manifesting an interest in the marginalized and outcast. A number of women are often mentioned as among his most loyal followers. Though some considered him a political leader, it appears that he shunned that cloak, presenting himself as a spiritual leader, teacher, and bold interpreter of Israel's sacred texts and emphasizing a radical message of divine love that would characterize the Reign of God that was soon to come. His Golden Command crystallizes his main teaching concerning God's law: "In everything do to others as you would have them do to you; for this is the law and the prophets" (Matthew 7:12). His famous "Beatitudes"[10] promised to turn the world upside down by elevating the meek and the lowly, thereby stripping the mighty of their privilege (Matthew 5:5-12):

---

[8]Christology refers to the dimension of theology that focuses on the person, life, activities, and meaning of Jesus Christ. Soteriology refers to the doctrine of salvation, a topic with different approaches in different religions.

[9]See, e.g., Heikki Räisänen, *The Rise of Christian Beliefs: The Thought World of Early Christian* (Minneapolis: Fortress Press, 2009).

[10]Matthew 7:12 and 5:5–12 quoted from the NRSV.

5:1   When Jesus saw the crowds, he went up the mountain; and after he
      sat down, his disciples came to him.
2   Then he began to speak, and taught them, saying:
3   Blessed are the poor in spirit, for theirs is the kingdom of heaven.
4   Blessed are those who mourn, for they will be comforted.
5   Blessed are the meek, for they will inherit the earth.
6   Blessed are those who hunger and thirst for righteousness, for they
      will be filled.
7   Blessed are the merciful, for they will receive mercy.
8   Blessed are the pure in heart, for they will see God.
9   Blessed are the peacemakers, for they will be called children of
      God.
10   Blessed are those who are persecuted for righteousness' sake, for
      theirs is the kingdom of heaven.
11   Blessed are you when people revile you and persecute you and utter
      all kinds of evil against you falsely on my account.
12   Rejoice and be glad, for your reward is great in heaven, for in the
      same way they persecuted the prophets who were before you.

From Galilee (at the age of *c.* 30), Jesus traveled to Jerusalem, entered
the city on the day Christians remember as Palm Sunday, and taught at the
Temple.

After a Passover meal with his disciples and a time of prayer in the
Garden of Gethsemane (on the Mount of Olives), he was betrayed by one
of his own, Judas, and subsequently denied by his first disciple, Peter. After
being condemned to death by the Roman procurator Pontus Pilate, he
was executed by crucifixion and then buried in a nearby tomb. All four
of the canonical gospels mention women followers as being present at the
crucifixion and its aftermath. Since the Sabbath was beginning, the tomb
was left unattended until early on Sunday morning, when some of those
women, among whom were Mary of Magdala, Mary Salome, and Mary of
Clopas, found the tomb empty; they became the first messengers of the heart
of the Christian proclamation—the message of Jesus's resurrection.

On this witness and memory a Christian church was founded: Jesus's
followers continued to share their experiences and knowledge of Jesus, and
some began to baptize new members into their community and to celebrate
the Last Supper in the memory of Jesus who was believed, and experienced,
to continue to live and who promised to include his followers in eternal
life. He was going to come back and claim his own, when the time was
right. The early Christian church was founded on this sense of in-between
time: between the announcement of the coming of the reign of God and the
return of Jesus (his *parousia*). Although this *parousia* did not manifest as
the earliest Christians expected, expectation of Christ's return has remained
one of the pillars of Christian faith, essentially tied to Christian hopes for
resurrection and eternal life.

The New Testament canon—the official list of sacred Christian writings—was the end result of decades of debate and compromise among bishops and teachers of the emerging churches in the second and third centuries, who had to decide how best to preserve the record and message of Jesus and his movement and which writings would be included and which would be excluded. The first to propose a New Testament canon was the mid-second-century teacher, Marcion of Sinope, who produced a short list of books, containing an abbreviated version of the Gospel of Luke and abbreviated versions of Paul's letters. In addition, Marcion's intention was that this list of Christian books (and in the form in which he presented them) would constitute the sole Christian scripture, thus displacing or eliminating the Jewish sacred scripture altogether for Christians. Marcion's intentions would not win the day, as the church ultimately decided on a two-volume Bible, containing the Jewish sacred scripture in its Greek translation (the "Old Testament") and the twenty-seven-book Christian collection (the "New Testament").

Whereas the Scriptures have served as the foundation for Christians' teaching of Jesus, the Creeds became an important tool for the teaching of the theological meaning of Christ. The wording of the ecumenical Creeds gives a condensed version of the information on Jesus cherished by early Christians. What is included in the Creeds' statements is considered the core truth, the non-negotiable, on the basis of which Christians are called to interpret the meaning and ongoing presence of Jesus Christ in the lives of individuals and faith communities.

True God, True Human—The Chalcedonian Definition

The third article in *Augsburg Confession* concerns explicitly the Son of God. It gives a synopsis of Jesus's path to humanity, the reality of his humanity and death, his unique position as the true God who reigns the universe and will return as the final judge. The statements draw directly from the Creeds. The location of the article signals what is the utmost concern with Lutheran teachings of Christ. The article about Christ (AC 3) comes immediately after the article two (AC 2) that addresses the immensity of human sin and right before the pivotal article four on how human beings are made right with God. Article three on Christ, then, has a clear soteriological point to make: first, what all is necessary vis-à-vis Christ in order for the human beings to have hope, and second, what can—and need—be known about the Trinitarian God in the face of human fallibility and finitude.

Following the wording of the Creed, the article starts with the question of Christ's nature: "Likewise, they teach that the Word, that is, the Son of God, took upon himself human nature in the womb of the blessed Virgin Mary so that there might be two natures, divine and human, inseparably conjoined in unity of one person, one Christ, truly God and truly human being" (AC 3:1–2). In few short words, Melanchthon's *Apology* simply restates the agreement with the "opponents"

> that there are two natures in Christ, namely, that the human nature was assumed by the Word into the unity of his person; and that this same Christ suffered and died in order to reconcile the Father to us and rose from the dead in order to rule over, justify, and sanctify believers, etc., according to the apostles' Creed and Nicene Creed. (Ap. 3:1)

(It may be noted that he does address the role of Mary in the conception of Jesus.)

A central statement is the affirmation of Christ's inseparable two natures, divine and human. Christ is one person, a true God and a true human. As both human and divine, Christ has journeyed from a human birth, from a woman, through suffering to death, until resurrection and continues living in the unique dual realm of Christ, as only God can. Christ's two natures are necessary for Christ's life, death, and resurrection to matter for the human beings.[11] In his journey in life, death, and resurrection, Christ has immersed himself in the existence of human beings, in most mysterious and real ways. Thus, "we believe, teach, and confess that God is a human being and a human being is God."[12] The article continues to paraphrase the creedal statements about Christ's birth from Mary, his suffering, death and burial, his descending into hell before resurrection and ascending to heaven, and promising his return to judge the living and the dead. Before that, the Creed signals, Christ will "reign forever and have dominion over all creatures" (AC 3:1-6).

Two considerations. First is the question of God-knowledge: what human beings know about God in terms of God's disposition toward human beings and God's will for human beings' fate, in the deepest sense, is based on the story of Jesus. Jesus has come, lived, died, and reappeared to make a point to human beings, who were and are like him; he has always been God, has come from God, and would bring human beings with him to God as well.

---

[11]Reaffirming the Chalcedonian teaching (FC VIII:4–5), confessions argue for Christ's presence for human beings in the sacraments. Christ's divine and human natures, each retaining its own characteristics, are united while not blended together (ibid., 5–6). The divinity of the omnipresent Christ is characterized with words "almighty," "eternal," "infinite." As a human being who surrendered to suffering and dying, Christ is a bodily creature, flesh and blood, finite and circumscribed (ibid., 7–8). On the cross, it was "no mere human who suffered, died, and was buried ... ascended into heaven" (ibid., 13). His dual nature makes Christ's real presence in the communion possible (ibid., 17–8). "Christ is and remains for all eternity God and human being in one inseparable person, which is the highest mystery after the mystery of the Holy Trinity ... In this mystery lie our only comfort, life, and salvation" (ibid., 18).

[12]"daß Gott Mensch und Mensch Gott sei" (FC Ep. VIII:10, footnote 60, in Kolb and Wengert, *The Book of Concord*).

Jesus makes God's presence in human life personal and real. Another way to say this is that in Jesus God has been revealed, and God's immanence in the midst of human life is demonstrated in flesh and blood.

Second is the question of why. Christ's life and death are believed to be necessary for the human beings to have the chance of redemption and life eternal as God has designed it. Without Christ, human beings would be helpless in the face of death. Without Christ, human beings would surrender to death and all that destroys life. In the face of the immense dangers and troubles humanity encounters, as mortal humans, Christ offers hope beyond hope and a lifeline to God the source of life. The statements about Christ's two natures explain how Christ can do this and how Christ is what is called in Christian terminology the savior or the redeemer.

Christ, the Spirit, and the Consummation of God's Work

The end of the article notes what Christ does: "He will sanctify those who believe in him by sending into their hearts the Holy Spirit, who will rule, console, and make them alive, and defend them against the devil and the power of sin" (AC 3:5–6). And, "The same Christ will publicly 'return to judge the living and the dead'" (AC 3:6). Christ's divinity makes this possible; Christ is God who connects human beings with the Trinity; this happens by sending of the Holy Spirit. Not just a dose of God's spirit is sent but rather the statement promises that, because of Christ's doing, God enters the human life in the Holy Spirit. The presence is not ornamental or a vague blessing. Rather, it armors one against the fundamental enemies of life. It would seem most proper for the following article to focus on the Holy Spirit but, as noted earlier, there is no such separate article. The Holy Spirit's role is returned to later in the confession when explicating the rationale of the Christian community of faith charged to proclaim the promise of Christ.

The absence of a separate article on the Holy Spirit in the *Augsburg Confession* could be speculated like this: article one already said enough to say what had to be said about how God was understood doctrinally and creedally. Perhaps it was best to say less about the Holy Spirit to avoid associations with the sixteenth-century radical groups with a stronger emphasis on the Holy Spirit and thereby setting themselves further from the confines and structures of the institutional church; namely, those groups were vehemently persecuted by both the Catholic and Protestant groups. Sans the explicit focus on Spirit-led religion, theologically speaking, references to the Holy Spirit can be found throughout the Lutheran confessions, especially in Luther's *Catechisms*, which combined are a thorough treatment on the many aspects of the work of the Holy Spirit in human life and communities. In contemporary exploration of Lutheran theology, and when orienting toward Lutheran spirituality for today, further attention to the Holy Spirit is warranted. This is also ecumenically fruitful; attention to the Spirit gives common ground for religious talk and practice.

In addition to omitting a more substantial article on the Spirit, another curious decision is that the article three ends with a cliffhanger with its last statement about Christ's return to judge. The topic is returned to later in the article seventeen: "They teach that the consummation of the world Christ will appear for judgment and will bring to life all the dead. He will give eternal life and endless joy to the righteous and the elect but will condemn the ungodly and the devils to endless torment" (AC 17:1–3).[13]

This conclusion has been shared since the witness of Jesus's resurrection among Christians who have waited for his return. The language of judgment and about the ungodly, as common as it has been in Christian writing, raises problems for the contemporary reader. For one, the very questions of who are godly and ungodly and what the end of times can mean warrant reconsideration. But for now, the attention here is what is stated about Christ at the beginning of the politically charged Lutheran confession. The point is clear: Christ is the lord, of the now and of the future. This is the foundation for hope. As a whole, the article three affirms the creedal teaching of Christ and is built on the doctrine of the Triune God, explicated in article one. As a fortification of this, the article defends Lutherans' orthodoxy with condemnations of any heresies and alternate opinions that in any way would diminish either Christ's divinity or humanity and therewith his capacity for lordship over human life and death and from hereafter, which is, for Luther, the heart of the matter.

Christ's Lordship—A Perspective from the *Catechisms* and *Smalcald Articles*

With Luther, Lutheran theology promises not to divert from the content of the creedal theology about Christ but rather offers a reorientation to the interpretation of the meaning of what is known of Christ for the human beings. In this spirit, in his *Large Catechism* Luther addresses the second part of the Creed notably briefly. He reiterates the words of the second part of the Apostles' Creed:

> And [I believe] in Jesus Christ, his only Son, our LORD. He was conceived by the Holy Spirit and born of Mary the virgin. He suffered under Pontius Pilate, was crucified, died, and was buried. He descended into hell. On the

---

[13]On Christ's descent into hell (FC IX:3), "For it is enough that we know that Christ descended into hell and destroyed hell for all believers and that he redeemed them from the power of death, the devil, and the eternal damnation of hellish retribution. How that happened we should save for the next world, where not only this matter but many others, which here we have simply believed and cannot comprehend with our blind reason, will be revealed" (FC IX:4).

third day he rose from the dead. He ascended into heaven and is seated at the right hand of God, the Father Almighty. From there he will come again to judge the living and the dead. (LC 356)

Then Luther zooms in on one sentence: "We shall concentrate on these words, 'in Jesus Christ, our LORD'" (LC 356).[14]

In contemporary theological imagination, the word "lord" or "lordship" evokes many negative connotations of, e.g., male-centeredness, patriarchy, and domination. The term has prevailed, regardless, as a commonly used name or indicator in Christian speech about God and Christ in particular. The rationale for the term arises from doctrinal determinations about the supreme power and sovereignty of God over all life, including human, and thus also God's reign over matters infinite and finite, such as death. Luther found it a helpful description for what Christ does for the human beings' security and hopes and for confessing human beings' fundamental reliance on the one God in terms of life and what all it entails.

Luther addresses Christ's lordship as something without which human beings would remain under the wrath of God and feel condemned by God. He writes: "What is it 'to become a lord'? It means that he has redeemed and released me from sin, from the devil, from death, and from all misfortune. Before this I had no lord or king, but was captive under the power of the devil. I was condemned to death and entangled in sin and blindness" (LC 357).[15] Luther underscores the key belief about Jesus, who has the power to transform a person's life with freedom: freedom from fear and freedom from the humanity's worst scenario by the only being with the power to alter the course of the universe and any human destiny.

Speaking from his own experience, Luther concludes: "Let this be the summary of this article, that the little word 'LORD' simply means the same as Redeemer, that is, he who has brought us back from the devil to God, from death to life, from sin to righteousness, and keeps us there." The rest of the articles clarify how this was accomplished: by Christ becoming a human creature, to suffer and die, be buried to pay my debts. "And he did all this so that he might become my LORD" (LC 357–8).[16] In this regard, the Creeds offer a grammar about Christ on which Luther adds nothing but rather renews the reader's focus on what is the personal meaning of Christ for the living and breathing human beings.

It could be said that much of Luther's production is about his ongoing deliberation on the meaning of Christ, which is also at the heart of Christian proclamation and identity beyond Luther, who is aware of the complexity

---

[14]See also Kolb and Wengert, *The Book of Concord*, LC 434:25, 26.
[15]See also Kolb and Wengert, *The Book of Concord*, LC 434:27; 434, 25.
[16]See also Kolb and Wengert, *The Book of Concord*, LC 434:31.

and of what is at stake. "Indeed, the entire gospel that we preach depends on the proper understanding of this article. Upon it all our salvation and blessedness are based, and it is so rich and broad that we can never learn it fully" (LC 358).[17] To Luther, Christological questions are not theoretical but existential, pastoral, and spiritual and utterly relevant for faith communities and individuals who join them because of the meaning they find in the proclamation of Christ.

When speaking of Christ and his relevance on a personal level, in addition to the word "lordship," another word Luther employs is "justification." For Luther, "the first and chief article" is that of Christ, the second part of the Creed (SA 429).[18] Similar to his statement on the Trinity in the same book, Luther seeks to add nothing to the doctrinal content already established but steers the attention to what it is that Christ does for the human being. Referring to Paul (Romans 4:25), he aims the focus with Christ's death on justification of human beings.

The word "justification" emerges here with a particular point Luther wants to make about Christ and justification as the life and death focus. Christ with his death took away the consequence of sin in terms of damnation. With Paul's words in Romans 3:26 Luther underscores the belief that human beings in need of justification are justified—freely— because of Christ and his death specifically. This is a pivotal matter of faith (SA 429). Had there been another way, Christ would have died in vain! This Luther thus insists as a nonnegotiable article of faith and one not to have any doubt about (SA 429).[19] Luther's justification-by-faith logic explains his uncompromising insistence on what to believe, a tone that is not too helpful in contemporary discourse on these matters. Similarly problematic for contemporary reader may be his use of lordship in his Christological argumentation. One suggestion is to consider the content of what is being communicated and reframe the meaning of the sentence. Instead of speaking of Christ's lordship over one's life and for the purposes of justification by faith that Christ has merited for human beings, this also could be said: the life and death of Jesus Christ offer the window to imagine the premises of one's life in a personal relationship with the Divine who is immanently and intimately present in finite human existence and in whose omniscient vision both the sorrows and joys, fears and hopes are gathered. Phrased this way, Jesus's lordship suggests God's all-encompassing presence for all that belongs to human life and therefore speaks of the God incarnate as the ground of being that holds human existence in divine care beyond which nothing exists or occurs.

The word "freedom" could replace both terms. As the Christ story gives theological roots for the human right called freedom, his lordship could

---

[17]See also Kolb and Wengert, *The Book of Concord*, LC 435:33.
[18]See also Kolb and Wengert, *The Book of Concord*, SA Part II art. 1:1–2.
[19]See also Kolb and Wengert, *The Book of Concord*, SA Part II art. 1:4–5.

be understood as existential freedom of fear and death he guarantees with what he has done with his life and death. Justification merited by Christ is a term to name the internal freedom, from fear of damnation and of death as the end, and from regrets. Such freedom promises a grounding and orientation for life that is positive, oriented with hope, and equips one to care for other living beings in compassion; that is where the fruits of what is meant with justification manifest. To use the notable twentieth-century Lutheran theologian Paul Tillich's[20] famous wording *the ground of being*, one could say that the words "lordship" and "justification" both point to the source of life and source of freedom, the source of hope, God and God's omnipotent and all-seeing presence. Luther's questions about God aim to wake up individuals to reckon this God in their lives and live accordingly.

Christ–God–Spirit—The Trinitarian God as the Source of Being

One of the fundamental beliefs about God expressed in the Creeds that Lutherans uphold is that God is the source of what exists, i.e., creator. By the same token, God is considered the ongoing source for what is needed in human life. This belief offers a particular orientation to life, to one's existence, relations, and duties. The starting point is that of gratitude and— to use German thinker Friedrich Schleiermacher's terminology—a feeling of ultimate dependency. While the idea of dependency may strike negative connotations in current culture where freedom implies independency broadly conceived, a Lutheran lens sees this as positive: if all beings depend on one divine source of life, this equalizes the situation and supports the idea of equality in life and promotes humility versus arrogance, all of which are ingredients for building webs of human communities where harmful power dynamics and hierarchies are kept in check.

Succinctly, Luther gives words for this position in his *Small Catechism:*

> I believe that God has created me together with all that exists. God has given me and still preserves my body and soul: eyes, ears, and all limbs and senses; reason and all mental faculties. In addition, God daily and abundantly provides shoes and clothing, food and drinking, house and farm, spouse and children, fields, livestock, and all property—along with all the necessities and nourishment for this body and life. God protects me against all danger and shields and preserves me from all evil. And all this is done out of pure, fatherly, and divine goodness and mercy,

---

[20]See, e.g., Paul Tillich, ed. F. Forrester Church, *The Essential Tillich* (Chicago: Chicago University Press, 1999).

without any merit or worthiness of mine at all. For all of this I owe it to
God to thank and praise, serve and obey him. This is most certainly true.
(SC 354:2–355)

Luther parses this out in more detail in *Large Catechism*: "'I believe
in God, the Father almighty, Creator of heaven and earth … ' This is the
shortest possible way of describing and illustrating the nature, will, acts,
and work of God the Creator" (LC 353). Furthermore, Luther asks: "What
kind of person is God?" … "How can we praise or portray or describe God
in such a way so we may know God?" (LC 353).[21] The Creed explains this
as a response based on the First Commandment. Luther makes the integral
connection between what is considered the basic expectation set by God
for humanity—know who your God is—and the confession of faith that
reckons this God, and that knows this God, already from the bare existence
of life itself (even if in limited fashion).

In the *Large Catechism*'s explanation of the Commandments, Luther
returns to the definition of God: "'You are to have no other gods.' That is,
you are to regard me alone as your God. What does this mean, and how
is it to be understood? What does 'to have a god' mean, or what is God?"
Luther answers:

God is that in which we are to look for all good and in which we are to
find refuge in all need. Therefore, to have a god is nothing else than to
trust and believe in that one with your whole heart. As I have often said,
it is the trust and faith of the heart alone that make both God and an
idol. If your faith and trust are right, then your God is the true one …
Anything on which your heart relies and depends, I say, that is really your
God. (LC 300)

The bottom line is, "to have a god is to have something in which the
heart trusts completely" (LC 301).[22]

The most rudimentary Lutheran argument for the existence of God is in
the heart and desires of a human being. Both can lead one astray to false
gods, looking for joy, sustenance, and grounding in what one covets and
defends. These objects of one's desire and the sources of one's trust, however,
are finite. The *Large Catechism* points to the infinite source of life and
sustenance, the real God, who wants to be reckoned for who God is and,
furthermore, who wants to be desired and loved. God emerges to the human
being in a personal and communal relationship between the creator and the
created. The God of the Creeds wants to be known like that, personally, just
as this God engages in the finite world. The creedal faith in God the creator
thus is less of a theoretical or cosmological statement about the existence

---

[21]See also Kolb and Wengert, *The Book of Concord*, LC 432:9–10.
[22]See also Kolb and Wengert, *The Book of Concord*, LC 386:2–4; 387:10.

of the Divine and more a personal admission or a recognition of creatures knowing their creator—in their gut, in their amazement of life in its many facets, and from the Scriptural revelation.

The God in question is not a distant deity but one intimately involved in the creation's affairs. Luther's explanation of the word "creator" and the realm it involves, cosmically and in the life of the individual, encompasses all that is essential for life in all forms.

We should emphasize the words "creator of heaven and earth." What is meant by these words or what do you mean when you say, "I believe in God, the Father almighty, creator," etc.? Answer: I hold and believe that I am God's creature, that is, that God has given me and constantly sustains my body, soul, and life, my members great and small, all my senses, my reason and understanding, and the like; my food and drink, clothing, nourishment, spouse and children, servants, house and farm, etc. Besides, God makes all creation help provide the benefits and necessities of life—sun, moon, and stars in the heavens; day and night; air, fire, water, the earth and all that it yields and brings forth; birds, fish, animals, grain, and all sorts of produce. Moreover, God gives all physical and temporal blessings—good government, peace, security. (LC 354)

"Thus we learn from this article that none of us has life—or anything else that has been mentioned here or can be mentioned—from ourselves, nor can we by ourselves preserve any of them, however small and unimportant. All this is comprehended in the word 'Creator'" (LC 354).[23]

Obviously, in contemporary theological reflection it behoves to embrace current scientific knowledge of reality. In the reformation period, the theologians of the day reacted to the sciences of the day and boldly entered the current reality talk. For them, theology remained the queen of sciences and tested any (other) scientific discovery against their theological framework and proofs. Today Christian thinkers can honor healthy distinctions between the different sciences, theology being one of them, each using different proofs and arguments. Relatedly, beliefs versus evidence questions point to the centuries-old tension, since the beginning of Christian theology really. Faith and reason have often been set opposite in theological debate, with varying emphasis.[24] The most satisfying solutions have been the ones that have not excluded one in favor of the other but have sought for ways to operate with and within the tension.[25]

---

[23]See also Kolb and Wengert, *The Book of* Concord, LC 432:13–433:16.
[24]Faith-reason tension characterized the medieval scholastics' deliberations, e.g., Anselm of Canterbury negotiating the relation between the two.
[25]See, e.g., *Astrotheology: Science and Theology Meet Extraterrestrial Life*, eds. Ted Peters, Martinez Hewlett, Joshua M. Moritz, Robert John Russell (Eugene, OR: Cascade Books, 2018).

The invitation for Lutheran discourse today is to imagine God bigger than historical doctrines that in many ways may clash with the most recent scientific vistas. Developing a new grammar for God can start with the creation thought, without making that the scientific premise but rather a religious cosmological orientation that regards life as is, and as a gift, and, in that, holiness beyond human comprehension or expressions. Also, the environmental crisis of today, the suffering of earth, air, and water, and different living beings, caused by the human-impacted climate change, presents an emergency to all who engage in religious thought and speech. It is imperative to readjust the theological language about God and creation to enhance the sense of holiness of all life, the godliness of the care of creation, and therewith alter human beings' attitudes towards the creation: so that instead of using and abusing it, human beings would be committed to caring for the creation. Christian faith about believing in God who exists, and sustains and cares for all the living beings certainly is poised to promote this kind of holistic and wholistic orientation in life.[26]

Luther tenderly reflects that since "everything we possess, and everything in heaven and on earth besides, is daily given, sustained, and protected by God, it inevitably follows that we are in duty bound to love, praise, and thank God without ceasing, and, in short, to devote all these things to God's service, as God has required and enjoined in the Ten Commandments" (LC 355).[27] The application opportunities of such an orientation are many. In sum, in the spirit of Lutheran catechetic teaching, a Christian can honor life as holy and therewith embrace human beings' call to protect life, in all its forms. This involves resisting the selfish tendencies. Luther's diagnosis of human beings' suffering from the tendency to always turn toward themselves (*incurvatus se*) is devastating in itself. It can become a positive term when using it as an impetus to shift human beings' selfish tendencies vis-à-vis nature to attitudes of caring and loving, turning outward, in other words.

The Catechisms addressed the impact of the creator in one's life beyond that of the origins and sustenance:

> Moreover, we also confess that God the Father has given us not only all that we have and what we see before our eyes, but also that God daily guards and defends us against every evil and misfortune, warding off all sorts of danger and disaster. All this God does out of pure love and goodness, without our merit, as a kind father who cares for us so that no evil may befall us. (LC 354)[28]

---

[26]See, e.g., Grace Ji-Sun Kim and Hilda P. Koestner, *Planetary Solidarity. Global Women's Voices on Christian Doctrine and Climate Justice* (Minneapolis: Fortress Press, 2017); Cynthia Moe-Lobeda, *Resisting Structural Evil: Love as Ecological-economic Vocation* (Minneapolis: Fortress Press, 2013).

[27]See also Kolb and Wengert, *The Book of Concord*, LC 433:19.

[28]See also Kolb and Wengert, *The Book of Concord*, LC 433:17–18.

In other words, Luther underscores God's sovereignty over all that is, including trouble, hurt, and suffering, as a doctrine of comfort and hope.

The wording seems to promise a trouble-free life for the believer, yet that is hardly the reality. The *Large Catechism* rather points to the certainty of God's reality and presence for the individuals in all of their lives, and deaths, and experiences. Also, an affirmation is given of a divine purpose for the design of one's life and experience and stimulus for an ensuing orientation that is filled with hope and calm rather than distress and hopelessness. A belief in God who cares, sees it all, and has ultimately all in God's gaze is presented by Luther as a freeing belief; similar emphasis can be seen in the theology of his fellow reformer Jean Calvin, famous for his teaching on God's sovereignty and omniscient care for the human life. Such a belief as a foundation in life offers freedom from paralyzing fear of non-existence—as Tillich[29] names the utmost abyss for the human being—and freedom that equips one to see hope even against hope, even life beyond death.

These are no minor things. Duly, Luther exclaims, "This article should humble and terrify all of us" (LC 355). But more important than the holy terror is the call to action:

> [W]e ought daily to practice this article, impress it upon our minds, and remember it in everything we see and in every blessing that comes our way. Whenever we escape distress or danger, we should recognize how God gives and does all of this so that we may sense and see in them God's parental heart and boundless love toward us. Thus our hearts will be warmed and kindled with gratitude to God and a desire to use all these blessings to God's glory and praise. (LC 355)[30]

The article sets human being in a proper position in relation to the source of life, that of adoration and gratitude. Listing a broad spectrum of life's necessities and God as the provider, Luther's words need not imply that all is well in the world and nobody is never wanting anything. Belief in God as the source and the sustainer and the protector is a fundamental belief about God's intention and motivation toward people, which is love. The same belief orients human beings to love their God and their neighbor.

Such, very briefly, is the meaning of this article. It is all that ordinary people need to learn at first, both about what we have and receive from God and about what we owe God in return. This is knowledge of great significance, but an even greater treasure. For here we see how we have received all of creation along with God's very being, so that we are

---

[29]Paul Tillich, *The Courage to Be*, 4th ed. (New Haven: Yale University Press, 1963, 2000).
[30]See also Kolb and Wengert, *The Book of Concord*, LC 433:22–3.

abundantly provided for in this life, in addition also to showering us with inexpressible eternal blessings through the Son and the Holy Spirit, as we shall hear. (LC 355–6)[31]

The Agency of the Holy Spirit and Holiness Prospects

The Lutheran confessions do not explicitly articulate nuanced teaching on the Holy Spirit, as noted above. Yet the sources are hardly silent about the Spirit. The most abundant engagement with the Spirit can be found in Luther's *Catechisms*. There Luther features the distinctive work of the Holy Spirit in the lives of Christian individuals and communities—building on the fundamental convictions about God's oneness and relating to human beings in three persons.

In other words, God works in this world in the Holy Spirit through whom God is really present, and that makes a difference in all aspects of life. This was Luther's solid conviction, one that shaped his outlook on life and his theology and how he operated. Spiritually, his whole being was wrapped in the experience of being held in God's Spirit. His words in *Small Catechism* illustrate this, offering an orientation for Lutheran spirituality.

> I believe that by my own understanding or strength I cannot believe in Jesus Christ my LORD or come to him, but instead the Holy Spirit has called me through the gospel, enlightened me with his gifts, made me holy and kept me in the true faith, just as he gathers, enlightens, and makes holy the whole Christian church on earth and keeps it with Jesus Christ in the one common true faith. Daily in this Christian church the Holy Spirit abundantly forgives all sins—mine and those of all believers. On the Last Day the Holy Spirit will raise me and all the dead and will give to me and all believers in Christ eternal life. (SC 355–7:5–6)

When reading Luther's *Catechisms*, it becomes evident how important the Holy Spirit was for Luther, personally and theologically, and professionally. What he experienced in his faith journey makes no sense without recognizing the involvement of the Holy Spirit. His theology of grace and justification would not work if the essential role of the Spirit was out of the equation. His method of reading the Scriptures assumed the revelatory work of the Spirit. His vision and actions as a reformer were fueled by his sense of the Holy Spirit calling for a change and empowering individuals to serve as agents of this Spirit in their place.

---

[31]See also Kolb and Wengert, *The Book of Concord*, LC 433:24.

Luther's statement of faith agrees with the creedally expressed doctrine: the one God is Triune God who relates to human beings in three persons and three distinct actions: "I believe in God the Father, who created me; I believe in God the Son, who has redeemed me; I believe in the Holy Spirit, who makes me holy" (LC 353; also LC 365). The third article of the Creed identifies the consequence of Jesus's lordship in human lives. "I believe in the Holy Spirit" means "I believe that the Holy Spirit makes me holy" (LC 360). That is the special office of the Holy Spirit, who "has made us holy and still makes us holy" (LC 359).[32]

Holy Spirit's mission is to make human beings holy and unite them with God. Luther simplifies: "Therefore being made holy is nothing else than bringing us to the Lord Christ to receive this blessing, to which we could not have come by ourselves" (LC 360). Holiness, justification, and freedom lend themselves thus as inter-exchangeable words to describe what happens when God encounters the human being in the ways only Spirit can facilitate. The Creed names particular venues with which the Spirit works grace and holiness into human lives: "I believe in the Holy Spirit, one holy Christian church, the community of saints, the forgiveness of sins, the resurrection of the flesh, and the life everlasting. Amen" (LC 358, 358–60).[33] In all this, the Word is the key.

Here is a foundation for the church, in the Lutheran view. The explanation of the article three in the Creeds names the foundation, dimensions, means, and hopes of the Christian community called church. In Lutheran view, church is understood as the nurturing ground for holiness and the playing field for the Holy Spirit. The church is the space for the Holy Spirit operating within and from. There are two main ingredients for the Spirit to work with, namely the Word and the means of grace. Without the Spirit's involvement, neither of these would have the power to effect what they promise in human life, namely holiness and hope.

A few reasonings here: First, human beings could not come to Christ or believe what he has acquired for humanity unless the gospel about Christ was "bestowed on our hearts through the preaching of the gospel by the Holy Spirit" (LC 360). To bring this gift to people, "God has caused the word to be published and proclaimed, in which God has given the Holy Spirit to offer and apply to us this treasure, this redemption" (LC 360). Second, the collaboration between the Holy Spirit and the Word is vital: "For where Christ is not preached, there is no Holy Spirit to create, call, and gather the Christian church, apart from which no one can come to the Lord Christ" (LC 361). Third, the church is crucial for "making us holy" as the place where the Word is preached.[34]

---

[32]See also Kolb and Wengert, *The Book of Concord*, LC 432:7; LC 440:67; LC 436:40; LC 435:36.

[33]See also Kolb and Wengert, *The Book of Concord*, LC 436:39; LC 435:34; LC 436:36–7.

[34]See also Kolb and Wengert, *The Book of Concord*, LC 436:38; LC 436:38–9; LC 436:45.

People need church as a channel of grace, according to Luther. The church consists of people who form a holy community of saints and sinners. "I believe that there is on earth a holy little flock and community of pure saints under one head, Christ. It is called together by the Holy Spirit in one faith, mind, and understanding" (LC 362). The main purpose of the church is the proclamation of forgiveness, just as being forgiven is what holiness of the daily experience ultimately entails. The forgiveness of sins "takes place through the holy sacraments and absolution as well as through all the comforting words of the entire gospel" (LC 363). Luther's seemingly exclusive stand points to the importance of the regular dose of Word and Holy Spirit for the daily experience of forgiveness (LC 363).[35]

To repeat, how does the salvation—or justification, to use another word—happen for human beings? According to Luther, it "is the office and work of the Holy Spirit, to begin and daily increase holiness on earth through these two means, the Christian church and the forgiveness of sins" (LC 364). When the Word is preached, in the community, faith is stirred and increased, with the affirmation of the forgiveness of sins (LC 364). This is so willed by God who created human beings to make them holy (LC 364–5). The Creed, Luther points out, "tells us what God does for us and gives to us" (LC 365). The Spirit, in Luther's experience, is the key intermitter and transmitter and communicator in this process, and not just once but on an ongoing basis.[36]

The Holy Spirit and the *Augsburg Confession*

Even if there is no separate article on the Spirit in the *Augsburg Confession*, several statements are made about the Holy Spirit in the articles. First, the Holy Spirit is first of all discussed and introduced in the articles expressing who is God—i.e., as part of the statement of faith in the Trinitarian God. *Augsburg Confession* article one talks about God as one divine essence—eternal, incorporeal, indivisible, of immeasurable power, wisdom, goodness, creator, and preserver of all things, visible and invisible; Spirit is understood as coeternal and of the same essence as the other persons of the Trinity, while distinct. Second, the Holy Spirit is introduced as the integral person making God known to human beings and making Christ's work come live and relevant to people—that is, making human beings united with God. It is only by faith that forgiveness of sins and grace are apprehended. Moreover, because the Holy Spirit is received through faith, consequently hearts are renewed and thereby human beings are able to do good works.

---

[35]See also Kolb and Wengert, *The Book of Concord*, LC 437:51; LC 438:54; LC 438:56, 58.
[36]See also Kolb and Wengert, *The Book of Concord*, LC 439:59; LC 439:62; LC 439:64; LC 440:67.

Third, the Holy Spirit is introduced as the person/agent that brings about oneness with God in the godly realm and, with that, empowers human beings for holy good life in this worldly realm. A most interesting point is made about the impact of the Holy Spirit: human beings need to be born again with Holy Spirit (AC 2). Christ will sanctify those who believe in him by sending into their hearts the Holy Spirit, who will rule, console, and make them alive and defend them against the devil and power of sin (AC 3). Fourth, the Holy Spirit is introduced as the agent that brings about faith and salvation "for and in us" and as the agent that makes Word alive in and for human beings. Articles (AC 5:2–3) remind of Luther's teaching that the Holy Spirit does not operate without the external Word but specifically works through Word and sacraments; these in turn are the very instruments through which the Holy Spirit is given and effects faith (AC 18:2–3). By the same token, without the Holy Spirit, free will has no power to produce righteousness of God or spiritual righteousness. God's righteousness is worked in the heart when the Holy Spirit is received through the Word. Fifth, the Holy Spirit is introduced as the heart of the church and Christian community, as the master, the mother, the birth giver, the preacher, the one who makes human beings belong in Christian community in this world and who includes human beings on the final day among those with God (AC 13:1–2).

In conclusion, the Holy Spirit makes Christ's work possible and effective for human beings. The Holy Spirit evokes and nurtures faith through the Word and Sacraments and, specifically, in the space serving the community of believers. Last but not least, the Holy Spirit makes human beings holy and whole, uniting them with God. In his explanation of the Creed, Luther summarizes his understanding of justification through the function of the Holy Spirit. His pneumatology intertwines with what in other contexts is often called sanctification.

To offer a brief synopsis: First, God has designed both the creation and the redemption of human beings and the Holy Spirit is integrally involved with all of that and everything between. It is through the Holy Spirit that God brings human beings to God and "sanctifies" or "makes holy." Second, when Christians confess that "I believe in the Holy Spirit who makes me holy" (LC 353), they affirm their trust in Christ and his saving work. Namely, "being made holy is nothing else than bringing us to the Lord Christ to receive this blessing, to which we could not have come by ourselves" (LC 360). Third, with their faith in the Holy Spirit Christians acknowledge their need for a divine teacher, on the one hand, and for the divine gift of faith, on the other. Holy Spirit, Christ, and faith belong together in a sense that (LC 360) human beings would know nothing relevant about Christ nor could they believe in Christ or receive Christ without the Holy Spirit preaching and bestowing the gospel, the gifts. Fourth, Luther names the crucial space for the work of the Holy Spirit in the community of faith where the gospel is proclaimed and the sacraments are offered, as means for the Spirit's operations (LC 361).[37]

It is important to notice how Luther explains the tools and venues of the Holy Spirit and locates the Spirit's work in the church. In *Large Catechism*, Luther explains how the Holy Spirit effects that human beings are made holy through "the community of saints or Christian church, the forgiveness of sins, the resurrection of the body, and the life everlasting" (LC 360). Luther's view of the spiritual space is important to recognize: the space is expansive and involves human beings connected and concerned about one another. The Word breathes and effects grace in these relations for which the community of faith gives a concrete foundation. The spiritual space does not rely on the nature or characteristics of the human beings involved or their goodness or holiness. Rather it relies on the life-giving and transforming energy that works through the pores and cracks and relations: the Word. The gift this Word brings along is about communicating the gospel about freedom and consolation.

Against false assumptions that Lutheran teaching is vague about spirituality or that Lutheran theology would be light on pneumatology, just a brief look into the *Catechisms* reveals that the opposite is the case. Spirituality is a most apt word to describe the interconnectedness and mutual support of Christians who are gathered and fed with hope by the Holy Spirit who involves communities in communicating the liberating word of the gospel. "All this, then, is the office and work of the Holy Spirit, to begin and daily increase holiness on earth through these two means, the Christian church and the forgiveness of sins" (LC 364).[38] The core of Lutheran theology and the heart of Lutheran proclamation and spirituality are expressed with this promise about the Holy Spirit. Luther's view of spirituality thus begins with Holy Spirit.[39]

Mary, the Mother of God

In the context of reflecting on the creedal language of God, this is an opportune moment to draw attention to Mary, who is notably mentioned in the Creeds, in conjunction of setting the parameters for God-talk, specifically about Christ.[40]

A reader might ask, though, why talk about Mary at all in a Lutheran book, given the nearly invisibility of Mary in Lutheran tradition, liturgy,

---

[37]See also Kolb and Wengert, *The Book of Concord*, LC 432:7; LC 436:39; LC 436:38; LC 436:43.

[38]See also Kolb and Wengert, *The Book of Concord*, LC 439:59.

[39]See, Stjerna, *No Greater Jewel*, 2020, and Kirsi Stjerna and Brooks Schramm, *Spirituality: Toward a 21st Century Understanding* (Edina, MN: Lutheran University Press, 2004).

[40]See FC VIII: 6–8 on Christ and Mary.

and spirituality? Compared to Catholic and Orthodox Christian traditions, Lutherans' Mariology appears thin if not nonexistent. Lutherans' general knowledge of Mary is limited as she has not been central in Lutheran piety and spiritual life. And yet, theologically speaking, Mary has always been at the center of Lutheran theological emphasis, standing right behind—and explicitly behind—Christ, on whom much of theological attention has focused.

In the past Lutheran theologians have lacked serious interest in encounters with Mary, starting from the confessional sources; for example, there is no special article on Mary in the *Augsburg Confession* or any of the other documents. Yet she is not absent but very much present in the theology that is communicated with the texts. Looking beyond the sixteenth-century Lutheran sources, Mary's presence in Western culture and religion has been obvious and multifaceted: she has been present in Christian art, music, and in general in Christian imagination and prayer life. It is pivotal that she is named in the Creeds, thereby having a firm place in Christian theology, also Lutheran. In the ecumenical theological scene with the ancient Creeds as the framework, Mary needs to be counted in.[41]

Luther personally appreciated Mary. Mary had served an important role in his spirituality, as she was a central figure in medieval practice of Christian faith. However, in his effort to redirect Christians' attention to Christ, Mary received less attention from Luther in his writings. His *Magnificat* (1521)[42] presents Mary in the context of cross and Christology as exemplary in faith and humility. Luther reminds that in "sacred hymn of the most blessed Mother of God," "she really sings sweetly about the fear of God" and about how God deals "with those of low and high degree" (Magnificat, 314–15). Nobody can understand God's mind and Word without the guidance of the Holy Spirit; Mary exemplifies that.

> When the holy virgin experienced what great things God was working in her despite her insignificance, lowliness, poverty, and inferiority, the Holy Spirit taught her this deep insights and wisdom, that God is the kind of Lord who does nothing but exalt those of low degree and put down the mighty from their thrones, in short break what is whole and make whole what is broken. (ibid., 316–17)

Luther does not consider Mary divine on a par with the Trinity and most definitely cautions against undue veneration and prayers addressed to Mary, when Christ should be the object of such holy attention. At the same time, in her humility and with her faith, and in her listening to the guidance of the Spirit, Mary deserves honor and affection. She stands tall as the exemplary

---

[41]Beverly Roberts Gaventa and Cynthia L. Rigby, eds., *Blessed One: Protestant Perspectives on Mary* (Louisville, KY: WJK, 2002).
[42]*The Magnificat*, 1521, ed. Beth Kreitzer, in *The Annotated Luther*, Vol. 4 (2016), ed. Mary Jane Haemig.

model of one whose heart believes and discerns God's will in her life. "The tender mother of Christ does the same here and teaches us, with her words and by the example of her experience, how to know, love, and praise God" (ibid., 319).

Mary also models how loving and knowing God looks like. First, one needs to know "God who looks into the depths and helps only the poor, despised, afflicted, miserable, forsaken, and those who are nothing." Mary in her lowliness, and instructed by the Spirit, had eyes to see where God's affection really was, and in that knowing her heart leaped of joy. In her knowing God in lowliness she loved God (ibid., 318). She also found the peace all humans should aspire for: "There is no peace except where it is taught that we are made pious, righteous, and blessed not by any work or external thing but solely by faith, that is, a firm confidence in the unseen grace of God is promised us" (ibid., 323). "We pray God to give us a right understanding of this Magnificat, an understanding that consists not merely in brilliant words but in glowing life in body and soul. May Christ grant us this through the intercession and for the sake of his dear mother Mary!" (ibid., 381). Luther's bottom line is relatively simple: Mary deserves to be remembered as a model for Christian life for her humility and obedience. Mary's love for God manifested uniquely in her willingness to give birth to the Word, God incarnate.

Over the centuries Mary's role had grown to an important go-between for people to whom God seemed distant. Mother Mary became the more familiar face of divinity, one who cared for the human beings' travails, who would whisper prayers to God's ears, and who was there to receive the person to God in the end of their life. For the Queen of Heaven to have these powers, in medieval imagination of the male theologians, she needed to be pure. Her virginity became a proof of her holiness and closeness to God. The concern over Mary's virginity became a dogma, to be affirmed by consequent other dogmas, to make sure that the birth-giver of Jesus the Savior of the humankind was not born in "ordinary human ways" and from an ordinary woman's body that felt the joys of sex. Luther was far less interested in the issue of Mary's virginity and yet he was fascinated by the autonomous nature of the holy birth.

Luther writes in *Smalcald Articles*, "That the Son became a human being in this way: he was conceived by the Holy Spirit without male participation and was born of the pure, holy Virgin Mary" (SA 428).[43] In other words, Mary's active role was necessary for Christ to be born. With all the things believed with the Creeds about Jesus, something important is simultaneously believed about Mary: that she was the mother of God. Mary with her pregnant body is a key player in the Christ story, and, as Luther points out, no human male was involved in Mary's pregnancy.

---

[43]See also Kolb and Wengert, *Book of Concord*, SA Part I.

Traditionally thinking this conviction underscores the miraculous conception of the Child of God. Naming Mary as pure and holy and Virgin is in perfect line with the Catholic and Eastern Orthodox teaching of Mary's human body as a vehicle for the holy birth. Since the decision at the Council of Ephesus in 431, Jesus's mother has been titled *theotokos*, a God-bearer; this continues to be a Lutheran teaching as well, with an emphasis on Christ's divinity, not Mary's.

The teaching on *theotokos* is a good example on how the decisions about Mary were made around Christological questions, in discernment of Christ's true nature as human and divine. He was the focal point. The title *theotokos* for Mary was not settled without a debate: not everyone in the early centuries favored this title but would have been happy to call Mary as Christ-bearer, *christotokos*. Her virginity and purity were shared concerns for the male theologians (many of them monks with vows to live a celibate life) who could not have conceived a way that a normal, sexual, and sexually active woman could have had anything to do with the birth of God.[44]

In Catholic tradition, several other Mariological definitions have followed since the early centuries' decisions. These are the most important Catholic teachings on Mary: (1) that Mary is *theotokos*, the Mother of God (431); (2) that Mary is *aeiparthenos*, with perpetual virginity (by 553), that Mary's own birth happened without sin via immaculate conception (1854); and (4) that Mary in her death has already been assumed into heaven in body and soul (1950). For Lutherans, the first one is a given, the second one receiving different levels of attention. The last two teachings, both elevating Mary's special status and her rise to the Queen of Heaven status, are not embraced by Lutherans or other Protestants. Another doctrine on Mary has been lobbied in the Catholic scene already for some time, and that is to declare Mary co-redemptrix to highlight her role in the salvation story as Christ's mother. Although it is not an official teaching, in people's imagination and spiritual practice, Mary has lived as a vital persona shepherding people to grace and to God. With Lutherans, Mary has never had that role. Instead, she has stood out as the model of humility and faith and an example for ordinary Christians in her exemplary willingness to serve God.

Today the question of Mary is generating new excitement, mostly because of friendlier ecumenical relations and increasing familiarity with Catholic and Eastern Orthodox traditions' teaching on Mary, but also as a result of feminist deliberations. Whereas the topic of virginal birth generates less excitement and is not held as a necessary doctrine about Mary, more interest occurs in unfolding the meaning and impact of the physical fact that Jesus

---

[44]In the early church, different parties supported either *christotokos* or *theotokos* as the most appropriate title and description for Mary as mother of Jesus Christ. Both had implications to how Jesus's own human/divine nature was understood, as well as the status of his mother.

was born from and fed by a real flesh-and-blood woman. Not Mary's sexual abstinence or intactness but her actual womanness and bodiliness draw attention both in terms of scholarship and in people spiritual imaginations. Mary the real birth-giver and a mother who knew joys and sorrows with her children becomes a more relatable figure who can indeed draw attention to the Christ story and the impact of Christ's incarnation for the human existence. In other words, contemporary Lutherans' curiosity about Mary and her humanness, and her body, can lead to an increasingly, and much needed, body positive theology and celebrating life in its holiness in the mundane and the physical, just as in the birthing story of baby Jesus.[45]

In conclusion, the hopes that the creedal faith expresses about the divine presence in human life and the spectrum of human destiny in this life and beyond have their foundation in the conviction about the existence and disposition of God. With their unwavering Trinitarian monotheism, Lutherans have demonstrated their orthodoxy and Catholicity in the most fundamental issue. Today, this foundation still stands, with this caveat or adjustment: instead of limiting the conversations and imaginations about God to the doctrinal detail and discernments of the past, it is fruitful to listen to a variety of languages and experiences about the Divine. With a humble humility about the limits of all human language regarding the Divine, Lutheran God-language can employ the ancient vistas, while exploring the meaning of this faith on a personal and communal level as a source of grounding, orientation, and freedom.

---

[45]See, e.g., Elina Vuola, *Virgin Mary across Cultures: Devotion among Costa Rican Catholic and Finnish Orthodox Women* (Abingdon, Oxon; New York, NY: Routledge, 2019).

I. Central Topics and Learning Goals

1. The ecumenical foundation for Lutheran theology of the Triune God.
2. Christological foundations for the doctrine of justification.
3. Pneumatological foundations for the Christian life.

II. Questions for Review, Reflection, and Further Reflection

1. Theological rationales for inclusive language about God.
2. What is or can be meant with Jesus's "lordship"?
3. What does it mean that Lutheran theology is Christ-centric?
4. What are the implications of the connection between the Spirit, faith, and Word?
5. What role can Mary have in Lutheran theological imagination?

III. Keywords

Creator, Creeds, God, Jesus, Holy Spirit, lordship, Mary, *theotokos*, Trinity.

IV. Readings with the Chapter

The Ecumenical Creeds. AC 1, 3, 17. (Skim Ap., 1, 3, 17.)
LC Explanation of the Creed in full.
Also LC, 1–3 Commandments, LC, Lords Prayer, petitions 1–3.
SA Part I. SA Part II art. 2. FC VIII–IX.

6

The Human Condition, Sin, and Hopes

Sin as a Starting Point?

Grace-talk, with statements about justification by faith, is one of the Lutheran hallmarks. It could be expected that one of the first articles in the *Augsburg Confession* would be on grace or justification, but that is actually not the case. After the foundational and unifying statement on what kind of a God Lutherans believe in, an article on sin follows. Not just any kind of sin but what is called the original sin is addressed immediately after the statement on God and before the article concerning the Son of God (AC 1, 3). Sin language starts the portrayal of the human condition and God-human relation and, also, sets the tone for what hopes and options are imagined for human beings on theological grounds. The pivotal issue on which Christians have presented different views over the centuries is this: do human beings have the ability to not sin, to want right, and to have an active role in what is called salvation or redemption of the God—human relationship? The questions of sin and freedom are essentially interwoven and Lutherans have a particular point to make.

There are reasons why this article is among the first. It is the recognition of the human condition in its fragility that gives Lutheran hermeneutics its specific lens. If human beings were considered capable of being good and finding holiness on their own and with capabilities for a life without regrets and hurt, then the very word "sin" would lose its purpose, as would the word "grace." But the human reality is not like that. Lutheran theology, with

---

Read AC 2, 18, 19. (Skim Ap. 2, 18, 19.) Recommended SA Part III art. 1–2, 3–4. FC I–II, XI; LC, Ten Commandments and Lord's Prayer, petitions 4–7.

its emphasis on God's loving relating with the creatures, assumes that the human life includes unavoidable experiences of sin and even more—a certain disposition that cannot be shaken off. On this basis, Lutheran theology facilitates a look at human reality as it is, in all its fragility, while setting eyes on elsewhere for hope and remedies—God. In that light, having God in the horizon from the start, sin can be seen in proper perspective and not with a pessimistic, fatalistic sense. The topic is difficult, however, and the Lutheran position since the time of the Reformations has been an extraordinary one. It has caused controversy also among Lutherans themselves, one that had to be sorted out on several occasions, including in the *Formula of Concord* that starts with the article on sin (FC I).

What is it then that Lutherans teach about sin and the human condition?

> Likewise, they teach that since the fall of Adam all human beings who are propagated according to nature are born with sin, that is, without fear of God, without trust in God, and with concupiscence. And they teach that this disease or original fault is truly sin, which even now damns and brings eternal death to those who are not born again through baptism and the Holy Spirit. (AC 2:1–2)[1]

Furthermore, as with articles one and three, the opposing views are rejected: "They condemn the Pelagians and others who deny that the original fault is sin and who, in order to diminish the glory of Christ's merits and benefits, argue that human beings can be justified before God by their own powers of reason" (AC 2:3). Proper teaching on sin correlates thus with proper teaching on God.

An Inherited Disposition

The article expresses a conviction that there is something seriously off in God-human relationships and that human beings suffer from a condition that makes them prone to want, orient, and act in ways that lead to a heartache and suffering. The German word "*Erbsünde*" for the original sin underscores the innate nature of it. The Latin term "*peccatum originalis*" points to the origins and the beginning of (all) sin. Such a sin is considered as the root of the problems in human condition, with different manifestations of sinning. Sin is named as a false inclination that leads one away from

---

[1]For the sake of comparison, the German version reads: "Furthermore, it is taught among us that since the fall of Adam, all human beings who are born in the natural way are conceived and born in sin. This means that from birth they are full of evil lust and inclination and cannot possess true fear of God and true faith in God. Moreover, this same innate disease and original sin is truly sin and condemns to God's eternal wrath all who are not in turn born anew through baptism and the Holy Spirit" (AC 2:1–2).

enjoying life as God would have intended it for the benefit of the human being. It is called a disease, as something that is contracted at birth and is thus unavoidable. Ultimately the word refers to the human condition and orientation as being without the appropriate fear of and trust in God. With all this, it becomes a fault, a form of guilt that one needs purging from.

The words "evil lust" and "*concupiscence*" paint definitely negative associations, especially in the mind of a contemporary Christian who might not ordinarily apply such expressions in their faith language (not to mention persons with a different religious background). The word "concupiscence" can be translated as ardent, sensual longing, and desire; it could be understood as a neutral drive as such and without considering sensual and desire as tainted per se. That said, in Christian language it has come to bear overwhelmingly sexualized and negative meanings, used misleadingly as a synonym to a disorderly sexual lust.

It is unfortunate that in the Christian tradition, including the Lutherans, the associations with these words have often been sexualized, with the impact of viewing sexual desires and human and erotic love as sinful. This direction of thought was immensely influenced by the most influential theologian of the early church, Augustine, the Bishop of Hippo, who regarded all human love, other than love toward God, as of lesser value, if not plain sinful. Augustine, who wrestled with his own demons in this regard, had struggled mightily with his erotic impulses. He sought to control his human passions in light of the Christian philosophies of the time and operating very much under a dualistic mindset that devalued bodily and sexual. He came to set a particular Christian language that preserves enjoying and pleasure love (*frui*) for the love of God only, whereas seeing other objects worthy of only user love (*uti*).[2]

Lutheran teaching of sin does not quite fall into these parameters while it is heavily influenced by them. As with many other theological concepts, Lutheran position on sin stands on Augustine's foundation, but with its own distinctions, and both simplifying and intensifying the medieval teaching on the matter. The confessional texts also reveal that Lutherans themselves have not agreed on the details regarding sin.

The term "sin" (*peccatum, Sünde*) is maintained in Lutheran parlance, while departures are taken from how the Catholic tradition understood it. The reformers took an issue with the medieval scholastics' teaching of sin having two dimensions: the lack of righteousness (Anselm of Canterbury), i.e., that something essential was missing from human life, and the concupiscence as *fomes peccati* (Peter of Lombard), i.e., that something extra had been added to human nature. Reformers also challenged the idea of different statuses of human nature (*status integrae, lapsae* and *gratiae*)

---

[2]Augustine's autobiographical *Confessions* is a recommended reading as a personal and theologically illuminating narrative of him developing a Christian view of sin and human nature, including deliberations on sin and love.

defined by the degree of sin's impact versus that of grace. The Reformers dismissed these distinctions and simplified to state that original sin, which was indeed a real sin, consisted fundamentally of the lack of fear of God and the lack of trust in God. Nobody would ever be free from it, not even with baptism, which would remove guilt and the damnation sin brought about, but not sin itself.

To explain the reality and the ongoing impact of the original sin, the term "concupiscence" was maintained, as Melanchthon explains in his *Apology*: "So when we use the word 'concupiscence,' we understand not only its act or fruits but the continual tendency of our nature," a real sin (Ap. 2:3). Furthermore, in agreement with the "scholastic opponents," the word refers to the "so called material element of original sin" and thus "concupiscence must not be left out of the definition" (Ap. 2:4). Original sin is about more than "only a subjection to or a condition of mortality that those descended from Adam endure through no fault of their own"; it is a real fault that has consequences. "With the best of intentions we identified and diagnosed it as a disease because human nature is born corrupt and faulty" (Ap. 2:5, 6).

From the Lutheran side, then, there is a fundamental agreement on many essential points about original sin. However, Melanchthon proceeds to point out the scholastics "trivialize" the teaching of original sin inherited from the Fathers. Considering it a "tinder of sin" or a weakness only,

> they have suppressed the main point. Thus, when they speak about original sin they fail to mention the more serious defects of human nature like being ignorant of God, despising God, lacking fear and confidence in God, hating the judgment of God, fleeing this judging God, being angry with God, despairing of his grace and placing confidence in temporal things, etc. ... For what else is the ability to love God above all things with one's own power and to keep the commandments than original righteousness? (Ap. 2:7, 8, 9)

In other words, sin is about losing one's righteousness, or one's ground of being, to phrase it differently. Sin of this magnitude goes beyond individual wrongdoings to humankind's disorientation on the most fundamental things in life.

In other words, sin is about more than an individual's occasional transgression. Unlike in the Catholic teaching, which makes distinctions between different transgressions and forgivable venial and mortal sins,[3] the Lutheran position is streamlined: the foundational sin, the root of all sins,

---

[3]Catholic moral theology, drawing from the Scriptures, has defined venial sins as lesser transgressions, done more or less unknowingly and carelessly, whereas mortal sins involve intentional, knowingly committed, and voluntary act of a grave transgression (such as murder), which turns one away from the love of God. Remedies and return to grace, if and when feasible, would involve serious remorse, conversion, and acts of repentance.

is that human beings do not trust and believe in God and they look for God from all the wrong places. More important than what all is meant with concupiscence, according to Melanchthon, is the lack of "fear of God and faith." This out-of-balance reality is behind the experience human beings have of being drawn to different directions that may lead to unsatisfactory if not damaging outcomes.

With their desires and needs, human beings tend to look for happiness and security from a variety of sources, many of which fail to offer what they are looking for, not to mention to provide the ground of being and fuel for hope. The word "concupiscence," or "desire," was used in the reformation century for this tendency and searching. Today better-fitting words might be "orientation" or "impulses," the main point being that sin describes human beings' tendency to cling on false sources of hope and dangers of becoming distracted and losing sight of God's presence in the lives of their own and their neighbors, which in turn leads to different experiences of unhappiness and suffering. As much as the reformers emphasized the reality of this sin, as a force, they also importantly underscored that it is a shared burden. This tendency, this sin is *our* sin, the reformers argued, focusing attention on this primary sin as something shared by humanity rather than seeing the value of dwelling with deliberations between different individual transgressions that, everyone knows, are many (AC 2:3, 4, 5).

Major refocusing thus occurred with the teaching of sin. At the same time, the notion of sin intensified as sin was conceived as more immense and an ongoing condition complicating human existence in all levels and relations. The *Augsburg Confession* characterizes the human condition with a fundamental ontological problem that requires God's attention and initiative for a remedy. Without God's first move to cure the situation, human beings and their world would be lost to this disease that is "our" sin and "our guilt" (AC 2:5). Nobody is immune or untouched by it. An egalitarian view holds that all human beings are in this bondage to sin and cannot free themselves (words frequently used in Lutheran liturgy as part of the confession of sin). Human beings cannot shake it, but God can and will offer a cure of lasting value. Just as God in God's wisdom has allowed sin to enter the human existence and to persist there, God has foreseen a way forward: the cure is Christ and his life and death, and the redeeming and healing impact of this is brought to human beings by the Holy Spirit. After naming the "real" sin that involves all human beings, the *Augsburg Confession* proceeds to explain how with baptism and the Holy Spirit one can expect to receive a new grounding in God and a new orientation with a renewed hope.

Sin, Will, and Non-freedoms[4]

As already noted, Lutheran view of the original sin draws heavily from Augustine who gave the Western church a grammar to speak of the chronic human condition so grave that God needs to design and determine the human beings' fate and remedies needed. With terms *"privatio boni"* and "concupiscence" he argued that human beings were unable to not sin, and therefore God surely would not be expecting human beings to make right choices or be responsible for their fate. The gravest impact of sin was thus the inability to choose, or to choose well, or, to begin with, to have the freedom to choose to not be in bondage to sin.

Augustine had developed his arguments when conversing with his contemporary Pelagius, whose followers are condemned in the *Augsburg Confession* article two. A similar debate took place centuries later between Luther and Erasmus of Rotterdam, a famous humanist scholar at the time.[5] Like Pelagius, Luther's contemporary Erasmus had a more positive view of the human nature and human beings' ability to choose with the help of grace. Both Pelagius and Erasmus had deemed it an unreasonable view that God would be so utterly unjust to design a life for human beings with unattainable expectations. Thus there had to be space for the freedom of choice.

The logic expressed in the article two required further elaboration. Later in article eighteen, the matter of free will is addressed again, right before article nineteen seeks to name the cause of sin. A question arises about God's involvement with sin and all the ills it entails. To clear God from any fault, and to refute imaginations that God would deliberately cause sin, evil, and suffering, article nineteen offers an explanation: "Concerning the cause of sin they teach that although God creates and preserves nature, nevertheless the cause of sin is the will of those who are evil, that is, of the devil and the ungodly. Since it was not assisted by God, their will turned away from God" (quoting John 8:44) (AC 19). Who are the ungodly? In light of the basic teaching of sin, all human beings fall into this category. All human beings are at fault, starting from the first ones. At the same time, the article prompts the possibility that there is such ungodliness and evil in humanity that goes even beyond that. With whom, where, and how such an unredeemable sin might exist—that is a question that the Lutheran reformers left open. That was not to be the preoccupation of mortals with a limited vision.

Similar to Augustine, the reformers taught it was enough to proclaim grace, name the sin, and invite faith community together around the gospel

---

[4]Read AC 18–19, 2. (Skim Ap. 18–19, 2.)

[5]Pelagius (354–418), an ascetically oriented theologian and a major challenger of Augustine's views on human capabilities vis-à-vis grace and salvation. Erasmus of Rotterdam (1466–1536), a Dutch humanist scholar and a key figure in (particularly Northern) European renaissance.

of Christ and therewith draw a mixed community to dwell together, trusting that God sees into the hearts of people like no human can and that some affairs simply belong to God's purview and not for human beings to get obsessed with. Human beings cannot see to each other's souls or make judgments of anyone's holiness or lack of it or internal well-being. Human beings' charge is to worry about sharing the good news of grace, with confidence, with all, and let God do the rest. Besides, a contemporary reader could suggest that just as sin is assumed to involve everyone, also God's grace pertains to everyone. In short, labels of ungodly and evil people render themselves irrelevant, as remnants from medieval vocabulary.

That said, that the article eighteen points to the will as the root of the problem is worth paying attention, especially when it is presumed, with Luther, that human will is bound in matters concerning the salvation and godly matters and is seriously compromised in all matters of choice. From the Latin text, this is said: "they teach that human will has some freedom for producing civil righteousness and for choosing things subject to reason. However, it does not have the power to produce the righteousness of God or spiritual righteousness without the Holy Spirit because 'those who are natural do not receive the gifts of God's Holy Spirit' [1 Cor 2:14]" (AC 18:1–2).[6]

But not to despair, help is already there: instead of trusting the feeble human will and ability to make right choices, the help comes from the outside by the act of God (AC 18:3). "But this righteousness is worked in the heart when the Holy Spirit is received through the Word" (AC 18:3–4). With Augustine, Lutherans profess that "all human beings have a free will that possesses the judgment of reason. It does not enable them, without God, to begin—much less complete—anything that pertains to God, but only to perform the good or evil deeds of this life" (AC 18:4). With good deeds the writers refer to normal daily affairs like going to work, getting dressed, having friends, marrying, etc. (AC 18:5). That is the only area where humans have freedoms to choose, and yet even there, the freedom is compromised with the competing helpful and unhelpful inclinations and calculations that remain a real force in human decision-making.

The *Augsburg Confession* adds a condemnation of the Pelagians and those "who teach that without the Holy Spirit by the power of nature alone, we are able to love God above all things and can also keep the commandments of God" (AC 18:8). The bottom line is the human being's absolute dependency on God's grace in these matters. "Although nature can in some measure produce external works .... Nevertheless it cannot produce internal movements, such as fear of God, trust in God, patience, etc." (AC 18:9). The German text in translation (AC 18:2) phrases it

---

[6]In comparison, the German text reads that (AC 18:1) "human being has some measure of free will, so as to live an externally honorable life and to choose among the things reason comprehends."

poignantly: "However, without the grace, help, and operation of the Holy spirit a human being cannot become pleasing to God, fear or believe in God with the whole heart, or expel innate evil lusts from the heart."

This brings to mind Luther's original theological argument he presented at the *Heidelberg Disputation* in 1518 in the presence of his fellow Augustinian monks. His life-changing theological discovery was exactly this point that human beings cannot and need not make themselves pleasing to God. In the words of his thesis 28, "God's love does not find, but creates, that which is pleasing to it. Human love comes into being through that which is pleasing to it" (*Heidelberg Disputation*, 104).[7] The other side of the coin is his insistence on the absolute bondage of the human will in this regard, most profoundly articulated in his watershed 1525 work *On Bondage of the Will*.[8]

In that famous text Luther speaks of two opposite kingdoms. One is ruled by the Satan, he says, and one by Christ. Human beings exist in the middle. Luther describes the internal and external battles human beings encounter with forces around and inside them, identifying the role of the human conscience in how one sees or feels about oneself and one 's choices. "I should not wish to have free choice given to me." Luther says,

> [E]ven if I lived and worked to eternity, my conscience would never be assured and certain how much it ought to do to satisfy God. ... there would always remain an anxious doubt whether it pleased God or whether God required something more, as the experience of all self-justifiers proves, and as I myself learned to my bitter cost through so many years. But now, since God has taken my salvation out of my hands into God's hands, making it depend on God's choice and not mine, and has promised to save me, not by my own work or exertion but by God's grace and mercy I am assured and certain both that God is faithful and will not lie to me, and also that God is too great and powerful for any demons or adversities to be able to break God or to snatch me from God. (*Bondage of the Will*, 251)

Luther's argument arises from his view of salvation and his notion of God's omnipotence. "Moreover, we are also certain and sure that we please God, not by the merit of our own working but by the favor of God's mercy promised to us, and that if we do less than we should or do it badly, God does not hold this against us, but in a parental way pardons and corrects us. Hence the glorying of all the saints in their God" (ibid., 251). The question would receive more attention from the new generation of Protestant

---

[7]Dennis Bielfeldt, *Heidelberg Disputation*, in *TAL*, Vol. 1, ed. Timothy Wengert (Minneapolis: Fortress Press, 2015), 67–120.
[8]Volker Leppin, *The Bondage of the Will*, in *TAL*, Vol. 2, ed. Kirsi Stjerna (Minneapolis: Fortress Press, 2015), 153–258.

teachers, most notably from the Genevan reformer Jean Calvin, who in the midst of persecutions taught about predestination as a comforting doctrine pointing to the Sovereignty of God.

Luther's main point is about who God is and what are the premises for the delivery of grace. "For if we believe it to be true that God foreknows and predestines all things, ... that nothing takes place but as God wills it ... then on the testimony of reason itself there cannot be any free choice in human being or angel or any creature" (ibid., 255). Luther gives several arguments from the human reality of sin and the function of Satan against the possibility of free will: (ibid.)[9] "To sum up: If we believe that Christ has redeemed human beings by his blood, we are bound to confess that the whole human being was lost; otherwise, we should make Christ either superfluous or the redeemer of only the lowest part of humanity, which would be blasphemy and sacrilege" (ibid., 255). The bottom line for Luther is this: "This omnipotence and the foreknowledge of God, I say, completely abolish the dogma of free choice" (ibid., 229). Luther is protecting his view of salvation by grace alone, by God's doing alone, as a gift to receive only.

If Luther's extreme point proved impossible to agree upon to many of his contemporaries, his viewpoint is not any easier to access today. In a world where individual freedom and choices are of great value, a theological language denying freedom of choice in the ultimate concern matters is hardly appealing and rather is hard to digest. For a contemporary reader, perhaps a helpful opening to this tackle is to look at the intended emphasis: God, God's goodness, and mercy in his bull's eye, Luther sought to lift the burden from the individuals to try make themselves worthy and to free those oppressed under the self-condemnations or feelings of failing. Human beings of any era can at least on some level relate to the experience of burdens, which might be a better term to unfold the therapeutic potential of Luther's insights into the struggles of the human soul. Human passivity or activity specifically in God-human relation may not be the most enticing angle for contemporary Christians, whereas questions pertaining to self and the webs of relations individuals are involved in would offer a plenty of turf to plow from the perspective of freedom/bondage.

The bottom line with the *Augsburg Confession* in the matter of salvation and the restoration of the God-human relationship is this: God does the work, God pulls one in, and the Word is the medium. Human beings cannot want to choose God but they most certainly can be chosen by God. Lutherans' grace-based reasoning left many details open to debate, though. It is hardly surprising that the *Formula of Concord* begins with discussion on sin, which

---

[9]"Similarly, if we believe that Satan is the ruler of this world ... then again it is evident that there can be no such things as free choice." "Similarly, if we believe that original sin has so ruined us that even in those who are led by the Spirit it causes a great deal of trouble by struggling against the good, it is clear that in a human being devoid of the Spirit there is nothing left that can turn toward the good, but only toward evil" (ibid., 255)

is the knot involving the different threads of argumentation: about God, about human life and nature, about freedom of will, about expectations for human life and for justification, about expectations for Christian life *coram deo* and *coram hominibus*, and about church and sacraments. Lutherans' bold teaching of the bondage of the will and irresistibility of grace in conjunction with their teaching of original sin had opened up a can of worms, touching many nerves in medieval Catholic theology, as well as religious practice, including that of sacraments. By the time of writing the *Formula of Concord*, enough conversations had taken place with also different Protestant views on the matter, and yet another angle needed attention: since it was taught that human being is "not free not to sin" and that human will conducts itself *pure passive* in terms of salvation (FC I, II), the topic of predestination warranted returning to (FC XI) but still did not get much space in Lutherans' writings. The case was different with the second-generation reformer Jean Calvin and his followers—amid serious persecutions—who gave more attention to it as a doctrine of comfort, drawing from the conviction of God's sovereignty and trust in God's grace.[10]

Illumination from the *Smalcald Articles* and the *Catechisms*

What the *Augsburg Confession* briefly but firmly states about sin is later affirmed in Luther's *Smalcald Articles* from 1537 (Part III:1–2) that gives a clear exposition of how Lutheran teaching of sin differs from that of the Catholic. Luther's earlier work, the Large *Catechism*, also teaches about sin to a different audience, offering a rich canvas on how sin manifests in human life more concretely. Of all his writings, it could be said, his last lectures on the Book of Genesis offer his final exposition on the matter of sin, taking the reader to the Garden of Eden to explain the origins of sin. From there Luther draws the big picture and the cosmic drama between God and the devil, a war he felt in his life and the experience of which connected him to the first parents (as he understood Adam and Eve, in accordance with the Christian tradition) and their transgression. Unbelief, doubt, and idolatry— with these words Luther strives to explain the existence of sin that has meta historical roots, in light of the biblical narrative, but is ultimately a timeless experience of the breakdown between human beings and their source of life.

---

[10]For Jean Calvin, who had to flee his home in France and who emerged as the leader of reformations in his new home Geneva, which under his leadership welcomed religious refuges for support and training, the doctrine of predestination was about God's sovereignty and eternal degree. It provided comfort for the persecuted Protestants, while it was not the central piece in Calvin's own theology, whereas after him in what is known as "Calvinism," the doctrine was extrapolated further to explicate human beings' total depravity, unconditional election, limited atonement, God's irresistible grace, and perseverance of the saints (t.u.l.i.p).

While the study on Genesis lectures is beyond the scope of this discussion, a few words can be offered to point to the uniqueness of Luther's interpretation. Analyzing the discourse between Eve and Adam and the serpent—also a creature of God, important to notice—Luther zooms into the fundamental breaking point in God-human relations: the experience of sin originates from human beings' aspiration to be like God in a wrong way, the desire to know more than they could handle and, most egregiously, to doubt God's word. Unbelief, not believing God's Word given for human beings specifically, led the first parents to let themselves be lured to buy the devil's lie. Luther's fresh interpretation of the role of Eve stands in contrast to the more traditional readings that considered women the weaker link and more susceptible to a temptation. Neither with Eve nor with the matriarchs that followed would Luther hold woman as the primarily responsible party; rather, his treatment of the biblical texts draws an integral connection from Eve to Mary to illuminate God's manifold working through women as the promise-bearers in the story of creation and salvation.[11]

In the *Smalcald Articles*[12] Luther reminds the reader that sin comes from the original disobedience of Adam and Eve against the fundamental vital command to not eat from the tree of knowledge. Their disobedience manifested their ill-directed desire, their wanting what was against their best and against what God had intended, all of which had devastating consequences. The disobedience earned the humankind the condition called original sin which in turn leads to acts that Luther calls evil works. Reflecting on the Ten Commandments, Luther provides a plenty of examples on how deep and broad the impact of these sinful impulses is in human life and relations.

Luther's language is colorful.

The fruits of this sin are the subsequent evil works, which are forbidden in the Ten Commandments, such as unbelief, false belief, idolatry, being without the fear of God, presumptuousness, despairing, blindness, and, in summary, not knowing or honoring God. Beyond that, there is lying, swearing [falsely] by God's name, not praying or calling on God's name, neglecting God's Word, being disobedient to parents, murdering, unchastity, stealing, deceiving, etc.

---

[11]Luther's last lectures focused on Genesis, over the last ten years of his life. In many ways they present the rich summa of his theology and biblical interpretation. See the introductions and annotated revised translations of Genesis 1–3 by Jussi Koivisto, Kirsi Stjerna, and Else Marie Wiberg Pedersen, in *The Annotated Luther*, Vol. 6, ed. Euan Cameron, 2017. Also, Kirsi Stjerna, "Grief, Glory and Grace: Insights on Eve and Tamar in Luther's Genesis Commentary," *Seminary Ridge Review* 6/2 (Spring 2004), 19–35.

[12]References to *Smalcald Articles* are taken from *The Annotated Luther*, Vol. 2, ed. Kirsi Stjerna, 2015, introduced, revised, and annotated by Kurt Hendel.

Furthermore, "Such inherited sin is such a deep, evil corruption of nature that reason does not comprehend it; rather, it must be believed on the basis of scriptural revelation in Ps. 51[:5] and Rom. 5[:12]; Exod. 33[:20]; Gen. 3[:6ff.]" (SA Part III art. 1).[13]

Then he launches into attacking the errors of the "scholastics," that is, medieval theologians. His main issue with their teachings was with their optimism regarding what has remained intact or capable in human nature after the Fall. He rejects the teaching that "each human being possesses by nature sound reason and a good will," that "the human being has a free will, either to do good and reject evil or, on the other hand, to reject good and do evil," and that "the human being is able to keep and carry out every command of God by using natural powers" (SA Part III art. 1). He refutes any teaching that would imply that "if human beings do as much as is in their power, then God will certainly give grace to them" (ibid.).[14] And there it is, his main point, his central teaching that grace is free and cannot be earned. Grace must be free, just as sin is real and prohibits human beings from reaching grace. Expecting human beings to draw from their natural powers and goodness would return to the teachings he was trying to reform. With his teaching on the incapacitating power of sin, and with that the immensity of God's free grace, Luther knows he is presenting an unpopular position. He is critiquing rational efforts to explain this issue called original sin and makes a striking statement: this (too) is a matter of belief. It does not make sense, but so it is.

While Luther, in his own assessment, was not really adding anything new doctrinally but staying within the Augustinian parameters in thinking about sin and freedom issues, his emphasis on grace is extreme and unyielding; there is his uniqueness among theologians before and after. His peers and followers had difficulty following in his steps in this regard. This shows already in Melanchthon's *Apology* and its long treatment on the article two, and the fact that the youngest book in the confessions had to return to the article after several controversies split Lutherans on this matter.

The Synergistic Controversy and Lutherans in Discord

Disagreements among Lutherans on the matter of sin were serious and led to controversies[15] that threatened to split the constituency. Synergistic controversy is the name for the intra-Lutheran debate about the limits of

---

[13]See also Kolb and Wengert, *The Book of Concord*, SA Part III art. 1.
[14]See also Kolb and Wengert, *The Book of Concord*, SA Part III art. 1:4–8.
[15]On the controversies, see *The Formula of Concord*, 1577 in Chapter 3.

will and freedom of choice vis-à-vis grace and Christian life. The actual question for the most was not about theory but a practical matter on how this scenario of being saved by grace alone in faith with no works or effort from their part and with no free will to make the first move toward God would show in real life. How this new status and situation would manifest in Christian life, and what could be expected as a result of this miraculous event?

Formula of Concord had to judicate between different opinions on the matter with affirmative and negative theses. The cause of debate is stated in the first article: is original sin "really, without any distinction, the corrupted nature, substance and essence of the human creature"? Or is there "a distinction between the human substance, nature, essence, body and soul, and original sin" so that human nature and original sin are distinct and not identical? (FC I:1). This question is logically prompted from the strong teaching of the pervasiveness of the original sin in human life, desires, and decision-making.

As a solution, it is proposed that there is a difference between the originally pure, God-created nature of human being and the original sin. "The difference is as great as the difference between the work of God and the work of the devil" (FC I:2). God is the creator of all nature, all bodies, before and after the Fall; thus this goodness and distinction cannot be forgotten (FC I:4). Furthermore, as the most convincing proof: Christ took on himself this nature, all of it. "But he did not create, assume, redeem, or sanctify original sin." Therefore, they write, "From all this, it is easy to distinguish between the corrupted nature and the corruption which is embedded in this nature—through which this nature is corrupted" (FC I:7).[16]

In other words, in Lutheran view, God creates good, and only good. The wrong, the evil, the bad in the good creation is not God's doing. In this view, human being's substance can never be equated with something called evil and bad. Sin, in a way, is the unwanted guest who does not leave. The impact of the sin is real and felt in every human life, while this sin has not replaced human beings' godly created existence; there's the difference. At the same time, the document continues to address the gravitas of the situation: this sin "is a corruption so deep that there is nothing sound or uncorrupted left in the human body or soul, in its internal or external powers" (FC I:8). This goes clearly beyond human logic. "The damage is so indescribable that it cannot be recognized by our reason but only from God's Word. The damage is such that only God alone can separate human nature and the corrupt of this nature from each other." How does this separation happen? Not in this life. It happens at the resurrection, through death, at God's doing (FC I:9–10). The final conclusion is the affirmation of

---

[16]Words "substance" and "*accidens*" are used to make a distinction between what makes an entity what it "is" in its core and the changeable and unessential characteristics of it.

the goodness of the human nature and flesh, namely, at the resurrection "I will be covered in my own skin, and in my flesh I shall see God" (quoting Job 19:26–7). From this resurrection belief one can, at least in part, comprehend how the original sin that is so real and damaging in one's life is not the final word or the real essence of the human being, created by God, whose creation is good.

It is not a coincidence that the article immediately following addresses the free will, another *status controversiae*. Of all the different situations for human will—in creation before the Fall, after the Fall, after the new birth, and at the resurrection—it is the second that requires further deliberation: "What kind of powers do human beings have after the fall of our first parents, before rebirth, on their own, in spiritual matters?" "Are they able ... to dispose themselves favorably toward God's grace" and prepare themselves to receive the Spirit, offered in Word and in sacraments (FC II:1)? In line with the earlier article, this is the answer: that human reason is blind to spiritual matters (FC II:2), and furthermore, human will "has become God's enemy" as "it has only the desire and will to do evil". Therefore, the goodness and competence of human beings in spiritual matters always come from God (FC II:3).

Quite startling words are used to describe this passive standing: those who are "spiritually dead" because of sin cannot raise themselves any more than a dead corpse could make itself to live again (FC II:3). The imagery makes the point clear about the absolute necessity of grace and the absolute passivity of the human being in spiritual matters. The article rejects several other view points on freedom vis-a-vis human abilities and sin. The writers "condemn" suggestions that human beings could, "on the basis of their own natural power", obey God and prepare their will and themselves for grace. That is not how grace works, they surmise. Besides, sin makes any such movement from human beings' part impossible. (FC Ep. II: 7–19.)

The preceding article (FC I) characterizes sin as a fundamental enmity of God and uses colorful expressions to describe the "inherited guilt," "horrible disease," and "total corruption"[17] that is so deep that only God can heal the un-regenerated will. The emphasis is on the activity of God. Since human beings are unable to will themselves toward God or even want God, there really is only one solution for the problem of sin and salvation: God must take care of things. The Lutheran document affirms God's power to save— that being the gospel—and that it is in God's acting through the Word that human beings would not plug their ears but receive the gospel (FC II:5) and, importantly, the Holy Spirit, "who alone accomplishes the conversion of the

---

[17]FC Ep. I:1–10. II:5–7, 9–11, 33, 60. The impact of sin in will is addressed in several articles, also in FC Ep. III on righteousness.

human being." The article quotes John 15:5, "Apart from me [Christ], you can do nothing." The question of predestination is evoked here preliminarily, and it is returned to later. That is a difficult topic Lutherans have spent very little time on, and for a reason. Similarly difficult topic is that of conversion and rebirth, which the article touches upon.

After rejecting several teachings of the medieval Catholic church, namely, the article concludes, "[I]t is correct to say that in conversion God changes recalcitrant, unwilling people into willing people through the drawing power of the Holy Spirt and that after this conversion the reborn human will is not idle in the daily exercise of repentance, but cooperates in all the works of the Holy Spirit which he [the Spirit] performs through us" (FC II:17). Luther is explicitly evoked to support the point made:

> Likewise, when Dr. Luther wrote that the human will conducts itself *pure passive* (that is, that it does absolutely nothing at all), that must be understood *respectu divinae gratiae in accendendis novis motibus*, that is, insofar as God's Spirit takes hold of the human will through the Word that is heard or through the use of the holy sacraments and effects new birth and conversion. For when the Holy Spirit has affected and accomplished new birth and conversion and has altered and renewed the human will solely through his divine power and activity, then the new human will is an instrument and tool of God the Holy Spirit, in that the will not only accepts grace but also cooperates with the Holy Spirit in the works that proceed from it. (FC II:18)

Just as this statement raises the question of the freedom of the will, that had been repudiated earlier, a clarification follows: there are "only two efficient causes, the Holy Spirit and God's Word as the instrument of the Holy Spirit" that effect human being's conversion. People need to hear the Word about grace, but human beings "cannot believe and accept it on the basis of its own powers but only through grace and action of God the Holy Spirit" (FC II:19). After it is all said and done, the *Formula of Concord* adds little clarity to the question of free will and sin. It rather reveals the ongoing tensions and different leanings with the question, even among Lutherans defending Luther's views. Also, it opens up the door to discuss predestination.

The word "predestination" refers to a view that God has foreseen and predetermined human beings' eternal faith. Essentially the doctrine of predestination is about the Sovereignty of God, as the Genevan reformer Jean Calvin proclaimed. Given the debilitating sin, in divine mercy God has prepared a person's path to grace and salvation. Grace is the agent, and human being receives divine care, as God has planned it and seen good. In his context in Geneva, where many a persecuted Protestant found their way for safety, it was a comforting doctrine to know that all lives, and deaths, were in God's hand. Luther held a similar view, in the tradition of

Augustine, but preferred to say very little about it. He did not see it wise or necessary for human beings to try to probe the question of God's mind. Unlike Calvin, Luther did not want to speculate on the rationales for God not wanting to save someone. The so-called double predestination view, that God predestines some people to salvation and not others, was of little interest to Luther. The same was true with speculations on the difference between God foreseeing versus God predetermining.

Even if the question of predestination was not a primary concern for Lutheran reformers generally speaking, the second-generation reformers in particular needed to clarify their position on it, if for no other reason than at least in response to Calvin's theology. The topic receives its own article in the Epitome and Solid Declaration of the *Formula of Concord*. Article eleven states that there is no dispute on this article of "comfort." The authors offer a Lutheran orientation to this question, by explaining the terminology used. A distinction is made between God's foreknowledge and predetermination of human fate: First, *praescientia*, foreknowledge, means "nothing else than that God knows all things before they happen." It is not simply the cause of sin or evil (for the latter God sets limits rather) (FC Ep. 3). Second, *praedestinatio*, God's eternal election, "extends only to the righteous, God-pleasing children of God. It is a cause of their salvation, which God brings about" (FC Ep. XI:5). Beyond this one should not try to probe it (FC Ep. XI:6). The glue and the heart for opinions on predestination is what was believed about Christ, who was both chosen and voluntarily offered himself for the salvation of the humankind. Given that his offer pertained to all, just as God's grace does, the reason for any condemnation then must lie in people not hearing God's word and plugging their ears—something that God sees but does not cause (FC Ep. XI: 8, 12, 13, 15). It appears that the more the confessions writers attempted to say about predestination, the more complicated the matter became, with more questions than answers emerging. Luther's advice of "don't go there" had its reasons!

The sixteenth-century Lutheran solution to the question of predestination could be concluded from the *Formula of Concord*'s interim wording: "God undoubtedly also knows and has determined for every believer the time and hour of calling and conversion. However, because this has not been revealed to us, we must obey his [God's] command always to cling to the Word and to commend the time and the hour to God" (FC SD XI:56). In other words, the Lutheran orientation is that of trust in God's care as revealed in the Scriptures and not worrying about what is not for humans to worry about. Rather than occupy their minds with the question of election, Christians should remember this: that God wants to be active in human beings with the Holy Spirit and "through the Word, when it is preached, heard, and meditated on, to convert hearts to true repentance, and to enlighten them in true faith" (FC SD XI:17). From this foundation it makes sense to talk about predestination as a comforting doctrine:

If we are content to remain with and hold to the mystery of predestination insofar as it is revealed to us in God's Word, it is a very useful, salutary, and comforting teaching. For it confirms most powerfully the article [43–9] that we become righteous and are saved apart from all our works and merit, purely on the basis of grace, solely for Christ's sake. (FC SD XI:43)

Sin in Daily Life—Perspectives from the *Catechisms*[18]

Luther's *Large Catechism*[19] brings the teaching of sin to home with its explanation of the Ten Commandments, in particular. The Ten Commandments could be read as a mirror to the human sinful condition and how sin manifests in daily life and human relations.

First, with his instruction on the first three commandments, Luther explains the basic sinful orientation of human beings. Not knowing who one's God is or putting one's trust elsewhere but God and not honoring God's name and presence in one's life is at the root of the human problems. One's values and orientation are just off, and that has consequences. From there on, it is to be expected that human beings will falter in other relations as well. Luther steers attention to the sins of neglect, the sins of tongue and hurting others, as well as the sins of neglect towards those in need. These are the kinds of transgressions people should be worried about, in his opinion, in their daily lives, where sin and its impact are experienced concretely. At the same time, in these areas, human beings have clear expectations and (some) freedoms to make choices toward the benefit of their neighbor. With the word "sin" Luther explains the difficulty with those choices and why people against their better judgment in many ways fail not just the expectations of God and their neighbors' but their own as well.

Commandments seven to ten cover basic human affairs in light of the expectation of love and respect of the other: For example, whereas holy life would entail no stealing or "sinful and forbidden" coveting after other people's belongings, or spouse, or honor, most humans find this an impossible rule to follow (LC 348); human beings do steal, and hurt, and betray, and get into other people's lives in ways that are improper and unhealthy and unethical. Also, and most definitely, human beings sin on daily basis with their tongue and words shot to hurt others. Talking about others and their business,

---

[18]With the publisher T&T Clark's permission, the text in this section draws from chapter 3.3 "The Large Catechism (1529), Martin Luther (1483–1546)," in *Reading Christian Theology in the Protestant Tradition*, eds. Kelly M. Kapic and Hans Madueme (London, New York, Delhi Sydney: Bloomsbury T&T Cl ark, 2018), 351–61, pages 352–4 in particular; with endnotes deleted and citations adjusted.

[19]References to and quotations from the *Large Catechism* are from *The Annotated Luther*, Vol. 2, ed. Kirsi Stjerna, 2015.

especially in a negative sense, is an absolute no-no for Luther. It is a clear commandment from God, he points out (LC 341–7). "So you see that we are absolutely forbidden to speak evil of our neighbor" (LC 344). Yet that is exactly what human beings do, and this is one of the most devastating sins humans commit against one another. Luther says, "There is nothing around or in us that can do greater good or greater harm in temporal or spiritual matters than the tongue, although it is the smallest and weakest member" (LC 347).[20] The word "concupiscence" and the reformers' logic about the irresistible nature of sin make sense with this particular manifestation of it: even if one rationally knows of the harm done with words, lies, and gossip, the human heart is not immune to feelings and impulses that lead to these transgressions.

Luther also points out another form of sinning: not caring for those in need. To ignore those in need would be similarly devastating. "But beware of how you deal with the poor" because "if you arrogantly turn away those who need your aid ... they will cry out to heaven ... [and] they will reach God, who watches over poor, troubled hearts" (LC 339–40).[21] This warning is as important today as it was in Luther's day, as the numbers of poverty are only rising while the wealth of the privileged increases—both in terms of individuals and countries—and the gap between those in need and those with means only expands. Seeing God on the side of the marginalized and needy, and addressing a concrete matter of injustice, such as poverty, is in line with Luther's theology of the cross. Notable contemporary theologians have powerfully extrapolated Luther's conviction of God's presence in the margins and in the suffering to apply theology of the cross as an approach to reality that is fueled by compassion and solidarity to eradicate different forms of injustice and poverty.[22]

The commandments guiding family relations are essential and dear for Luther. In his married experience, he knows there is enough of a holy challenge in the domestic scene to try not to break the commandments. No monasteries are needed for spaces to learn spiritual discipline—regular households will do just fine for that as a true testing ground (LC 316). Household chores and parent-child responsibilities outdo the "holiness and

---

[20]See also Kolb and Wengert, The Book of Concord, LC 425:293; LC 420–5; LC 422:274; LC 424; LC 425:291.

[21]See also Kolb and Wengert, The Book of Concord, LC 419:246.

[22]On Luther's theology of the cross—a topic that warrants its own book—the following authors contribute significantly: Vitor Westhelle, "Usus Crucis: The Use and Abuse of the Cross and the Practice of Resurrection," in Encounters with Luther: New Directions for Critical Studies, eds. Kirsi Stjerna and Brooks Schramm (Louisville, KY: Westminster John Knox Press, 2016), 85–95; Deanna A. Thompson, "Becoming a Feminist Theologian of the Cross," ibid., 96–108; John Douglas Hall, "The Theology of the Cross: A Usable Past," ibid., 173–84; Anna Madsen, "Suffering and the Theology of the Cross from a Feminist Perspective," ibid., 241–9. Also, Arnfridur Gudmundsdottir, Meeting God on the Cross: Christ, the Cross, and the Feminist Critique (Hardcover, 2009). See a few comments in Chapter 9, Conclusions.

austere life of all the monks," Luther proclaims, like no other theologian before him (LC 322).[23] True happiness begins from a happy household where faith and love rule, Luther believes.

An ex-monk married to an ex-nun Katharina von Bora (1525) and a father of six children, Luther describes parenthood as a holy vocation and also an area of daily challenge: "God has given this walk of life, fatherhood and motherhood, a special position of honor, higher than that of any other walk of life under it" (LC 314). Yet the proper honoring and respect does not necessarily happen. Young people need to be taught to love and honor their parents. "It must therefore be impressed on young people that they revere their parents as God's representatives, and to remember that, however lowly, poor, feeble, and eccentric they may be, they are still their mother and father, given by God. They are not to be deprived of their honor because of their ways or failings" (LC 315). Using words like "lowly," "feeble," and "eccentric" is a gentle way to talk about the many failures any parent may experience. He does not call these experiences explicitly as sins but points the dynamics between parents and children as areas where sins fester. As for children, obedience is the "great, good, and holy work" expected from them (LC 316).[24] Contemporary reader can remember Luther's context of a patriarchally ordered society, the hierarchy of which was mirrored in domestic relations, and contemporary reader can appreciate his intent of maintaining peace and order and his care for the children's well-being. For him, obedience to parents entailed also parents' reasonable relating to the children and mutual care. In that light, his advice makes sense. In light of the abundance of experiences where parents have terribly failed or hurt their children, such advice, from any figure, need critical assessment. Perhaps words "respect" and "responsibility" could communicate better Luther's intent with his concerns about parent-child relations.[25]

Marriage itself is praised in the *Catechisms* as the most honorable walk of life, protected by the sixth commandment: one must not dishonor one's spouse with adultery (LC 331) but cherish the spouse given by God (LC 335).[26] God is involved in all the aspects of marriage and parenting; these vocations are the cradle of holiness—and also of the gravest of temptations. This would be an opening for a rich conversation on Lutheran theological perspectives on humanity, human relations, and sexuality. For now, let it just be noted that this is the realm of urgencies for today's Lutheran theological

---

[23]See also Kolb and Wengert, *The Book of Concord*, LC 401:112; LC 406:146.
[24]See also Kolb and Wengert, *The Book of Concord*, LC 400:105; LC 401:108; LC 402:116; LC 401:112.
[25]Luther's love for the children and the theological attention he devoted to children is notable; he also has firm words on those who hurt children; for example, see Kirsi Stjerna, "A Lutheran Feminist Critique of American Child Protection Laws: Sins of Sexual Nature," in Ronald Duty and Marie Failinger, eds., *On Secular Governance: Lutheran Perspectives on Contemporary Legal Issues* (Grand Rapids, MI: Eerdman, 2016).
[26]See also Kolb and Wengert, *The Book of Concord*, LC 413:200; LC 415:219.

deliberation where religious views have a concrete impact on human beings' quality of life, dignity, and freedoms.

Contemporary Considerations: Freedom in Non-freedom

The reformers explained sin as an inherited disposition and a chronic desire that was destructive and aiming wrong, not orienting one's concerns toward God and one's neighbors and their benefit. Perhaps today one could reconsider the sin-talk as a way to name a basic human experience on a very rudimentary, instinctive level. Human beings do not always want or do what they should. Human beings make questionable choices, often, and against their best intentions. Human beings hurt one another, and themselves, and the world around them. Human beings fail to live their lives in ways that would manifest trust and honor and love with God as the ground of being. There is a certain relief in naming this experience with sin, and yet, a contemporary person cannot help but ask whether the sin-talk is really necessary. For the time being, Lutheran faith language presumes so.

There is a therapeutic value in looking at one's life from the perspective of "it is ok, it is not (all) your fault, and you are forgiven, you are free from self-imposed burdens, or from those set for you by others." That said, Luther's adamant, excessive, extreme insistence on the bondage of the will is harder to swallow, especially in today's climate where freedom and individual choices are valued. Perhaps, to propose, it is enough to appreciate the emphasis Luther had, and for good reasons, that one does not need to try to make oneself worthy, which is beyond anyone's hands. Luther believed that God makes people worthy, just as God gives people life. Taking this as the starting point would underscore the immensity of underserved grace, and it would allow one to adore the mysterious God who would want and grant such a thing—against any human reasoning! Also, it would allow an opening to consider what happens next: what all is possible for and with people who are so free.

Luther's and Lutheran insistence on the bondage of the will does not negate the attention to the responsibilities and possibilities of individuals with faith in their current conditions, quite the contrary. As long as it is remembered that no good deed, no good will, no good disposition is required or would make one better than the person nearby, then active language about the parameters of Christian life is more than welcome. This is so especially in light of the ills of the world. It would appear that the personal obsession with sin and the sin-language inherited from Luther can be put in a new perspective in contemporary situation. Rather than viewing sin as something that only taints or problematizes one's self-worth and relationship with one's God, it would seem timely to recognize sin in human beings' external relations and in the different structures of human life and, importantly, not remain there but embrace boldly and compassionately the ethical and spiritual challenges that grow from such awakening.[27]

I. Central Topics and Learning Goals

1. Lutheran notion of sin and original sin.
2. Lutheran view of the bondage of the will.
3. Perspectives on human nature and hope.

II. Questions for Review, Discussion, and Further Reflection

1. What would be the benefit or disadvantage of starting with the recognition of sin in human life—is there any wisdom in that?
2. What are the challenges and the potential of "bondage of the will" premise?
3. How does the article on sin lean on and illustrate the teaching of justification by faith?
4. Intersections between the ideas of sin, church, and sacraments.

III. Keywords

Concupiscence, forgiveness, freedom, guilt, hope, original sin, predestination, sin, suffering, will/bondage will.

IV. Readings with the Chapter

AC 2, 18, 19. (Skim Ap. 2, 18, 19.) Also SA Part III art. 1–2, 3–4. FC I-II, XI. LC, Ten Commandments. LC, Lord's Prayer, petition 4–7.

---

[27]See Cynthia Moe-Lobeda, *Resisting Structural Evil: Love as Ecological-economic Vocation* (Minneapolis: Fortress Press, 2013).

7

Communities of Faith and Means of Grace

Christian Lutheran Communities and Their Reformation Roots

Who are evangelical or Lutheran Christians? How do these Christians continue to live with that identity outside the mother church, the Catholic church, after the Reformations? What would be the parameters for a new church or a new branch? What about the old church, what in it needed reforming, and what could still work? The sixteenth-century Protestant ancestors pondered upon these questions that strike a chord with contemporary Christians, who find themselves similarly assessing what would be the point with the institution called church. What does it stand for, for whom, and what constitutes a church? Also of contemporary relevance is the question of what all is needed for unity in order for the diverse groups to call themselves Lutheran.

Lutheran Christians were exiled from the Catholic church as a danger to the empire since the 1521 papal bull that had declared Luther, and his associates, a heretic—a crime that could lead to death. This theological condemnation has not been officially lifted, not even with the historic ecumenical signing of the *Joint Declaration on the Doctrine of*

Read AC 5, 7–8, 14–15. (Skim Ap. 5, 7–8, 14–15.) Recommended SA Part III art. 4, 12, 5–15; Part II art. 2; FC V, X. LC and SA citations are from *The Annotated Luther*, Vol. 2, ed. Kirsi Stjerna, 2015. LC references also given in footnotes to Kolb and Wengert, *Book of Concord*.

Justification (1999).[1] Institutionally and politically, it was not until the Lutherans' 1530 *Augsburg Confession* was accepted at the 1555 Peace of Augsburg that any other than Catholic form of Christianity was a legal option in the Holy Roman empire in the West. Since the watershed imperial decisions in the fourth-century Roman empire, after the Emperor Constantine's conversion and his successor's decision to declare Christianity the only accepted religion, the catholic Christian faith had unified citizens from East to West.

Three watershed periods can be noted as times when the unity of the church became seriously challenged: First, after the expansion of the Roman empire to the East in the fourth century with Emperor Constantine, the Byzantine with its new capital Constantinople (modern day Istanbul) grew independent until the invasions of the Turks in the fifteenth century. Second, the mutual independency of the East and the West became solidified with the 1054 dramatic split, caused by a variety of political, theological, cultural, and geographic factors; from thereon, Christianity was practiced in the East and the West in distinctive forms, while still sharing the faith of the ecumenical Creeds.[2] Third, in the West, the next major transformation took place with the sixteenth-century Protestant reformations. Lutherans, as the foremost instigators, laid roots for a new direction for the practice and teaching of the Christian faith and in many ways were setting a new stage in Europe with multiplying denominations and religious diversity.

When assessing the actions of the first reformers, it needs to be noted that until the 1555 legal acceptance of the Lutheran faith in accordance with the *Augsburg Confession* as a viable form of Christian religion in the empire, restructuring and reforming efforts could be judged as a form of transgression and punishable as such. That said, transgressors as they were, the Lutheran reformers were not interested in causing political revolution. Generally speaking, individuals worked hard to avoid chaos in the matters of religion. Their intent was not to cause disorder, but, being passionate about their faith, they were willing to take risks to make sure that the Christian faith continued to be practiced with the (in their assessment) right teaching and proper sources and means. They believed Christian communities were

---

[1] *The Joint Declaration on the Doctrine of Justification* (JDDJ), a major milestone in ecumenical dialogue between Lutherans and Catholics, was signed in 1999 and has since then been joined by the Reformed, Anglican, and Methodist church bodies. The document takes a critical look at the teachings from both sides and evaluates the past—as conceived—disagreements and concludes on the shared Christian teaching of salvation being from God and a gift of grace.

[2] The Eastern Orthodox Church, or the Orthodox Catholic Church, is the oldest continuous expression of Christian faith, with about 260 million members, most of them Russian-speaking. Unlike in the Catholic church with the Pope as its head, the Orthodox churches are organized by local synods and bishops with the Ecumenical Patriarchate of Constantinople as the "first among equals." Christological issues since the council of Chalcedon (451) had already caused divisions, the 1054 mutual excommunication of the Christian leaders of the East and the West leading to the most significant, and lasting, split.

instrumental for the well-being of the citizens of the society. In negotiating the reforms for the health of such communities, the German reformers sought ways to maintain a workable situation within the political system, focusing on religious reforms, while knowing that some of those would have impact outside the church walls as well.

The questions about the church—what it is, for what, and for whom— were both theological and practical. Lutherans had to consider what would be the proper parameters for the new or rather reformed church that aimed to return to the most original ways. Would there be a need for liturgy and if so, what about it? How would the Word be proclaimed, who would preach and with what, and why? Would there be need for holy rituals known as sacraments, and how would those be decided about? How about leadership? Who would do what in the church, and where would the power reside? In the end, how would this faith community look like, and would all the Lutheran faith communities (need to) look alike?

The reformers set up quite general and, in their view, realistic expectations. They discerned it best not to dismiss all of the old ways, as that had not been the intent of the reforms to begin with. Going back to the fundamental understanding of what was needed for the church and what was its primary and ultimate function, the reformers stayed within the broader parameters that had structured the life of the church in the preceding centuries. Unlike the more radical reforming groups, Lutherans sought to maintain much of the old order for Christian communities. They considered faith communities important for the nurturing of Christian life and in fueling its members in their vocations in the society. Church would be the place where to teach the Christian faith, with a Lutheran interpretation, to practice it and to come together for the proclamation of the Word and for the celebration of the sacraments and mutual support. There should be individuals duly called to serve the church and the gospel, on behalf of all, while all the baptized were included in the priesthood expressed in different aspects of life. There should be sacraments as the heart of what the church would offer, but newly defined and used in accordance with new revised rationales. The worship, the Mass, would continue as a staple in its reformed format.

This vision for the church and its functions and offices is briefly explained in the *Augsburg Confession* articles five, seven, and eight and with more flesh in the *Large Catechism*, particularly with the third part of the Creed. Also the *Smalcald Articles* add to the definition, reminding of the initial reasons for the reforms and summarizing the revised teaching of the sacraments and their use.[3]

---

[3]On Luther's teaching on church and the sacraments, see *The Annotated Luther*, Vol. 3, ed. Paul W. Robinson (Minneapolis: Fortress Press, 2016). See the *Large Catechism*, the *Confession of Faith*, and the *Smalcald Articles*, in *The Annotated Luther*, Vol. 2, ed. Kirsi Stjerna, 2015. Also, Cheryl M. Peterson, *Who Is the Church. An Ecclesiology for the Twenty-First Century* (Minneapolis: Fortress Press, 2013).

The Making of the Church and Its Purpose[4]

In Lutheran understanding, the church exists and functions because of faith. The *Augsburg Confession* explains the Lutheran view of the church in articles five, seven, and eight with a noteworthy order.

Article five about the ministry of the church comes right after the main article four about justification by faith. The conviction that human beings are received into grace and are reckoned and made holy rests on what is understood with faith: faith is the agent, the energy, with which grace alters the status and the orientation of the human being. The church and church callings are instituted for the purposes of generating such faith in human beings. This happens with the mighty help of nothing less than the Holy Spirit.

In Lutheran teaching, the Holy Spirit comes to human beings in the Word and Sacraments that the church is caring for and with (AC 5:1–3). In Lutheran emphasis, it is always God who effects faith and always via Word. Specifically, the Holy Spirit, received through Word and sacraments, "effects faith where and when it pleases God in those who hear the gospel" (AC 5:2–3). Other scenarios are rejected, such as those that teach that human beings would be able to prepare themselves for grace without the Word (AC 5:4). With their emphasis on the external Word, the confession writers defend their view of grace being free and human beings not needing, nor being able, to earn it or even prepare themselves for it. This has implications for how the function of the church, and its welcome, is understood: in the church people can expect to encounter God the Spirit, in the Word and in the sacraments. No prerequisites are set for entering this community of the Spirit. The church is meant for human beings in need of God and of one another, in whom the Spirit of Gods dwells.

The following article six brings "new obedience" as the consequence of justification and encountering the Spirit in the Word that justifies: the faith received by the Spirit's work is bound to produce good works. Referring to ancient authors, the article, again, underscores that salvation, and in that the forgiveness of sins, is a gift received by faith alone and not in any shape or form merited by these works of new obedience (AC 7:3). The article seven that follows returns to the definition of the church as the vital nurturing place for the Spirit and the Word to birth and feed the faith that justifies.

The one holy eternal church, article teaches, is a community of saints. For the unity of this assembly it suffices that the word is proclaimed and sacraments are administered. "Likewise, they teach that one holy church will remain forever. The church [*ecclesia*] is the assembly of saints [*congregatio sanctorum*] in which the gospel is taught purely and the sacraments are administered rightly" (AC 7:1, Latin).[5] Here is the simple

---

[4]Read AC 5, 7–8. (Skim Ap. 5, 7–8.) Recommended SA Part III art. 4, 12.
[5]In German, *die Versammlung aller Glaubigen*, the assembly of all believers.

definition of the church, one that leaves freedom for quite different local customs in praxis. "It is not necessary that human traditions, rites, or ceremonies instituted by human beings be alike everywhere" (AC 7:3, Latin). This flexibility has allowed the Lutheran world to expand in different directions and have a different face in different contexts. One thing is considered a given, though: there is no Lutheran church, not even in theory, where proclamation and sacraments would not be offered. Also, the words "rightly" and "purely" carry weight; in the interpretation and proclamation of the Word and in the practice of the sacraments, the specifically Lutheran teaching of justification was (to be) employed and practiced with no exceptions.

A Community of Sinners and Saints

Who belongs to the assembly of saints is the next question. In the turmoil of reforms and as regents and regional governments had a say and an investment in the affairs of the church in their land, membership became a live question: who belongs to the Protestant communities of faith? Article eight (AC 8:1) answers broadly that the church is "the assembly of believers and saints … " [*societas sanctorum et vere credentium*]. In a language that is less palpable for contemporary discourse, the article names hypocrites and "evil people" (AC 8:1–2, Latin), "public sinners" and "false Christians" among those who worship in these communities (AC 8:1–2, German). In other words, sacraments that the church administers belong to all. The Lutheran view of the church is broad and inclusive. It is a place for sinners. The word "sinner" needs to be understood in light of the Lutheran conviction that all human beings are sinners and nobody is free from sin.

Lutherans' inclusive view of church and sacraments speaks of the firm belief in God's action and rises from the fundamental teaching of justification by faith alone. Building on the teaching of Augustine, Lutherans clearly and definitely refute the so-called Donatist heresy: a view point that had gained traction in fourth-sixth centuries in the church of Carthage in particular. In the aftermath of the persecutions of Christians, the Donatists sought to protect the purity of the church and tied the sacraments' effectiveness to the goodness and purity of the priest performing them. Named after the North African bishop, Donatists considered invalid the ordinations of those priests and from those bishops who had crumbled under the persecutions, and thereby the sacraments they would administer would lack validity. They also desired to keep the Christian church pure and exclude known sinners. In a decisive battle of words, Augustine's opposing view prevailed. In his teaching, church is a mixed community of sinners and saints for whom the sacraments effect grace by the work of God without the prerequisite of the flawlessness of the clergy administering them or the person receiving them. Article eight reiterates that conviction.

The article also reaffirms the Lutheran position on the value of external signs. The writers reject alternate views that place a lower value on such rituals; for example, the Anabaptists and the Enthusiasts are rejected—a label given to the more radical and explicitly Spirit-led and world-rejecting reforming movements.[6] The differences regarding the holy rituals speak of important disagreements in how the sacraments work vis-à-vis faith. Lutheran view of sacraments rests on how God's action is understood and how the means of grace are tied into what is believed about Christ's work. The effectiveness of the means of grace is not tied to the recipients' or administerers' purity or evidence of their sanctity. The emphasis is on their effectiveness *extra nos*, beyond human effort or performance, resting solely on God. Also on a theological basis, Lutheran invitation to the sacraments is open and inclusive, just as the membership in a faith community is open and without prerequisites in accordance with the doctrine of justification by faith alone because of God's grace.

In contemporary church practice, the Lutheran principle of inclusivity is of utmost importance. It may be one of the most important principles moving forward as a church committed to proclaiming grace. The communion practice and regulations around that may serve as the most revealing litmus test for how aptly Lutheran doctrine of justification is exercised in the life of the faith communities. Is the core of Lutheran teaching (still) theology of unconditional grace, or are any conditions put on that grace in practice? Thinking of the contemporary situation, amid the many questions about the future of Lutheran church, a fundamental question springs from the perspective of hospitality and inclusivity: are there limits to the welcome? Sound sacramental theology, building on the historical emphasis on the undeserved, freely gifted grace, would be the most powerful welcome sign with a possibly life-changing impact.

Sacraments and Hospitality with Grace[7]

One of the major reforms pertained to the practices with worship and sacraments. How would the new worship look and sound like, and how many sacraments should be administered? What would be the basis for any sacraments, and was there a need for a new definition? The decisions on these questions were pivotal and would draw the lines between different faith communities, Catholic and Protestants, and between different Protestants.

---

[6]Anabaptists: a radical sixteenth-century Protestant radical movement, teaching, e.g., baptism of believers, separation of church and state, and refusal of bearing arms or giving oaths. The *Schwärmer* or Enthusiasts: a derogatory label for the Protestant groups emphasizing and actively seeking for the experience of the Spirit.
[7]Read AC 9–13. (Skim Ap. 9–13.) Recommended SA Part III art. 3, 5, 8; LC on Baptism, Confession, Lord's Supper.

Sacrament can be defined in various ways. The most basic definition names sacrament as a religious ritual that was commanded by Christ and that serves as a means or symbol for grace and spiritual realm per scriptural evidence. The medieval Catholic church had concluded on seven sacraments to administer: baptism, the Lord's Supper, penance, confirmation, anointing the sick, matrimony, and the holy orders. The Catholic church today maintains these seven means of grace, all performed by the duly ordained clergy.[8] The number was settled during the High Middle Ages at the 1215 IV Lateran Council, where many of the central medieval Catholic teachings and practices were ratified.[9] For the evangelicals wishing to argue for all their practices with the Scriptural basis, the decision on the number was decided on account of Jesus: only those ceremonies should be maintained that had a history with Jesus, that he himself participated in, and that he commanded his disciples to do also, with a promise.

Only two such rituals could be argued with the Scriptures: baptism and the Lord's Supper. For a while, some ambiguity remained about the possibly third one, the confession. Today Lutherans follow the resolution of the sixteenth century that ties confession with baptism and the Lord's Supper, as a way to live out and personalize the two sacraments' meaning. Baptism, Lord's Supper, and confession each have their own short article in the *Augsburg Confession*'s first part and are returned to in the later part too. Baptism is treated more fully in Luther's *Catechisms*. Otherwise, it was a topic of lesser controversy as a ritual that explicitly tied Lutherans to the practices of the early church.

Article thirteen states that sacraments are not only marks of faith or confession, but "signs and testimonies of God's will toward us, intended to arouse and strengthen faith in those who use them" (AC 13:1–3). Proper use of sacraments is one that increases the faith (AC 13:3). Those are condemned who teach that faith is not important and that sacraments work *ex opere operato*; this is a direct criticism of the Catholic teaching of the sacrament's

---

[8] In the early church, sacraments were communal signs of thanksgiving. Augustine gave the definition for the visible word, "addit verbum ad elementum et fit sacramentum," i.e., "adding word to the element makes a sacrament." In medieval church, the number of sacraments was settled at seven and their administration became tied to the office of the priests.

[9] The most important council between the first seven ecumenical councils (that articulated the Creeds) and the Council of Trent in the sixteenth century (that decided on the responses to the Protestant reforms), the fourth Lateran Council (twelfth in order of ecumenical councils in the West), was called by the most powerful Pope of all times, Pope Innocent III. During the time of the Crusades, in the gathering of 400 bishops, 800 monks and representatives of kings in Europe, doctrinal and practical issues for the sake of the reform of the church were settled with decisions lasting for centuries, if not even till modern days, for example, the number of sacraments, the doctrine of transubstantiation, and the stipulations for the Eucharistic practices. The recovery of the Holy Land from the hands of Muslims was also in the agenda and a desire that momentarily united the otherwise warring European Christian constituencies.

efficiency as tied to the clerical office.[10] Promise is an essential part of the sacraments that are never just rituals but holy symbols that convey real grace and personally so. How?

The definition of the sacrament, inherited from church father Augustine, is that when the Word—the scriptural basis with a command and a promise—joins the element, a sacrament is thus formed. The element conveys the word of grace to the receiver in a tangible means. Both parts are needed, the word and the matter. In other words, water, or bread and wine themselves would not offer anything special unless they are served with the proclamation of the Word about what and why they effect grace. How they work this, and to whom, is more ambiguous. For Luther and his peers the main emphasis was not "how" but "that": the sacrament works what is promised, and this must be believed. It is easy to see how important a role the community of faith has in this as the holy space for offering the rituals and for proclaiming the Word and teaching the recipients about "what is."

The sacraments' rationale and formula for effectiveness rely on the fundamental principle of evangelical theology: justification by faith by grace alone. Initially, this emphasis extended a broad welcome to the sacraments: one could come without fear to receive, just as one was, simply believing in the gift; this meant believing that grace is real and is offered "for you." But as deliberations continued on the nuance of the evangelical teaching, the question of faith needed attention. Would the sacrament be efficient without explicit and cognizant faith? Or would sacrament mostly enhance, or birth, the faith? The faith-sacrament relation needed clarification. This would happen logically in the deliberation on baptism and particularly with infants and the role of faith there. With their "faith-alone" principle, Lutherans had much at stake in clarifying their unflappable position on the gift nature of grace—and of faith.

After defining the principles of the church, the *Augsburg Confession* moves on to make a statement on the number and the impact of the sacraments that can be defended with the Scriptures. The first in order is baptism, followed by statements on the Lord's Supper, confession, and repentance. With these short articles, from nine to thirteen, a Lutheran doctrine of the sacraments is presented. Some of the topics need further addressing later in the document and also in *Formula of Concord*.

---

[10]The expression *ex opere operato*, meaning, "from the work worked," or "performed," has been used in Catholic theology to describe how grace is conveyed through the sacraments because of the holy ritual itself, irrespective of the holiness or unholiness of the one who administers or who receives it. The Council of Trent affirmed this as a nonnegotiable canon, which in the context of the Reformation debates on church affairs also underscored the authority reserved for the duly ordained priests, that is, the sacrament "effects" by "the work worked" as long as the act involves an ordained priest and the correct ceremony.

Baptism[11]—Heavenly Water for New Birth[12]

Luther taught baptism is the "greatest jewel."[13] He approached it with all seriousness and as a life-and-death issue:

> Suppose there were a physician who had so much skill that people would not die, or even though they died would afterward live eternally. Just think how the world would snow and rain money upon such a person! ... Now, here in baptism there is brought, free of charge, to every person's door just such a treasure and medicine that swallows up death and keeps all people alive. (LC 396)[14]

Lutherans have, since the reformations, continued to practice baptism as a vital Christian ritual in which the central teaching of grace is enacted. In baptismal practice, Lutherans have decided to maintain the tradition of the early Christians in terms of baptism serving the initiation and inclusion into the Christian community. In line with Augustine's thought, Lutherans have taught baptism is necessary, for each Christian, including the children. In continuation with the medieval teaching, baptism has been deemed by Lutherans a sacrament with a special effect of grace conveyed through it. How the sacrament works, for whom, and why, these questions steered the particulars of the Lutheran position, especially vis-à-vis the topic of salvation and the role of baptism in that regard.

Historically speaking, Lutherans stand on the centuries-old tradition: Christians have always baptized. Baptism's rationale goes back to the Scriptures, to the evidence of Jesus's own baptism and his commendation on that to his disciples (e.g., Matthew 28:19 and Mark 16:16, Mark 1:9–11). It has been the most important signal of a person's Christian identity and an invitation to the Christian community. The practice of baptism actually gave stimulus to the formation of the ecumenical Creeds, as the baptized needed a symbol for the faith they were baptized into; the same symbol, Creed, served as the catechetical tool in the rigorous teaching involved in the preparation of the baptized. Augustine had an influence in underscoring the importance of learning the faith in the community and also via his teaching of baptism in light of his view of the humanity's chronic condition with sin and baptism as a means of grace to counter the impact of that sin. In medieval practice the sacrament of baptism was unproblematic. In the Holy

---

[11]Read AC 9–13, 22, 25. (Skim Ap. 9–13, 22, 25.) Recommended SA Part III art. 3–6; FC VII.
[12]Read AC 9. (Skim Ap. 9.) Recommended LC, Baptism; SA Part III art. 4 and 5.
[13]For suggestions on thinking ecumenically with baptism, see Kirsi Stjerna, "Seeking Hospitable Discourse on the Sacrament of Baptism," *Dialog: A Journal of Theology*, 53/2 (2014). Also, Kirsi Stjerna, *"No Greater Jewel: Thinking of Baptism with Martin Luther"* (Minneapolis: Augsburg Press, 2010).
[14]See also Kolb and Wengert, *Book of Concord*, LC 462:43.

Roman empire, where Christianity functioned as the catholic faith that encompassed everyone, baptism was not required on theological grounds only but also by the imperial code of law that governed all citizens.

As a sacrament, first of the seven recognized in the Catholic church, baptism had a secure and uncontested place. Being Christian meant being baptized, regardless of which corner of the empire one dwelled in. For individuals and families it provided a sense of security and belonging; not being baptized, not being a Christian, would have meant that one was outside the known parameters in life here and now, and, even a more scary thought, that they were outside the realm of salvation and God's care from here till thereafter.

When the reformations erupted, and since then, baptism has not stirred as vehement a debate as the Lord's Supper has, even if serious disagreements arose between the mainstream reformers and the radicals about the baptism of children versus adult baptism and rebaptism; differences in this regard continue to exist. The *Augsburg Confession* was written a year after the Diet of Speyer, where Anabaptists and adult/re/baptizers were condemned with a death penalty. (Just two years earlier, one of the leaders, Felix Manz, was drowned in Zürich.) As a matter of fact, that Diet reissued the 1521 condemnation of Luther as a heretic and set plans to extinguish all reforming movements. This background explains the tone of the article nine, where the Lutheran teaching of baptism is articulated as one in agreement with the Catholic teaching and disassociating Lutherans from the Anabaptists.

With the article nine Lutherans teach that God's grace is given through baptism, which serves as the medium. It is also taught, firmly, that children should be baptized so that they would be "received into the grace of God when they are offered to God through baptism" (AC 9:1–2). The same article rejects the views of those who refute infant baptism or teach that children would not need it for salvation. The question of salvation being necessary was important in the sixteenth-century religious realm and the reformers did not challenge that, while they sought to offer nuance to that teaching, on the foundation of their teaching of justification taking place by faith alone, with no work—not even baptism.

In harmony with the Catholic doctrine, the article agrees "it is necessary for salvation, that the grace of God is offered through baptism"; for this reason also children need to be baptized (AC 9:1–2, Latin). Or, in slightly different words, "it is necessary, that grace is offered through it." Children belong to this command, as in baptism "they are entrusted to God and become pleasing to him [God]" (AC 9:1–2, German). This invitation ends with a condemnation of those who do not baptize children. Several questions arise here, first of all, about the wording of necessity and the relation of baptism to salvation. Relatedly, the question of infant versus adult baptism is a live topic, still, with different practices in different faith communities. Lastly, the point of condemning other views is hardly a constructive approach, whereas the context of the words of the confessions illuminates the reasons. The question of the necessity of baptism opens up most constructively with the *Catechisms*' teaching on the practice of infant baptism.

Infant Baptism with *Catechisms*[15]

Luther teaches that God has instituted baptism with Jesus's command and promise that can be read in the Scriptures. This makes it a sacrament. For Lutherans, only two rituals meet this criterion. Because it is commanded by God, and because of the promise attached to baptism, "[i]t is of the greatest importance that we regard baptism as excellent, glorious, and exalted." In short, "it is a most precious thing" (LC 390), a visible word, as Augustine called it. "No greater jewel, therefore, can adorn our body and soul than baptism, for through it we become completely holy and blessed, which no other kind of life and no work on earth can acquire" (LC 396).[16]

Luther explains with a question: "What is baptism? Namely, that it is not simply plain water, but water placed in the setting of God's word and commandment and made holy by them. It is nothing else than God's water, not that the water itself is nobler than other water but that God's word and commandment are added to it" (LC 391). Luther calls it the "washing of regeneration" (LC 393) and "this washing takes place only through God's will and not at all through the word and the water" (SA 455). The Word thus is what makes the water a sacramental vehicle or a container. "It is not simply plain water, but water placed in the setting of God's word and commandment and made holy by them. It is nothing else than God's water, not that the water itself is nobler than other water but that God's word and commandment are added to it." Such holy God's water then "contains and conveys all that is God's" (LC 391).[17]

Luther poses the holy regard of the "glorious" baptism as something that God wants, also for children (LC 390). As a gift, baptism belongs to all. Because of the reality of sin, baptism is meant to be offered to all; Luther teaches on the basis of Augustine's reasoning of sin and grace. Luther's teaching of baptism for anyone, but also for children, thus boils down to two theological convictions: everyone is born in bondage to sin and cannot free themselves without the grace of God. Baptism, for Luther, is the vehicle for this grace. That said, since his doctrine of justification underscores that salvation is a gift and a matter of faith, in that regard nothing, not even

---

[15]References to *The Large Catechism* and *Smalcald Articles* are taken from *The Annotated Luther*, Vol. 2, ed. Kirsi Stjerna, 2015.

[16]See also Kolb and Wengert, *The Book of Concord*, LC 457:7–9; LC 462:46.

[17]See also Kolb and Wengert, *The Book of Concord*, LC 458:14; LC 460:2; SA 329:3; LC 458:14, 17–18.

baptism, can be a condition or the only and exclusive way. Faith is the nonnegotiable agent. "Where faith is present with its fruits, there baptism is no empty symbol, but the effect accompanies it; but where faith is lacking, it remains a mere unfruitful sign" (LC 400). Luther writes that those who believe and are baptized will be saved, whereas "[w]ithout faith baptism is of no use, although in itself it is an infinite, divine treasure" (LC, 394). If this is not confusing enough, Luther emphasizes that this is something that one's heart "must believe it" (LC 395).[18]

It is helpful to think of faith as a particular language Luther uses to describe what happens with baptism. It is also helpful to think of faith as trust and as a way to underscore the gift nature of justification and grace celebrated in sacraments. Luther is careful to maintain God's freedom to act, without any prerequisites from the human being, including efforts to produce or demonstrate a particular kind of faith. Faith as a saving force, just as grace, can only be a gift and best expressed from the human angle as a form of trust. It cannot be a precondition for receiving baptism. Rather, baptism is received in that trust that faith alone saves. Luther's view here differs, e.g., from the Anabaptists' teaching of a confession or expression of personal faith as a condition for baptism. Luther's consistent emphasis is that God is also the actor of faith that saves and in the baptism that embodies that trust. "To be baptized in God's name is to be baptized not by human beings but by God and God's own doing" (LC 390). The necessity of faith language does not refer to the right to receive or to a condition for the effectiveness of the sacrament but rather underscores the necessity to trust this gift. "For my faith does not make baptism; rather, it receives baptism. Baptism does not become invalid if it is not properly received or used, as I have said, for it is not bound to our faith but to the word" (LC 397).[19]

In addition to the question of validity, another area where Luther disagrees with other reforming groups is how they understand the impact of the sacrament. Unlike the Swiss reformer Uldrich Zwingli who taught baptism as a pledge of faith and a covenant with God, Luther saw baptism as a holy encounter for a multidimensional relationship with God and even more. With baptism Luther addresses the reality of God dwelling in human life via Word. More than a symbolic gesture, baptism highlights the reality change in human beings' ontological condition due to the presence of God. With all his affirmation of what happens in baptism, though, Luther would not suggest that God's action and presence would be bound to the ritual of baptism or anything else for that matter. But Luther is adamant: God has explicitly commanded this ritual, for people's sake and for the sake of their faith and spiritual well-being. God has seen

---

[18]See also Kolb and Wengert, *The Book of Concord*, LC 457:7; LC 465:73; LC 460:33, 34; LC 461:36.
[19]See also Kolb and Wengert, *The Book* of Concord, LC 457:10; LC 457:53.

it wise to set a concrete ritual as the means and support for the trust with which human beings knowingly receive God's gifts.

One of the most obvious gifts baptism communicates is forgiveness and the freedom that brings about. Baptism marks the gift of freedom from guilt and the burden of (feeling) being damned in one's being and for one's role in the (very real) calamities that plague humankind. In other words, baptism communicates about what happens in justification, when one is made right with God, one's ground of being (LC 391).[20] A shift in one's existential status and sense of self occurs when in baptism one receives the affirmation that the guilt of the original sin has been lifted and a person is freed from the damning impact of the original sin. Luther and most theologians of the past have used the word "salvation" to describe this shift and from the position of salvation being about one's relationship with the creator and the source of life. A contemporary focus might expand on the freeing impact of the experience of forgiveness and on how to effectively teach in the baptizing communities of faith the meaning of such a gift in terms of one's personal self-awareness and self-love, mutual relations, and overall functioning in the world.

Luther is describing a mystery with baptism, one beyond human comprehension, something that is, he repeats, a matter of faith.

> Just by allowing the water to be poured over you, you do not receive or retain baptism in such a manner that it does you any good. But it becomes beneficial to you if you accept it as God's command and ordinance, so that, baptized in God's name, you may receive in the water the promised salvation. Neither the hand nor the body can do this, but rather the heart must believe it. (LC 394–5)

Just as God has designed human salvation and deliverance so that faith only suffices, God has tied this promise to the life and work of God's child, Christ, and the Word about Christ. "Thus you see plainly that baptism is not a work that we do but that it is a treasure that God gives us and faith grasps, just as the Lord Christ on the cross is not a work but a treasure placed in the setting of the word and offered to us in the word and received by faith" (LC 395).[21]

This is why and how baptism is not only a special holy ritual but a special holy means of grace, a sacrament. It becomes a holy means when the Word and water work together for the benefit of the human's whole being.

> This is the reason why these two things are done in baptism; the body has water poured over it because all it can receive is the water, and in addition

---

[20]See also Kolb and Wengert, *The Book of Concord*, LC 458:18.
[21]See also Kolb and Wengert, *The Book of Concord*, LC 461:36; LC 461:37.

the word is spoken so that the soul may receive it. Because the water and the word together constitute one baptism, both body and soul shall be saved and live forever: the soul through the word in which it believes, the body because it is united with the soul and apprehends baptism in the only way it can. (LC 396)

Luther draws the mystery back to God and what God does, with the Word, God's preferred medium. Without the Word, water would be just plain water. The Word makes it a sacrament (LC 392). Not because of its "natural substance" but because "God stakes God's own honor, power, and might on it," baptism can be called "heavenly, holy word ... for it contains and conveys all that is God's" (LC 391).[22] Luther's teaching of baptism thus organically arises from and supports his view of justification by faith that entails both freedom in forgiveness (forensic justification) and a renewed union with God (effective justification).[23]

In accordance with Luther's teaching of the original sin, the new life with God following baptism is not trouble-free and sin-free. The burden of guilt is gone, though, and human being is invited to hang on to the promises of baptism. Baptism itself is a reminder of how much one needs constant reminders of God's true and personal presence in human beings' life. The baptized is invited to consider God in every aspect of human life, one's own and others', and live accordingly with the awareness of the holy - in oneself and in the others. In this vein, baptism signals freedom as the starting point for a human being's life, for each day. The struggle for the liberated sinner to live with the holy freedom is felt in many areas of life, perhaps most of all in failing to equip others with the life-giving freedom. Repentance that characterizes Christian journey could then be less about examination of one's personal issues and with more attention to one's interactions in the web of relations and human systems and how one fairs with the freed Christians' call to love and free others.

For Luther, baptism presents a "doorway" to another reality, to a new existence where death is not the end. It also is a doorway to a life lived with the promised relief of freedom in an existential sense. It also is a start-off for a lifelong battle with demons of all kind. "This is the simplest way to put it: the power, effect, benefit, fruit, and purpose of baptism is that it saves ... To be saved, as everyone well knows, is nothing else than to be delivered from sin, death, and the devil, to enter into Christ's kingdom, and to live with Christ forever" (LC 393). With the word "salvation" and describing the battle the baptized can expect, Luther as a medieval man is indeed believing there are demonic forces that attack every person and especially those in whom God dwells and who are baptized. Contemporary persons can take a broader

---

[22]See also Kolb and Wengert, *The Book of Concord*, LC 462:45–6; LC 459:22; LC 458:17, 18.
[23]On forensic and effective justification, see discussion in Chapter 4.

view on the meaning of demonic and devils and consider a broad spectrum of forces and factors that can threaten one's equilibrium and happiness. Life is full of battles and dangers; Luther speaks of a universal experience in that regard. He offers baptism as the shield of trust, a grounding for a hope-filled orientation, from which to face each day with its own challenges. Active remembering of one's baptismal shield matters. "Therefore let all Christians regard their baptism as the daily garment that they are to wear all the time" (LC 401).[24]

With these thoughts Luther sets the foundation for Lutheran spirituality. It can be characterized as baptism-centered and compassionate engagement in life with a concrete reminder of God's promises of a shield and real presence. Life nurtured with the sacraments and promise of God's dwelling in every corner of human existence, and also specifically with the individual, invites thoughtful introspection as well as inter-spection, guided so by active engagement with the Word. With a shield in baptism and the Word, it also entails active resistance to the many forces that conflict with the spirit of gospel, which is best summarized in one word: freedom. Lutheran spirituality starts with the sense of gratitude and joy, and it is oriented toward servanthood rather than staying with spiritual exercises aimed at personal improvement.

Lutheran spirituality, with baptism, underscores the importance of a community of faith where the Word is proclaimed and sacraments are administered with compassionate care toward one another and where the meaning of them and a proper respect toward them is taught. "Out of a sense of Christian commitment, I appeal to all those who baptize, sponsor infants, or witness a baptism to take to heart the tremendous work and great earnestness present here" (SC, *Baptismal Booklet*, 247–8).[25] The faith of the community is vital: even without an explicit expression of faith of the individual, the community of faith provides the space where infants can be baptized in and with the faith of the community.

There is no evidence that God would not approve of infant baptism; that is Luther's starting argument for infant baptism, as he writes that "the baptism of infants is pleasing to Christ is sufficiently proved from God's own work. God has sanctified many who have been thus baptized and has given them the Holy Spirit" (LC, 397). With that, Jesus's own model of relating to children and commanding the disciples to baptize "all" is about God's ordinance. Baptism, also of infants, is about following God's command that is more important than faith. This Luther argued against those who rejected infant baptism on the basis of children not having faith. He writes, "[B] aptism is simply water and God's word in and with each other; that is,

---

[24]See also Kolb and Wengert, *The Book of Concord*, LC 459:24–5; LC 466:84.
[25]SC citations from *The Annotated Luther*, Vol. 4, ed. Haemig, 2016. See also Kolb and Wengert, *The Book of Concord*, LC 372:2.

when the word accompanies the water, baptism is valid, even though faith is lacking" (LC 397).[26]

In other words, with people of all ages coming to baptism, faith "receives" but "does not make baptism." Similarly, "baptism does not become invalid if it is not properly received or used, as I have said, for it is not bound to our faith but to the word" (LC 397). If pushed further, Luther makes a radical point about infants' quite possible faith: "even if infants did not believe[27]—which, however, is not the case as we have proved—still the baptism would be valid and no one should rebaptize them" (LC 398). Luther does not want to dwell on this point, though, but underscores the vitality of the community of faith that believes for the child:[28] "we bring the child with the intent and hope that it may believe, and we pray God to grant it faith. But we do not baptize on this basis, but solely on the command of God" (LC 398).[29]

With his teaching on baptism, as with other areas of theology, Luther consistently insists on salvation being a matter of gift, grace given freely by God's own action, and human beings only able to receive in trust—the faith Luther highlights when unfolding the meaning of the sacraments in one's life. On the issue of necessity of the sacrament, he offers this: means of grace are for human beings' benefit, for their trust's sake. The way human beings are, in body and spirit, makes means like baptism necessary. Just as justification is necessary for the human condition, the means of grace are necessary for communities of faith to administer. Given the fragility of human beings' existence, sacraments are necessary with proper teaching for Christians' spiritual well-being and feeding their hope-filled orientation in life resting on the fundamental promise of freedom.

Luther's reflections on the question of necessity with baptism and the role of faith are remarkably flexible. Standing solid on his belief in justification being a matter of freely received grace, he can afford to be nimble and address the question slightly differently in different situations.

---

[26]See also Kolb and Wengert, *The Book of Concord*, LC 462:49; LC 463:53; LC 464:60–1.

[27]Luther writes on children's faith and baptism in his arguments against those practicing believers' baptism: "For even if I were not sure that they believed, yet for my conscience's sake I would have to let them be baptized. For it is much better that baptism be extended to children than that I abolish the practice. For if, as we believe, baptism is right and useful and brings the children to salvation, and I did away with it, then I would be responsible for all the children who were lost because they were unbaptized – a cruel and terrible thing." (*Concerning Rebaptism*, 1528, ed. Mark D. Tranvik, *The Annotated Luther*, Vol. 3, ed. Paul Robinson, 2016, 307) (also LW 40:254.)

[28]"For here in the words of these prayers you hear how plaintively and earnestly the Christian church brings the infant here, confesses before God with such steadfast, undoubting words that the infant is possessed by the devil and a child of sin and perniciousness, and through baptism so diligently asks for help and grace, so that the infant may become a child of God" (*Baptismal Booklet*, 248, in *The Annotated Luther*, Vol. 4, ed. Haemig, 2016; in Kolb and Wengert, *Book of Concord*, 372:2).

[29]See also Kolb and Wengert, *The Book of Concord*, LC 463:53; LC 463:55; LC 464:57.

Unless debating his fellow reformers on doctrinal points, typically his pastoral concerns steer his answers. Where this manifests most beautifully is when Luther was approached by grieving parents worrying about the fate of their unbaptized child who had died. In his *Consolation to Those Women Who Have Had Difficulties in Bearing Children* (1542) Luther is all about grace when comforting the parents about God's immeasurable grace beyond human means and comprehension. Children who have died before baptism should be presented to God with the consolation that God hears the "unspoken longings and has done everything better than we have been able to put into words." "The immeasurable does more than we either ask or conceive" (ibid. 180).[30] Parents should not worry for their infant or for themselves. Rather, "know that your prayer is pleasing and that God will do everything much better than you can grasp or desire" (ibid.).

To conclude with Luther, the traditional language of the necessity with baptism—and vis-à-vis what is meant by salvation in relation to baptism—most urgently requires adjustment in contemporary theological imaginations toward hospitable appreciation and enjoyment of the means of grace in today's world.

The Lord's Supper, the Real Presence of God "For You"[31]

Who Is Welcome and What Is Received?

The Lutheran reformers needed to distinguish their teaching on the Lord's Supper in relation to the Catholic tradition as well as other reforming views. With the short article ten, Lutherans teach that Christ's body and blood are "truly present" (in Latin) or "truly present under the form of bread and wine" (in German) and "distributed" and "received" by those partaking the supper. Other teachings are categorically and firmly rejected. The main opponents in mind are those who deny the real presence of the Christ in the actual event of the Lord's Supper. Also rejected are those who put any preconditions on those who wish to receive the benefits of the sacrament. The article does not offer a nuanced exposition of the Lutheran view but leaves room for interpretation.[32]

---

[30]*Consolation to Those Women Who Have Had Difficulties in Bearing Children* (1542), 180, in *Luther on Women: A Sourcebook*. transl. Susan Karant-Nunn and Merry Wiesner-Hanks (Cambridge: Cambridge University Press, 2003, 179–88); WA 53:206.12.

[31]Read AC 10, 15, 22. (Skim Ap. 10, 15, 22.) LC on Lord's Supper, Repentance.

[32]See Amy Nelson Burnett, *Debating the Sacraments: Print and Authority in the Early Reformation* (Oxford: Oxford University Press, 2019).

The question of real presence became a cause of explicit controversy in the 1540s.[33] Already in 1529 at the Marburg Colloquy Luther had seriously clashed with the Swiss reformer Uldrich Zwingli on the meaning of "presence" in the sacrament; it became the breaking point in a possible alliance between German and Swiss reformers.[34] Later, in his eagerness to facilitate an alliance with the Genevan reformer Jean Calvin, Luther's close colleague Philip Melanchthon tweaked the wording on the real presence. Calvin was willing to sign the *Augsburg Confession* with the "altered" text. While this ecumenical agreement and alliance would have been momentous and with long-lasting impact in the Protestant relations and their unified front in relation to the Catholic side, the majority of Lutherans vehemently rejected this "altered" confession.[35] Luther's teaching of the real presence of Christ was reaffirmed.

This topic continued to generate disagreements. Lutherans needed to return to the lingering issues, already within the *Augsburg Confession* itself, and later in the *Formula of Concord* that aimed to solve the intra-Lutheran controversies that lingered.[36] In the following, the topic is addressed in light of the other documents in the *Book of Concord*, given its importance as the topic that both unites and divides Lutherans among themselves and Lutherans in relation to other Christians.

Whereas the *Augsburg Confession* article is short and sweet, Luther's Large *Catechism* offers more meat around the bones. Luther starts with an admonishment: because the sacrament is established by Christ, "everyone who wishes to be a Christian and to go to the sacrament should know them" (LC 402). The main thing to remember is that the sacrament is based on God's Word and command. "It was not dreamed up or invented by some

---

[33]Already in the Middle Ages, several debates evolved around the Lord's Supper and whether Christ's presence was to be understood as real presence, metaphorical, or something to remember (Ratramus, Radbertus, John Scotus Erigena); the doctrine of transubstantiation offered a compromise to describe a mysterious and holy change of the elements that allowed the teaching of real presence.

[34]In an effort to reach unity between the Swiss and Wittenberg reformers, Martin Luther and Uldrich Zwingli, Zurich, were called to Marburg Castle for a meeting. On the fifteen articles of faith discussed, one remained a cause of disagreement: the presence of Christ with the sacrament. The consequent traditions have upheld the differences, while recent ecumenical partnerships have found ways to honor each other's interpretations and practices and even finding table community, that is, sharing in the sacrament of the Lord's Supper and its administration.

[35]See *The Formula of Concord*, 1577 in Chapter 3.

[36]Rekindling the medieval debate, different reformers interpreted in their own way Jesus's words "This is my body" against the Catholic position that suggested a change, transubstantiation, in the elements, "This *becomes* my body" (transubstantiation). Andreas Karlstadt considered the words "*This* is my (physical) body" as a call for remembering. Uldrich Zwingli understood "This *is* (spiritually) my body" symbolically, and Jean Calvin with a different nuance as spiritual and real presence for the received. Luther shouted the weight of each word "*THIS IS (really) MY BODY*" to mean one thing only, real presence.

mere human being but was instituted by Christ without anyone's counsel or deliberation" (LC 402).[37]

What is it, then? "It is the true body and blood of the Lord Christ, in and under the bread and wine, which we Christians are commanded by Christ's word to eat and drink." To be sure, "the sacrament is bread and wine, but not mere bread and wine such as is served at the table. Rather, it is bread and wine set within God's word and bound to it" (LC 403–4). In line with Augustine's definition—*Accedat verbum ad elementum et fit sacramentum*—Luther states, "It is the word, I say, that makes this a sacrament and distinguishes it from ordinary bread and wine, so that it is called and truly is Christ's body and blood" (LC 404).[38]

Eyes on the main force, grace, Luther underscores the effectiveness of the "treasure and gift" for all who receive "Christ's body and blood" (LC 406). A most profound statement applies the Lutheran doctrine of grace: "Even though a scoundrel receives or administers the sacrament, it is the true sacrament ... just as truly as when one uses it most worthily. For it is not founded on human holiness but on the word of God." Instead of setting requirements for its effectiveness or reception, Luther reminds that it is meant explicitly for those feeling weak and for the strengthening of the conscience (LC 404).[39]

Luther describes the Eucharist as "food of the soul," as "daily food and sustenance," given for the strengthening of one's faith (LC 405). Human beings often feel pressures and the burdens of the world on their shoulders; the sacramental food is there to refresh and strengthen especially at those times "when our heart feels too sorely pressed" (LC 406). This is a most pastoral insight into the sacrament, emphasis being on its personal, real, unmerited impact toward human beings' real-life griefs. Then comes the twist: when asking who exactly receives such benefits, Luther notes the importance of faith: those who believe will receive (LC 407).[40]

Taken out of context, these words would suggest that the sacrament's reception and benefits would depend on the validity or power of the person's faith. But that is not what is meant here. Luther's argument that it can be received in no other way than by faith (LC 407) simply refers to the mystery of the gift that one can simply trust is true. Faith speaks of the importance of actively, and in trust, partaking in the mysterious meal even when feeling one's unworthiness and even when not fully comprehending the how and what happens in the holy ritual; trust that "it is so" and receiving in that trust the gifts "for me" is enough. Human beings' reason, or body, cannot "grasp and appropriate what is given in

---

[37]See also Kolb and Wengert, *The Book of Concord*, LC 467:2; LC 467:4.
[38]See also Kolb and Wengert, *The Book of Concord*, LC 467:9; LC 468:10.
[39]See also Kolb and Wengert, *The Book of Concord*, LC 469: 29; LC 468:12.
[40]See also Kolb and Wengert, *The Book of Concord*, LC 469:23, 24, 25, 27; LC 469:27; LC 470:33.

and with the sacrament. This is done by the faith of the heart that discerns
and desires such a treasure" (LC 407). Luther's teaching of the unmerited
grace crystallizes in the invitation. "The treasure is opened and placed at
everyone's door, yes, on the table, but it is also your responsibility to take
it and confidently believe that it is just as the words tell you" (LC 407).[41]

Catechism, a teaching tool, gives an exhortation to teach people to use
the sacrament frequently (LC 407). No force is to be used, though, under
any circumstances. Christ did not institute that kind of a model (LC 408).
Here Luther's tone is that of the *Invocavit* sermons from 1522, when Luther
had returned from his hiding in Coburg to preach and stopped the violent
implementations of the reformation teachings by his eager colleagues.
Going back to what Christ did and said, "DO THIS in remembrance of
me" means that anyone who "wants to be a disciple of Christ," says Luther,
"must faithfully hold to this sacrament, not from compulsion, forced by
humans, but to obey and please the Lord Christ" (LC 409). The word
"must" in this place is used to counter the person's feelings of unworthiness
and being unfit for the gift (LC 410). Luther's urging is to not give in to
those feelings but instead hold on to God's promise with a force. Going to
communion is about following Christ's command, which is the only force,
and about receiving the benefits of his promise when hearing the words
"This is my body, given FOR YOU" (LC 411). The sacrament is Christ's gift
and presence for the individual: "For in this sacrament Christ offers us all
the treasures he brought from heaven for us" (LC 411).[42]

Luther's invitational tone is intentional as he is countering the baggage
inherited from the medieval situation of people fearing the sacrament
or people not feeling worthy of it or being forced to receive it. Luther
repudiates these teachings as a form of spiritual torture and abuse of the
means that is supposed to bring comfort and consolation rather than evoke
fear. Reason and nature make people already feel unworthy and timid.
Luther has a colorful metaphor for such teachings: "[I]t appears like a dark
lantern in contrast to the bright sun, or as manure in contrast to jewels"
(LC 410). While he does address the situations when people are unruly and
callous and not ready to receive forgiveness with the sacrament (LC 410),
the bottom line in his argumentation is that if people were to wait until they
are ready and perfect and without blemish, the communion tables would
remain empty (LC 411). With the sacrament, thus, Luther's emphasis is
God's unconditional grace. "For we are not baptized because we are worthy
and holy, nor do we come to confession as if we were pure and without sin;
on the contrary, we come as poor, miserable people, precisely because we

---

[41]See also Kolb and Wengert, *The Book of Concord*, LC 470:34; LC 470:37; LC 470:35.
[42]See also Kolb and Wengert, *The Book of Concord*, LC 470–1:39; LC 471:42; LC 471:45; LC
472:55; LC 473:64; LC 473:66.

are unworthy. The only exception would be the person who desires no grace and absolution and has no intention of improving" (LC 411).[43]

The question of "unworthy" recipients still lingers, though, and is worth pausing for a moment. Luther admits that it is possible to eat the sacrament for one's damnation in the case of blatantly despising it while receiving. For those leading unchristian lives, he also speculated what it could do. He compares this to a situation of someone ignoring medical advice about what to eat and what not (LC 412). The only truly unworthy recipient would be "those who do not feel their burdens nor admit to being sinners" (LC 412). Their situation is quite different from that of those who feel weak and anxiously desire help: they are the ones who "should regard and use the sacrament as a precious antidote against the poison in their systems" (LC 412). In the sacrament one receives "from Christ's lips the forgiveness" which entails grace, God's Spirit, and the kind of protection against "every trouble," the kind only God's Spirit can offer (LC 412). Luther's advice is practical and compassionate: "Try this," "examine yourself, or look around a little, and cling only to the Scriptures." There is the affirmation of the gift that is true and available for everyone, guaranteed so by Christ himself (LC 414).[44]

In conclusion, the *Catechisms'* main points underscore the reality of the gift offered in the bread and wine, and the personal invitation, for all to come and receive. Later Luther returns to the topic in his *Smalcald Articles*, where he had a chance to summarize the main reforms, their rationale, and the theological clarifications the evangelicals had to offer. The debates never quieted down; rather more conversation partners entered the controversy around the sacrament, which was one of the reasons leading to the writing of the *Formula of Concord*.

Further Insights from the *Smalcald Articles* and the *Formula of Concord*

An important consideration in Lutheran thinking about sacraments is that, in the spirit of Luther, it always begins and ends with the gospel, the Word. Also, with Luther, the context for the questions about the sacraments is the life of the church, a faith community where the sacraments are used and their meaning taught. These discussions can, thus, never remain abstract.

Luther takes the opportunity to remind the readers that God has chosen to communicate grace with human beings with the Word and the sacraments. "Therefore we should and must insist that God does not want to deal with

---

[43]See also Kolb and Wengert, *The Book of Concord*, LC 472:56; LC 473:58–9; LC 473:60; LC 473:61.

[44]See also Kolb and Wengert, *The Book of Concord*, LC 474:69; LC 474:74; LC 474:70; LC 474:70; LC 475:83.

us human beings, except by means of his external Word and sacrament"
(SA 461). He sets the stage for sacramental considerations with an article
concerning

> the gospel again, which gives counsel and help against sin in more than
> one way, because God is extravagantly rich in his [God's] grace: first,
> through the spoken word, in which the forgiveness of sins is preached
> to the whole world, which is the proper function of the gospel; secondly,
> through baptism; thirdly, through the holy Sacrament of the Altar;
> fourthly, through the power of the keys and also through the mutual
> conversation and consolation. (SA 455)[45]

Then he checks on the major points of the Lutheran argumentation: the
real presence, the invitation to all to the full communion, and the importance
of confession as a proper preparation for all who need fortification.

First Luther makes a statement on real presence, refuting the doctrine
of transubstantiation with the sacrament of altar. "We maintain that the
bread and the wine in the Supper are the true body and blood of Christ
and that they are not only offered to and received by upright Christians but
also by evil ones" (SA 457). He confirms that he has "no regard" for the
teaching of transubstantiation, according to which the elements would lose
their natural substances, whereas the form of the bread and wine would
remain (SA 458). Then he returns to the question of the "both kinds" with
Christological arguments and with a most hospitable and inclusive view
about the participation. He writes, "[W]e maintain that only one kind in
the sacrament should not be distributed" (SA 457). He has no patience
for teachings that suggest that one is enough. "Even if it were true that
there is as much under one kind as under both, one kind is still not the
complete order and institution as established and commanded by Christ"
(SA 457–8).[46]

Years after the sacraments had been vigorously taught with the
Catechisms and defended with the Augsburg Confession and the Smalcald
Articles, the issue was returned to in the Formula of Concord. A major
controversy had been plaguing the Lutheran movement on the question
of Christ's presence. By now, the opponent was not the Catholic church
but the other Protestant groups, as well as those among Lutherans who
appeared crypto-Calvinist or closet-Calvinists (as they were called by their
opponents) in their sacramental theology. The debate was about whether
the real presence of Christ at the sacrament could be considered or spoken
of as spiritual presence and could therewith offer a position more distinctly
different from the Catholic teaching.

---

[45]See also Kolb and Wengert, The Book of Concord, SA 8:10; SA 4:1.
[46]See also Kolb and Wengert, The Book of Concord, SA 6:1; SA 6:5; SA 6:2; SA 6:5.

Article VII in the *Formula of Concord* "Concerning the Holy Supper of Christ" starts with a reference to the Zwinglians (FC VII:1). As the *Status controversiae*, the matter of controversy, in opposition to the "Sacramentarians,"[47] the *Formula of Concord* states the following debate: whether

> [i]n the Holy Supper are the true body and blood of our Lord Jesus Christ truly and essentially present, distributed with bread and wine, and received by mouth by all those who avail themselves to the sacraments—whether they are worthy or unworthy, godly or ungodly, believers or unbelievers—to bring believers comfort and life and to bring judgement upon unbelievers. (FC VII:2)

The Sacramentarians addressed here are of two kinds: those who consider the sacrament as simply a meal of bread and wine, and "the more dangerous kind" who speak of the "spirit of Christ" when addressing the questions of his presence with the sacrament. In contrast, in a specifically Lutheran view, the words of Christ are understood not symbolically but literally "that they are truly the true body and blood of Christ because of the sacramental union" (FC VII:7). In addition to the Scriptures, Luther's Christological stance is evoked: just as Jesus is essentially and truly both God and human, Christ after resurrection is ubiquitous, at the right hand of God but also wherever Christ wants. For God it is possible to be present in different places and spaces at the same time (FC VII:13–14).

The authors specify how the sacramental reality is possible exactly because it is God's doing and within God's realm of possibilities. "Concerning the consecration, we believe ... that neither human effort nor recitation of the minister effect this presence of the body and blood of Christ in the holy Supper, but that it is to be attributed solely and alone to the almighty power of our Lord Jesus Christ" (FC VII:8). Given the emphasis placed on the words pointing to God in the liturgical celebration, the words of Christ that give the foundation for the sacrament may under no circumstances be omitted. A belief is stated that "in the use of the Holy Supper the words of Christ's institution may under no circumstances be omitted but must be spoken publicly, as it is written, 'The cup of blessing that we bless ... ' (1 Cor 11 [10:16]). This blessing takes place through the pronouncement of the words of Christ" (FC VII:9).

After refuting the opposing views, this is the conclusion:

---

[47]*Sacramentarian* refers to those considering the sacrament as a symbol, without teaching a tangible presence of God in it or in its reception. Lutheran and Catholic views would be considered not-Sacramentarian, with their teaching of real presence and real reception of Christ.

[O]n the basis of the simple words of Christ's testament, we hold and teach the true, but supernatural, eating of the body of Christ and the drinking of his blood. Human reason and understanding cannot grasp this, but our understanding must be taken captive by obedience to Christ here as in all other articles of faith. Such a mystery cannot be grasped except by faith and is revealed alone in the Word. (FC VII:42)

In other words, two major points are made: first, the power and the agency of the Word of God, without which the ritual would not be a sacrament; and second, the real presence of Christ is a matter of faith, beyond reason, and a holy mystery, the meaning of which is revealed to the one receiving. The church contributes to this as the place where the meaning is proclaimed and where the beliefs are shared and confessed together.

Nothing new is doctrinally speaking added in the *Formula of Concord* to what was already said in the *Catechisms* and the *Smalcald Articles*. It is worth noting that in the *Augsburg Confession* the articles that follow the sacraments address the benefits of confession, which is an integral part of sacramental practice, whereas the *Formula* continues to deliberate on the person of Christ. All roads lead to Luther's central discovery: Christ is the lens, the hinge, the center for Christian faith and hope.

Other Holy Means: Confession,[48] Repentance,[49] and Mutual Consolation

Article eleven, also very short, urges the faith communities to teach that a private confession and absolution should be maintained, even if a minute enumeration of sins is no longer necessary. In accordance with the Lutheran convictions about the human nature and the prevalent tentacles of sin, efforts for complete enumeration of sins would be doomed to fail any way.

Relatedly, Luther speaks of confession in his *Smalcald Articles*. He ties the act of confession closely to the sacrament of the table, aiming to remove from it the feel of compulsion and teaching about it as a powerful tool to help the disturbed consciences and for education. Countering the—in his view distorted—medieval practice that had fueled the fear of the Lord without consolation, and where the power of the keys had been misused by clergy with stress on the detailed enumeration of sins as a prerequisite for absolution and communion, Luther presents confession and the use of keys as a form of consolation, primarily a tool of comfort rather than an instrument of fear and control.

---

[48] AC 10, 15, 22 (again 13, also 24). (Skim Ap.10, 15, 22, 13, 24.) Recommended SA Part III art. 3, 4, 6. FC VII (and VIII); LC on Lord's Supper, Repentance.
[49] AC 12. (Skim Ap. 12.) Recommended SA Part III art. 1–4, 13. FC V; LC, Ten Commandments.

Absolution, for Luther, eventually comes from God and it is about comfort. He speaks of the importance of the "keys" to absolve and issue of forgiveness as something Christ himself had instituted.[50] Therefore, this practice of confession and absolution "should by no means be allowed to fall into disuse." This is so particularly "for the sake of weak consciences and the wild young people, so that they may be examined and instructed in Christian teaching" (SA 458). Enumeration, however, is not necessary for the benefits of confession. People have freedom to discern what they wish or need to talk about in the confession (SA 459).[51] In other words, for Luther, confession is about soul care and pastoral care. Without dismissing the centuries-old practice, he targeted the effective communication of the consoling word that would provide a tormented soul with an experience of forgiveness and freedom from guilt and shame. Understood in this sense, thinking of today's Lutheran practices, confession has much promise and can serve as a powerful vehicle for liberation. It most definitely belongs, even if underused, to the application of Lutheran freedom theology.

The article twelve, which is slightly longer than the previous ones, concerns the practice of repentance in Lutheran teaching. It is treated separately from the act of confession, which is a departure from the Catholic teaching. In the Catholic tradition the sacrament of penance, which was required before partaking the Communion, included different steps: confession, contrition, works of satisfaction, and the absolution following. Private confession with the priest was a central part in the practice of the sacrament of penance and in preparing one for the sacrament of the Eucharist.[52] In Lutheran teaching, where only two sacraments have been practiced since the sixteenth-century reforms, repentance is placed in the midst of life as an orientation and a mood for the life of the baptized. Repentance in this fashion does not involve a priest, necessarily, but becomes an ongoing, personal expression of one's experience of sin and grace in one's daily life.

Namely, it is assumed that from their birth and even after baptism, people will falter and sin and thus in need of an ongoing reminder and affirmation of forgiveness. As in the previous article, the confession rejects the Anabaptists and others who hold that those who are made holy would not fall again or lose the Spirit. Similarly the article rejects an opinion that anyone would be able to avoid sinning in this life. One more condemnation is uttered:

---

[50]The power of the keys is used to name the special call and right that Jesus gave to his disciple Simon (Matthew 16:19, 18:18), and that is transferred to ordained clergy; this priest's authority to proclaim absolution, in Catholic teaching, serves the sacrament of penance—both are needed.

[51]See also Kolb and Wengert, *The Book of Concord*, SA 8:1; SA 8:2.

[52]In comparison, Catholic sacrament of penance involves, with the priest, contrition, confession, works of satisfaction, and absolution. In Luther view, confession has two parts: contrition and faith.

those who refuse to grant forgiveness (like Novatians)[53] or who place any conditions for the forgiveness (AC 12:10–11). The article expands on the central Lutheran teaching on the unavoidable original sin, on the one hand, and the unmerited grace on account of Christ, on the other.

In light of its mission, "the church should impart absolution to those who return to repentance." The practice of absolution is therefore retained from the medieval practice but in a simplified form from the point of view of the human being seeking for forgiveness: only contrition and faith are needed. Contrition refers to the remorse and terror that "strike the conscience when sin is recognized." These feelings prepare the way for the balm for the soul, namely, faith in the promise of the gospel that sins are forgiven—the faith that believes the forgiveness is not about right belief or knowledge but is about trust that "is brought to life by the gospel or absolution." Faith in the forgiveness "consoles the conscience, and liberates it from terrors." This is not the end, though. The fruits of this kind of terrifying remorse and liberating faith are good works, that is, good and loving actions.

In conclusion, Lutheran teaching of the sinful condition of the human beings and the teaching of unmerited grace lay the foundation for the invitation for confession and repentance. Also, the strong teaching of the reality in which human beings without a doubt will accumulate material for ongoing repentance has a significant therapeutic and spiritual value. In a way, the practice of confession and repentance expresses what the Lutheran teaching of sin and grace entails in person's life and thus the fundamental tenet of Lutheran spirituality. The *simul iustus et peccator* idea from Luther, the understanding that finite human beings are in constant need of mercy while resting in God's holiness already afforded, steers a particular kind of spirituality: one that calls for ongoing personal introspection and mutual affirmation of freedom from regrets and feelings of damnation (self-induced or from others).

Lutheran language of tension between the law and gospel proclamation, both needed for the well-being of the Christian and Christian communities, speaks to this reality as well: there is time to hear the urge to admit, face, and reveal one's brokenness, and there is time to hear affirmation of one's freedom from all that burdens or brings one down with an invitation to new beginnings. As alien as the *simul-simul* and law-gospel talk may sound to contemporary ears, at first, when pausing to see what is meant with them, one can quite probably relate. Everyone has regrets; everyone hopes for freedom from what binds and burdens. These convictions are behind the Lutheran confessions' urging to repent and live a life in repentance, in the spirit of hope and trust and stimulus to assist in relieving the burdens of one's neighbors as well. Freedom is contagious and binding! In contemporary use,

---

[53]Named after Novatus (200–58), an Italian priest and theologian, and an anti-pope, who taught that individuals who had surrendered under the Decian persecutions (*lapsi*, lapsed) should not be readmitted to the Christian communities of faith.

and in the spirit of the reformers, it is possible to make this invitation to repent a positive and warm welcome to seek for the nurture of the Word that holds God's promise of unending love, freedom from regrets with forgiveness freely already given, and grace abounding for new beginnings. The unfolding and communicating and embodying such a grace vision and freedom theology, then, is the task of the church.

Order and Call Questions in the Church[54]

Who has the right to offer this word of gospel and consolation? Article five simply names proclamation of the gospel and the sacraments as the important function for which the church as an institution was instituted. The church serves with the Word, which means that the Scriptures and their interpretation are at the center of all that the church does. *Augsburg Confession* article fourteen gives a brief rule of thumb on the order in securing that the church does what it is charged to do: "[T]hey teach that no one should teach publicly in the church or administer the sacraments unless properly called" (AC 14). The word "called" refers to the installation of the person through proper channels of authority; it does not refer to an internal discernment or the ritual.[55] This is a practical matter. Theologically speaking, to whom does the task to proclaim belong, the net is broad.

On the basis of the justification of all by faith, the holy and inclusive invitation is extended in the practice of baptism for all to care for and share the gospel. In the spirit of the reformation principle of equipping all people to engage the Word personally and the Word belonging to all, the so-called priesthood of all believers (or all the baptized) entails that all Christians are invited, charged, and authorized to proclaim with the Word. Luther explains the many dimensions of this in his *Smalcald Articles*.

The church's main agenda and treasure is the gospel; there are different channels for sharing from this treasure. Luther writes, concerning "the Gospel, which gives guidance" in these ways: "first, through the spoken word, in which the forgiveness of sins is preached to the whole world, which is the proper function of the gospel; secondly, through baptism; thirdly, through the holy Sacrament of the Altar; fourthly, through the power of the keys and also through the mutual conversation and consolation" (SA 455).[56] This paragraph succinctly describes how the community of faith shares with the Word in the priesthood of all believers.

It is worth reckoning that in the Lutheran texts, both the Word and sacraments are identified as means of grace. Proclamation is considered as

---

[54]Read AC 5, 7, 14, 27 (again 28). (Skim Ap. 5, 7, 14, 27.) Recommended SA Part II art. 3–4, Part III art. 7, 9–11, 14. Skim TPPP.
[55]See also footnote 81 in Kolb and Wengert, *Book of Concord*.
[56]See also Kolb and Wengert, *The Book of Concord*, SA 4:1.

the central and vital channel for communicating grace, as well as it is named as a duty for all in the faith community. Also, the sacraments proclaim in tangible ways the gospel on their part. At the core of Lutheran sacramental teaching stands that, in the priesthood of all believers, all are called to convey grace and the word of forgiveness and hope to one another. Proclamation is one of those shared duties even if it is also delegated, officially, as a job to some with an external call to the ministry of the Word and sacrament. This delegation is specified later in the *Augsburg Confession*.

As mentioned above, article fourteen on the church order simply states that only those who are "properly called" can teach publicly in the church or administer the baptism and the Lord's Supper. The Latin words *rite vocatus*, translated in English as "called," refer to an authorized calling by an established authority. The article therewith establishes the convention in church affairs, in general terms. Lutherans have valued order in church affairs and this has meant designing a system of managing whose responsibility it is to teach and preach regularly, as their specified call, and with which qualifications. In the early stages of the reforms, another path was possible, a more radical solution employed by the so-called radicals who valued direct personal communication with the Spirit, rather than setting a system of vetting the internal call with an external call process. Since the sixteenth century, Protestant churches have developed distinct processes to prepare and call individuals for different offices or roles in ministry.

As a rule, Lutheran ministers are academically trained, called, appointed by the bishop, and called to a local congregation within a specific synod or diocese or region. Affirmation for the call is sought from different constituencies. Globally, Lutheran communities have slightly different steps in the protocol but the principle is the same: one needs qualifications and preparation in accordance to the church's teachings and one needs to be called by a concrete, local community of faith. In Lutheran tradition nobody can decide to become a pastor on their own but a process needs to be followed in the spirit of the confessions that do leave room for different designs of the process in different contexts. This shows, e.g., in the matter of ordination that has some significant fluctuation from context to context: in some Lutheran contexts only bishops ordain, valuing the so-called apostolic succession,[57] whereas in other parts of the world bishops are not necessary or are explicitly omitted from ordinations or appointments.[58]

---

[57]Apostolic succession: a tradition of valuing the historical continuity with a theological rationale of ordaining pastors by bishops with a lineage tractable to the act of Jesus laying his hands on his disciple Peter (Matthew 16:18).

[58]The question of episcopal office and ordinations was one of the points first hindering the ecumenical agreement between the Episcopal Church of USA and the ELCA. Another issue was the traditions' different policies about the rights of gay and lesbian persons in the church. The agreement from 1999 *Called to Common Mission* brought the traditions to full communion, meaning, sharing in Eucharistic practices and services of the clergy.

This variation in practices is made possible by the positions outlined in the confessions. Melanchthon's *Treatise on the Power and Primacy of the Papacy* is most interesting in this regard and merits a brief visit.

When interpreting Jesus's words, "On this rock I will build my church" (Matthew 16:18), Melanchthon makes his case with the church fathers in pointing out that the word "rock" refers to Peter's faith, not any special authority given to him (TPPP 334:28). Those installed in the footsteps of Peter as leaders stand on equal footing and they share in spiritual authority (TPPP 334:31). The spiritual authority serves the human order but also has a specific function: "The gospel bestows upon those who preside over the churches the commission to proclaim the gospel, forgive sins, and administer the sacraments. In addition, it bestows legal authority," e.g., to excommunicate (TPPP 340:60).

Any other authority, such as that claimed by the bishop of Rome—who should be happy to be considered equal among equals—would be a matter of human decision and agreement. No bishop, including the bishop of Rome, enjoys special authority or superiority by divine right (TPPP 331:7–8). With these arguments, Melanchthon places the matter of episcopacy in the realm of human decision-making and order. This had immediate and concrete implications: if the Pope held no more authority than the other bishops and could be disobeyed—as Luther did—then also, as the reformers set agendas for changes that they considered crucial in light of the Scriptures and the current situation, they deemed it unnecessary to obey any bishop who was not with them.

This logic let to a standing that for new appointments of pastors, bishops would not be necessary (TPPP 340, 67). Communities could call their own pastors and arrange their ordination as seemed fit, as long as there was no "good" bishop available—that is, a bishop who led and taught in accordance with the reformed theology (TPPP 340:66–67, 341:72). With all this, Melanchthon set the stage for Lutheran ordinations and installations that can take different forms. It has been forgotten that with all these liberties that he argued for, Melanchthon also reminded that Lutherans could respect the Roman bishop as long as there was clear adherence to the gospel, which was the main reason for any form of ministry.

Bringing the considerations to this day, Lutherans have different sensitivities in the matter of authority and papacy. Regardless of the local and cultural variances, Lutherans have maintained a fairly structured system that involves higher education, examinations, and lengthy mutual discernment in who is called, internally and externally, to ministry; for example, ELCA practices a rigorous candidacy process with designated committees consisting of clergy and lay members before one is called to a designated ministry and then ordained and installed. In Finland, synodical postgraduate training serves the similar purpose for pastoral preparedness after ordination, with fewer steps prior the call and ordination. In the United

States, with the ELCA, for an individual to be called to preach and administer the sacraments, one needs to be approved in this process that takes a few years and intentional discernment and collaboration before proven readiness to appropriately and in due process be called to a synod and from there to a local congregation or other forms of ministry. The external call is highly valued and measured in the process. The placement of candidates involves bishops and the national church. The preparation includes seminary faculty, candidacy committees, bishops, and local congregations that nurture, support, and receive candidates. The person's internal call is a factor but not the one that determines the outcome. Lutherans like to vet the internal call and match it with an external call—thus the call processes that are followed. Furthermore, there are specific rules about being included and staying in the "roster" of called leaders. Currently there are two main tracks in the ELCA, one toward ordination for the ministry of Word and Sacrament and the other for consecration for the ministry of Word and Service calls.[59]

The following article fifteen on church rites or regulations sets the stage for how to negotiate what all goes in the church community and how to decide which rituals to observe and how. The bottom line is this: there is much flexibility in these matters and all "those rites should be observed that can be observed without sin and that contribute to peace and good order in the church." This includes festivals and celebrations with holy days. A reminder is added that none of this is a salvation matter. Whether one partakes or not in such ceremonies is not a matter of salvation or holiness. Ceremonies and celebrations are good as long as they do not "burden consciences" (AC 15:2). Fasting and observances that would require a vow—and therewith a sense of a requirement and an experience of failure if not able to keep the vow—are not in this category; for example, "vows and traditions concerning foods and days, etc., instituted to merit grace and make satisfaction for sins, are useless and contrary to the gospel" (AC 15:4). The key here is the function of the observance or ritual: the minute when a hint of hoping for merit or earned forgiveness with the said observance enters the mind—or the teaching of the observance—it becomes not only futile but even dangerous.

In his *Smalcald Articles* Luther launches in more detail about these imagined "dangers." He has critical words to say about "foundations" (associations,

---

[59]Melanchthon's treatise is the most detailed exposition in the *Book of Concord* of the history of episcopacy and particularly the Roman bishop's claims for superior status, which the reformers challenged. He also outlines the rationales and protocols for ordinations, as well as the functional division of authority in church affairs. He speaks of different callings that all serve the gospel in distinct roles and explains the relation between bishops and pastors and the stipulations regarding ordination. "However, since the distinction of rank between bishop and pastor is not by divine right, it is clear that an ordination performed by a pastor in his [her] own church is valid by divine right" (TPPP 140:66).

chapters, monastic groups) and monasteries that were originally established for educational purposes. These "should again be regulated for such use so that one may have pastors, preachers, and other servants of the church, as well as other people necessary for earthly government in cities and states, and also well-trained young women to head households and manage them" (SA 437). With furious words Luther accuses the papacy for the situation that Mass "has to be the greatest and most horrible abomination" (SA 430). Because, as it was practiced, Luther considered it clashed the central article about Christ justifying by faith alone (SA 427–8). One should not be misled to believe that Luther or Lutherans reject the Mass and the sacrament, quite the contrary. A refocusing is demanded, abolishing any teachings or practices that would allow one to believe that salvation and deliverance came from anywhere else but Christ. The reformer's shouting against the Mass demonstrates his passion to remind who the deliverer of sin is: "the Lamb of God alone should and must do this" (SA 430).[60]

Using colorful language, Luther calls the Mass "dragon's tail" that has "much vermin and excrement" and idolatries (SA 433).[61] He lists purgatory, relics, pilgrimages, fraternities, vigils, indulgences, and other well-known practices as unnecessary and harmful, his main argument being that the church had misled Christians to attach their hopes of deliverance and salvation on human inventions. He deemed the current practice of the Mass at the root of the problem: the parts in the Catholic Mass that suggested a rationale for a re-enactment of Christ's once-and-for-all sacrifice were deeply problematic. Such teachings would put the entire Christian gospel in jeopardy, this was behind Luther's furious words. With his rejection of the (in his view) distorted medieval teachings of what actually happens in the Mass, he was defending the gospel about Christ and his redeeming work. To enhance his point, he names several abuses, such as communing oneself and alone and buying and selling of Masses, all of which indisputably was practiced in the Catholic church.

Furthermore, while at it, Luther critiques the reverence of the saints, pilgrimages, relics, and the like, and this hits the nerve among people. Saints, Mary, relics, and pilgrimages were revered and well-established traditions; to touch these beloved poles of Catholic spirituality would mean trouble. At the same time, these questions invited much-needed fresh attention to spiritual practices and the rationales and hopes behind them. In Luther's view, it matters how Christian faith was practiced in the lives of men and women and children. These conversations, both doctrinal and practical, allowed Lutherans to set a new mood for what is called spirituality.

---

[60]See also Kolb and Wengert, *The Book of Concord*, SA Part II art. 3; Part II art 2; Part II art. 1; Part II art. 3.
[61]See also Kolb and Wengert, *The Book of Concord*, SA Part II art. 2.

I. Central Topics and Learning Goals

1. The Lutheran rationale for the church and its mission.
2. Lutheran definition of the sacraments and their proper uses.
3. Lutheran teaching of baptism and the rationale for infant baptism.
4. Lutheran teaching of the Lord's Supper and the emphasis on "real presence."
5. Lutheran view on confession and repentance.
6. Lutheran understanding of the office of (ordained) ministry and the priesthood of all believers.

II. Questions for Reflection, Discussion, and Further Reflection

1. Reflect on the mission for the church in contemporary context with hospitable uses of the means of grace.
2. What are the essentials for "unity" in the church? What decisions are *adiafora*?
3. How does the Lutheran teaching of sacraments draw from and apply the teaching of justification by faith?
4. What is the role of faith with sacraments?
5. Sacraments as tools in freedom theology.

III. Keywords

Bishop, confession, church, communion, faith, forgiveness, grace, hospitality, Lord's Supper, means of grace, real presence, repentance, saint, salvation, sinner, Spirit, vocation.

IV. Readings with the Chapter

(Church) AC 5, 7–8, 13, 14–15. (Skim Ap. 5, 7–8, 14–15.)
Also SA Part III art. 3–4, 12, 9, 5–15; Part II art. 2; FC V, X.
(Baptism, Confession) AC 9–13. (Skim Ap. 9–13.)
Also SA Part III art. 3, 4, 5, 7, 8; LC on Baptism, Confession.
(Lord's Supper, Repentance) AC 10, 12, 13, 15, 22, 24. (Skim Ap. 10, 12, 13, 15, 22, 24.)
Also SA Part III art. 3, 4, 6, 7. FC VII (and VIII).

8

Lingering Issues and Kindle for Future Fires

Last but Not Least—The Practical Matters

Whereas the first twenty-one articles in the *Augsburg Confession* pertain explicitly to doctrine, the last seven attend to reforms in practical matters, so indicates the document that, important to remember, was written for the audience that included the emperor and the German princes. The conclusion (AC Conclusion of Part I, p. 59: 1–2) says, "This is nearly a complete summary of the teaching among us. As can be seen, there is nothing here that departs from the Scriptures or the Catholic church or from the Roman church. ... The entire dissention concerns a few specific abuses, which have crept into the churches without any proper authority." A point is made that the bishops should have listened to the reformers and much trouble would have been avoided; the split would have been avoidable. They persistently defend their position with their self-assessment that "the ancient rites are, for the most part, diligently observed among us." Reformers, in their own words, simply wanted to continue in the spirit of the early church's ecumenical Creeds and with the ancient rites, toward which they deemed it necessary to correct those elements in religious life that were experienced as abusive and hurting the consciences of the human beings for whose sake the rites and practices had been developed in the first place.

The reader might assume that the last part of the text would be lighter and about issues less debated, but contrary is the case. In the latter part of the document several issues are on the table, ones that have since the Reformation days been a cause of contention, among Lutherans themselves, but also for Lutherans in relation to other Christians. Much ambiguity remains on several of the questions addressed in the last articles that are remarkably longer than many of the first doctrinal ones.

The German and the Latin versions of the preface to these articles slightly differ. The Latin text in translation states,

> Since the churches among us do not dissent from the catholic church in any article of faith but only set aside a few abuses that are new and were accepted because of corruption over time contrary to the intention of the canons, we pray that Your Imperial Majesty will graciously hear about the changes and our reasons for them, so that the people may not be compelled to observe these abuses against their conscience. (AC Introduction of Part II, p. 61:1)

For the sake of comparison, the German version promises that

> [n]othing contrary to Holy Scripture or to the universal, Christian church is taught in our churches concerning articles of faith. Rather, only some abuses have been corrected that in part have crept in over the years and in part have been introduced by force. Necessity demands that we list them and indicate reasons why correction is permission in these matters so that Your Imperial Majesty may recognize that we have not acted in an unchristian or sacrilegious manner. On the contrary, we have been compelled by God's command (which is rightly to be esteemed higher than all custom) to permit such corrections. (AC p. 60)

In other words, a strong point is made that the perceived dissension is not from the Protestant side who simply on the basis of the Scriptures, their guiding light and foundation, have valid concerns about the state of the Christian faith and teaching and thus urge necessary reforms in the church.

What were those issues needing correction, again? Questions concerning the Lord's Supper, marriage customs and calling, the purpose and proper use of the Mass and the use of confession, the value of monastic vows, the authority of the church and the ecclesial power, and discernment on fasting and other religious practices that may or may not be considered helpful in light of the revised teaching of faith. The articles then address areas where the evangelical interpretation of the gospel is very much lived out and applied, communally speaking, and in this space of lived faith, differences were—and have been—substantial enough to prevent a unified vision or collaboration. The practice and application of faith is the territory where the theological rubber hits the road and the divides and variations are to be expected. Sacraments, sexuality, and power in the church have continued to excite ongoing debate; also the current tensions are most palpable in these areas.

Just as sacramental practices and sensitivities still manage to divide faith communities and individuals, human sexuality is another area where Lutherans globally and locally speaking stand on fundamentally different places. It is fair to consider how the two issues and Lutheran approaches to them intersect, at least implicitly. That is, there well may be a correlation between how hospitable people are with their sacramental theology and practice and how respectfully and hospitably they approach the questions about the human body, relations, and sexuality, and listen to their neighbor's experience. In the past discourse, Lutherans have tended to distinguish between doctrinal questions and human interest or social issues. This has shown in, e.g., how and where the questions of human sexuality, sexual orientation and identity, and views on marriage have been deliberated on, as if in a different category of importance and not as theological urgencies and areas for reforms. The *Augsburg Confession* presents the opposite model: both topics are included, side by side, as questions meriting a confessing position with a theological rationale, on the one hand, and changes in practice, on the other. There is a connection.

Who Is Welcome to Communion?[1]

The main theological point about what happens in the sacrament of the Lord's Supper is made already earlier in the article ten. That of course is just the beginning of unfolding a complex issue with multiplying practical questions. With article twenty-two, there clearly was an urgency about the teaching of welcome and inclusivity of grace. One of the visible, most significant reforms was precisely the change to an inclusive practice that invited men, women, and children to receive both elements, bread and wine. The question of serving communion to the laity was enormously pertinent. The article twenty-two in the *Augsburg Confession* argues that the Bible clearly gives a command to offer to all both the bread and the wine. Quoting Matthew 26, a case is made that the laity can and should drink from the cup, following Jesus's own command. Also Paul's letter to Corinthians (1 Cor. 11) and other early teachers (e.g., Jerome and Cyprianus) are cited to prove that the early church included everyone—all the baptized—to the full meal.

In other words, a major reform is demanded from the Catholic practice of offering the communion to a lay person only in one form, the bread as body of Christ, and reserving the cup of Christ's blood for the priest only. This practice had crept into the church over the centuries and was decreed at the IV Lateran Council 1215 as the church's official practice. Reasons for this are ambiguous as the early church did not make such a distinction

---

[1] Read AC 22. (Skim Ap. 22.) Recommended LC, Sacraments; SA Part III art. 6.

between the recipients. Some of the reasons were the increased authority and special status of the clergy who, as it was taught, vicariously performed the sacrament and prayers for the laity, whose participation had decreased to that of an observant and receiver of the host—and often just once a year, that had been made a requirement.

Another reason for the practice of serving lay persons only the bread may have been the difficulty of storing wine that could spill or spoil. Yet another factor was the increased religious sentiment of adoration of the host and the fear of spilling of the blood of Christ. The Catholic teaching held, and still holds with the expression of *transubstantiation*, that when a duly ordained priest performs the proper rite, the substance of the mundane elements, bread and wine, is transformed, changed into the real body and real blood of Christ, while their appearances remain the same. The priest's role was essential in this mystery. At the heart of the practice was the conviction that the holy rite truly effects grace. The ritual was understood to work when performed in accordance with the church's stipulations: with the right ritual and an ordained priest, it worked *ex opere operato*, i.e., from the work done. Due to that action, the mysterious change called transubstantiation would happen. Assessing the space dedicated to the issue in the *Augsburg Confession*, it appears that the transubstantiation doctrine was not the primary headache for the reformers. They attended more to the issues of who was welcome and who could perform the sacrament. The question of the sacrament's effectiveness related to these questions and it included the role and position of the clergy.

The reformers were proposing changes in a context where the sacrament, for centuries, had been a clergy-performed ritual whose specific words, performance, and authority effected the sacrament's mysterious change in substance. Only clergy were authorized to perform the sacrament, clergy whose ordination was already a sacrament and a prerequisite for the effectiveness of the other sacraments. This special duty and privilege of the priest as the performer, combined with the teaching about the mystery of the ritual, contributed to the gap between people and the sacrament. Rather than inviting people to partake in the divine mystery, the ritual inspired veneration from the distance, with trust placed in the vicarious performance of the priests. The sacrament in its medieval practice, then, contributed to the already existing gap between laity and clergy, intended or not.

It is to be noted that these performers, priests, were all male and had to live under the rule of celibacy. The sexual abstinence was part of the imagination about the sacraments' effectiveness; this sentiment developed over time, while it was not the teaching of the early church. The male gender of the performing priest was a given. The question of women's ordination is still unsolved in the Catholic church. Also in Lutheran churches, globally, the question of women's ordination is answered differently; the arguments typically concern the models for ministry as gathered from the biblical evidence and its interpretation.

Much of the criticism the reformers with Luther expressed toward the church's sacramental practice had to do with their growing unease with customs that made the lay person feel less holy, less deserving, and less welcome. Also, with the Christological emphasis, the reformers grew weary of notions that would set the priest in the middle as the mediator, the middle person; that should have been unnecessary since Christ had already taken that place and opened direct access to God. With their convictions about grace belonging to all persons, for free, and everyone standing equal in the face of God and needing that grace, a sentiment grew to a conviction that the beloved sacrament was misunderstood, misused, and unduly withheld from the people.

Fired up with these ideas, Luther's colleague, former dean, Andreas Karlstadt of Bodenstein, originally had started with drastic measures to implement the ideas of equality and inclusivity, while Luther was still hiding in Wartburg as an exiled heretic and under the protection of Prince Frederick. "Brother Andreas," as he began to call himself, stripped off his clergy garb, led students by the river, and administered the sacrament there. Reciting the words in German, he also invited everyone to receive both elements, taking thus steps toward an egalitarian practice of the sacrament. These radical steps were inspired by Luther's teaching, but the changes were happening too fast, without important premeditation on the consequences and proper preparing of the soil—and souls. Also, it did probably not help that the first "Come all" Eucharist service by the riverside took place on Christmas Day. (Probably a good rule of thumb with reforms is to avoid the major holidays.)

Reformer Karlstadt with his eagerness to take the lead with concrete action found himself in hot waters with his colleagues and moved around between different Protestant constituencies, finally ending without a church or home base for his reforms.[2] Karlstadt's speediness and methods were criticized even by Luther, who had to rush back in town to restore peace. Namely, the reforming minds were not only changing communion practices but also rushed into churches with iconoclastic agendas, destroying church property and art as popish and unnecessary. Luther would have none of that. He hurried home, uninvited while still under the ban, during Lent in 1522, and gave eight s.c. *Invocavit* sermons.[3] He restored peace by proclaiming the importance of patience and mutual love over rush and compulsion, with any reforming acts, but most specifically with the Lord's Supper.

"Inclusivity" is a word that can be used here, a modern word but with roots in Luther's theological rationales with the sacrament. Another key word is "participation" versus "performance" when speaking of sacraments.

---

[2] See Amy Nelson Burnett, *Karlstadt and the Origins of the Eucharistic Controversy. A Study in the Circulation of Ideas* (Oxford/New York: Oxford University Press, 2011).
[3] See Luther's *Invocavit Sermons* (1522), ed. Martin Lohrmann, *The Annotated Luther*, Vol. 4, ed. Mary Jane Haemig (Minneapolis: Fortress Press, 2016).

Yet another Lutheran emphasis is the direct contact between the sacrament's gift and the receiver: the sacrament is given for the person ("for you"), not through the priest.

The article gives an argument with Scripture and a historical foundation for carving space where everyone is included to participate. The last sentence of the article points to participation as the key. Those elements should be omitted that would endorse ideas of performance and would keep the sacrament visual rather than a rite to partake with; this in mind, the Eucharistic elements were no longer to be carried in procession. The decision of forgoing the practice was not only a ceremonial preference or wanting to tone down the pomp that could make the ritual seem more as a performance act rather than a participatory event. As Lutherans were, slowly, departing from the teaching of transubstantiation and the related holy awe in the presence of the sacrament, their renewed focus was on equipping the receiving and participation. Teaching of the meaning of the gift "for you" became far more important than speculations on how exactly Christ's presence came about. And, as said, the priests' role in this was reconfigured from a mediator to a servant.

To conclude, changes with the Lord's Supper practices were among the major reforms implemented and the invitation for the laity to the full communion was one of the imminent and most visible signals of the community of faith being Lutheran. Today Lutherans draw from the same teachings of the *Augsburg Confession*, theologically, while their practices vary. Local and global differences can be observed in decisions on whether baptism is a prerequisite and what is the preferred age for the first communion, and whether a child can receive and at which age and with what kind of preparation. Typically such decisions are made by the faith community that has synodical (or in some cases national) guidelines to consider. Also, an evolving question is the role of clergy with the ritual and its administration. Whereas the reformers set theoretically broad parameters for lay leadership in the matter, they also explicitly preserved the role of the ordained clergy. There is some leeway in how the Lutheran theological standpoint regarding the sacrament and and the priesthood of all believers is interpreted today in different contexts vis-à-vis not-ordained person's role in the serving of the communion.

Lutheran communities of faith have freedom to exercise some decision-making in these matters, with the bottom line conviction that these are matters of human order, for the benefit of people and for the purposes of making sure the gospel of grace is proclaimed and communicated effectively and inclusively. In the ELCA, e.g., bishops can authorize lay leadership—properly trained individuals—in administering the sacraments. Congregations locally can decide on the proper age of the first communion. Congregations can also decide whether they place a clause in a bulletin about (only) all baptized Christians being welcome or whether to explicitly invite anyone. The latter practice would be more in the spirit of the *Augsburg Confession*.

Lutheran theological rationale makes it clear that practices with the Lord's Supper are about hospitality with grace. Everyone is invited to the table of grace, regardless of their faith, status, feelings, sense of worth, knowledge, etc.; even unbaptized individuals are to be invited. In Lutheran emphasis, the meal is about Christ, it is about a gift, it is about welcome to receive a gift of forgiveness, and it is about hearing personally the "for you" words of forgiveness and an affirmation of Christ's presence in one's life. What all happens in the meal, how mysteriously God becomes present "for you" is beyond human effort and construction and criteria. Theologically speaking, open table is a given.

Who Can Marry and Vocation Issues[4]

Another visible reform in the sixteenth century was that Protestants allowed—and very soon actually expected—their clergy to marry. Again, a most visible change, highly debated, and in the document the issue is tucked away toward the end. Whether it was Melanchthon's brilliant intention to tone down the anxieties or not, the question of marriage and matters pertaining to human sexuality could not be bypassed; theologizing on these matters would touch human lives directly. Decisions on human sexuality vis-à-vis holiness would be an important test on Lutheran teaching of equality among the baptized. It would also shape the emerging visions of diverse vocations and voices in the life of the church and how a community of faith can be a freeing space that honors the human experience in its multifaceted dimensions.

Before the writing of the *Augsburg Confession*, Luther had already argued on the basis of the Scriptures and in light of the contemporary laws about the rationale and the importance of the church supporting those who marry. His first arguments for the holiness of marriage were given in junction with his attack on the vows for celibacy, and these matters were included in his first published reformation agendas, such as the ones presented in the watershed work *On the Babylonian Captivity of the Papacy* (1520).[5] In addition to honoring marriage, with theological arguments, he saw the need to teach about the "how" when it came to the involvement of the church in these human matters. His *Small Catechism* includes "A Marriage Booklet for Simple Pastors" with short but concrete instructions for what should happen in a Lutheran wedding ceremony, with the understanding that the laws and regulations about the institution of marriage were decided by the laws of the land, not the church. These laws of the land could be quite different but

---

[4]Read AC 23. (Skim Ap. 23.) SA Part III art. 11. See in SC, *A Marriage Booklet for Simple Pastors*, 1529, ed. Timothy J. Wengert, *The Annotated Luther*, Vol. 4, ed. Mary Jane Haemig (Minneapolis: Fortress Press, 2016), pp. 242–6.

[5]*On the Babylonian Captivity of the Church*, 1520, ed. Erik H. Herrmann, *The Annotated Luther*, Vol. 3, ed. Paul Robinson (Minneapolis: Fortress Press, 2016), esp. pp. 96–107.

they would give the framework within which the church would be involved in marriage affairs. Luther is clear about the division of duties here and the distinction between the jurisdictions of the land and the realm of the church. Thus, he writes, "[B]ecause weddings and the married estate are worldly affairs, it behooves those of us who are 'spirituals' or ministers of the church in no way to order or direct anything regarding marriage, but instead to allow every city and land to continue their own customs that are now in use" (SC, "Marriage Booklet," 242). In other words, marriage is a civil contract, governed by the laws. This may seem odd to a contemporary reader but remembering that marriage was an important financial transaction and a contract between families as well as individuals, involving allocating property and assets, everyone involved needed to be protected by the laws. This is an important point to observe, also for contemporary conversations: marriage is a civil contract. It is not a sacrament and it is not governed by the church.[6] In no case should the church try to prevent a person from marrying.

Rather, Luther writes, "when people request of us to bless them in front of the church or in the church, to pray over them, or even to marry them, we are obligated to do this" (ibid., 242). In other words, church and clergy can only be involved in their proper role. For these reasons, to support people who wish to marry, and while being clear about the role of the church in the big picture, Luther gives advice for how to proceed in the spiritual support of the "godly estate." He hardly misses the opportunity to poke the monastics, and also here he remembers the festive consecrations of the monastics, when ruminating

> much more should we honor this godly station of marriage and bless it, pray for it, and adorn it in an even more glorious manner. For, although it is a worldly, nevertheless it has God's Word on its side and is not a human invention or institution ... Therefore it should easily be reckoned a hundred times more spiritual than the monastic station. (ibid., 243)[7]

Not only is the church's involvement in marking the solemn event important to correct misconceptions about holy and less holy vocations, this is especially for the education and benefit of the young so "that the young people may learn to take this station in life seriously". Luther expresses a deep pastoral concern for the people who wish to receive a blessing from God and prayers from the community (ibid.). He is convinced of the need for such blessings and prayers, having observed the misconduct, discord, and suffering caused by sexual behaviors and transgressions. He has a realistic awareness of the power of the sexual drive and he is not shy in naming devil

---

[6]See John Witte, Jr, *From Sacrament to Contract: Marriage, Religion, and Law in the Western Tradition* (Louisville, KY: Westminster John Knox Press, 2012).
[7]See also Kolb and Wengert, *Book of Concord*, SC 367:1–368: 2, 3.

as the great tempter, particularly in marriage. This is because it is God's institution and of course the devil would like to sabotage all that is holy.

> For all who desire prayer and blessing from the pastor or bishop indicate thereby ... to what danger and need they are exposing themselves and how much they need God's blessings and the community's prayers for the station of life into which they are entering. For they experience every day how much unhappiness the devil causes in the marital station through adultery, unfaithfulness, discord, and all kinds of misery. (ibid., 243–4)[8]

Contemporary readers may not want to name any devil as the culprit but can recognize the issues.

Article thirty-three continues in a similar line of argumentation, addressing the important question of marriage in light of the broader view of human sexuality and while presenting a renewed notion of vocation. Its arguments are inherently interwoven with those in a later article twenty-seven, on the monastic vows, where some of the same topics receive another look. The articles are thus best read together, also for the reason that both deal with the question of vocation, on which Lutherans have something fresh to offer.

Article twenty-three on marriage starts with the observation that there had been complaints and evidence of clergymen's gross misbehavior and not living up to the standards set for them. Quoting Pope Pius (fifth c.), it is acknowledged that there may be reasons for some not to marry but that there are stronger reasons for just the opposite. Most importantly, "God has commanded that marriage be held in honor" (AC 23:20). Building their case on the Scriptures and history, Paul is quoted in the reminder that "[i]t is also evident that priests in the ancient church were married" (AC 23:10–11). Looking at the evidence back to the fourth century, "[I]t can also be demonstrated from the historical accounts and from the writings of the Fathers that it was customary in the Christian church of ancient times for priests and deacons to have wives" (AC 23:10–11, German text). In other words, marriage was a normal choice for many, including the clergy, until the church's teaching in the Middle Ages began to underscore the importance of special chastity and calling for clergy whose ordination required vow to celibacy and gave them a special standing. Yet human nature being what it is with natural sexual urges and pleasure points, these ideals were hard to attain or maintain for any human being, ordained or not. It would seem that the strict regulations to suppress the basic instincts and needs in human nature would backfire, with hurtful consequences. Already in the Middle Ages, but continuing to modern days, sexual misconduct and

---

[8]See also Kolb and Wengert, *Book of Concord*, SC 368:4, 369:5.

abuse cases have involved alarming numbers of Catholic clergy men living under celibacy expectations.

Therefore, for the reformers, it made sense that "God instituted marriage to be a remedy against human infirmity." Statements like that imply that the reformers had a good sense of human sexuality and of the dangers of trying to deny or suppress its power (AC 23:15). Marriage is portrayed as opposite to celibate lifestyle, the latter considered an unfair human regulation leading to failures, the former a divine command and an institution in which one can find satisfaction and support, and a vocation. Proofs are drawn from the Scriptures and also from the knowledge that "laws in all well-ordered nations ... have adorned marriage with highest honors" (AC 23:20). It is suggested, in so many words, that Christian medieval Catholic teaching unduly denigrated the holy and good institution of marriage; it was breaking and attempting to nullify God's commands. As with other reformers, for the Lutherans, God's commands overrule human regulations; vows of celibacy that come with monastic life were deemed futile and against the human nature (AC 23:24). The articles condone freeing individuals from these vows and express special empathy toward the young who may have joined an order "before attaining the proper age" (AC 23:26).

It is hard to overemphasize the radicalness of the reformers' teaching of the goodness of marriage as an inherently good thing. In the reformation world, where celibacy and particularly celibate men had been considered worthier than those expressing their sexuality and finding love in human relations, affirmation of the goodness of the legally instituted marriage was a blessing. The Protestant proclamation of the holiness of marriage and related domestic vocations was very good news to many. People had not heard such proclamation and affirmation of their normal lives and the impact was exhilarating.[9]

Not everyone unilaterally rejoiced with the new preaching, and not all women jumped at the opportunity to marry. This becomes clear from some of the monastic women's reactions. As the convents were ordered to be closed and celibate lifestyle was judged unnecessary, if not harmful, for many women it still was or would have been the preferred option. The freedom not to marry was considered worth fighting for by nuns to whom convent was their home and place for calling that was theirs, just as for others hearing the affirmation of the holiness of marriage was freeing and affirming their sense of calling in the world. Correspondence from women who either left or decided to stay in their convent illuminates women's theological decision-making on the matters (e.g., Ursula von Münsterberg, Caritas von Pirckheimer).[10]

---

[9]Kirsi Stjerna, *Women and the Reformation*, chapter 3.
[10]See Merry Wiesner-Hanks, ed., and Joan Skocir, transl., *Convents Confront the Reformation: Catholic and Protestant Nuns in Germany* (1350–1650) (Marquette: Marquette University Press, 1996) and Kirsi Stjerna, *Women and the Reformation*, chapter 2.

Considering the impact of Lutheran teaching in this regard, some observations can be made from the perspective of women and how women's options have evolved. Whereas in the sixteenth century motherhood was presented as the highest of callings for all women, and marriage was the most common arrangement that provided women with bread and shelter, today women have ways to support themselves and other aspirations than motherhood. Parenthood today, beyond birth, is possible without the traditional involvement of a mother. There are many new considerations for the angles today when discussing Lutheran views on marriage.

One of the urgencies, still, among global Lutheran communities is how to ensure that the teaching of the goodness of sexuality and the right to marry include individuals with different sexual orientations and identities. In this regard, Lutherans still have much theological work to do, to rescue the reformers' liberating teaching on these matters from tendencies to return to the unnecessary limitations that Luther had originally criticized as simply wrong and cruel and not of the will of God.[11]

To conclude, what can be gleaned from the sixteenth-century statement as a stimulus for today is minimally this: a gospel-based theologically argued view of human beings' right to love and be loved and, if they so wish, be in a relationship that the church is called to bless. Luther's crucial point continues to be relevant today. Church should not stand on the way of marriage or other forms of committed relationships that the laws of the land regulate and support. Lutheran position, on theological grounds, honors such relations, calls the communities of faith to pray for people in love relations, and supports them. At the same time, with the modern knowledge of human sexuality and in the context of modern laws that do not require marriage, the other side of the coin in talking about marriage as a vocation needs further illumination and affirmation from the Lutheran front: the option not to marry.[12]

The article on marriage concludes, "In as much as the world is growing old and human nature has become weaker, it is fitting to exercise foresight so that no more vice creep into Germany" (AC 23:14). The statement about foresight, what all it might have implied back then, sounds reasonable today as well. If the aim with regulations for human conduct are to support safe, healthy, and satisfying lives of sexual human beings, and marriage for those who wish to marry, then foresight is good and wise, as is theological reasoning that learns from sciences pertaining to human life. Last but not least, in such fundamental matters in human life, decision-making could

---

[11]See Kirsi Stjerna, "Luther on Marriage for Gay and Straight," in *Encounters with Luther*, ed. Kirsi Stjerna and Brooks Schramm (Kentucky: Westminster John Knox, 2016).

[12]Contexts differ vastly on these matters, e.g., in Finland, a common law partnership is supported societally without the formal marriage agreement. Also for clergy and persons in training, this is a viable option. Currently in ELCA in the United States, this is a debated issue, particularly pertaining to those in rostered ministry.

not be left in the hands of just few but rather deliberately encompasses the wisdom arising from the varied human experiences, orientations, and identities. The world today is in a very different place from the reformation era in terms of understanding sexual orientation and identity. Also different is the role of marriage in the choices people have. Today marriage is not the exclusive, necessary, or the best option for everyone as a vocation or as a space for sexual relations. It is good to keep this development in mind when assessing the radical changes the reformation brought in teaching of marriage.

Monastic Vows, Celibacy, and Sexuality[13]

As noted, early on Luther attacked the church's imposition on its clergy to live in celibacy. The evidence from the lives of the priests under that oath—often not being able to remain celibate, some living with concubines and fathering children—revealed how untenable the rule was. As early as in 1521, just few years before his own marriage, Luther targeted the celibacy rule and the monastic vows with fire. His signatory 1520 reformation treatise *On the Babylonian Captivity of the Church* included a lengthy attack on the church's stipulations on the monastic and celibate life—and the impossibility of that.[14]

In the *Augsburg Confession* article twenty-seven the topic also receives a substantial treatment. Unlike the title suggests, monastic vows per se were just one, while a neuralgic, issue. This article starts with a brief look at the past. If the oath for celibacy had once upon a time been a voluntary step, and then a way to restore order and discipline, making it mandatory is deemed a wrong direction and a root of much misconduct and suffering. Originally a "harmless" practice opened a can of worms and led to unnecessary suffering, especially when "these chains were put on many of" young who, before legal age, had entered monastic life "mistakenly" (AC 27:1–2, 4–5).

The article addresses briefly a serious issue with women: how many women, girls, had been placed in convents against their own will, as a family decision, often for financial reasons, and were not free to just leave, because of the oaths given? The writers well knew that when a convent had become the home for a woman, for her to leave, she would typically need to marry or be received back by her family. Leaving a convent after vows was a serious step with penalties.[15]

---

[13]Read AC 27. (Skim Ap. 27.) Recommended LC, Commandments; SA Part III art. 14.

[14]*On the Babylonian Captivity*, ed. Erik Hermann, in *The Annotated Luther*, Vol. 3, ed. Paul Robinson (Minneapolis: Fortress Press, 2016), esp. pp. 96–107.

[15]Luther's wife Katharina von Bora had been placed in a convent by her impoverished family and she had taken her vows as a teenager. Her and eleven other sisters' leaving the convent was orchestrated, from the distance, with Luther's involvement, at the risk of serious penalties for those involved. Upon arrival to Wittenberg, Luther worried about her marriage prospects. The couple married in 1525 amid cheers and sneers.

The reformers expressed compassion to the lot of women in convents, even as they moved to close them, a process that took quite a long time. (Some convents managed to continue their operations, even with papal funding for a while, under the radar, as educational institutions for women.) Practical issues aside, Protestant women effectively lost a vocational option with the monastic orders; no longer could they opt for a life in an all-female community where the daily life and chances, e.g., for education looked quite different from how life was for a married woman whose realm of operations was home.[16]

The article recognizes that in "earlier times" monasteries and convents were rich places of learning. And indeed, monasteries have provided learning, also for girls, at times when educational opportunities were slim and reserved for the nobility. They were feeders for universities and fermentations for theological thought and places where countless valuable manuscripts were prepared and preserved. With the loss of convents, Protestant women in particular lost an important setting for learning and intellectual aspirations; before the universities opened their doors to women, centuries later, convents were the place of higher education, apart from the privileged noble women who enjoyed private tutoring. The reformers would begin to change this situation by designing curricula and public schooling that involved girls. Everyone had the right to education, peasants' daughters and all; everyone needed a proper education for their respective vocation in the world. In the same vein, reformers wanted to make it crystal clear that between these different vocations, there was no spiritual hierarchy.

The reformers deemed that monastics callings, to be abolished, were no better than the other vocations available to the average Christian. The claim that monastic life was "a state of perfection" was vehemently rejected. Besides, nobody could attain such unreasonable goals set for the monastics; vows in that regard would be futile and with no special merit. Most certainly, they do not "justify" or constitute special holiness (AC 27:61–2). On this basis, monastic lifestyle is on feeble ground with a false law-based theology and assumptions that vows had anything to do with the satisfaction for sins or that their "humanly invented observances constituted a state of Christian perfection" (AC 27:46). Warning against such distractions that pull one's attention away from Christ, the argument boils down to the Lutheran basic conviction against other, "ungodly" positions: justification by faith by grace is a free gift. "Moreover, although God's command concerning marriage appears to free many from their vows, our people offer still another reason why vows may be invalid: every service of God instituted and chosen by human beings without the command of God, in order to merit justification and grace, is ungodly" (AC 27:36). It would be scandalous to propose that any human act, choice, vow, or institution would justify human beings (AC 27:48).

---

[16]See Kirsi Stjerna, *Women and the Reformation* (2009), chapters 2 and 4 in particular.

In other words, the doctrine of justification is defended as well as applied to generate a vision for a Christian life that starts with the conviction about equality in grace reception and, thus, holiness. A new, inclusive definition of perfection is given:

> For Christian perfection means earnestly to fear God and, at the same time, to have great faith and trust that we have a gracious God on account of Christ; to ask for and to expect with certainty help from God in all things that are to be borne in connection with our calling, and, in the meantime, diligently to do good works for others and to serve in our calling. True perfection and true worship of God consist in all these things, not in celibacy, mendicancy, or shabby clothing. (AC 27: 49–50)

To conclude, the radicalness of this inclusive vision of spiritual perfection cannot be underscored enough. It has contemporary bearing, giving a language to affirm the value of natural, daily human life and different vocations. Today Lutherans do not condemn monastic life and special vows, while in Lutheran religious life there is no invitation or structure for such, per se. At the same time, among Lutherans, semi-monastic orders have been established in the modern era, with similar enough principles of ordered religious life in a community and rules for life, but without the expectation of oath to celibacy. An ambiguous expectation (implicit or explicit) for celibacy today may appear with Lutheran seminarians.

In terms of reviewing the past, particularly in light of women's experiences, there is an increasing appreciation to the contributions of monasteries over the centuries, especially as places of learning and as all-female communities for women. The women participants bring an important perspective for the assessment of the Reformations' success in terms of the wider population and with the variety of freedom concerns. A lesson to be learned from this is the importance of a variety of human experiences to be included in the theological discourse. Given how much Christian theology has been written on the basis of male experiences, and with heteronormative starting points, Lutheran theology does well in intentional encompassing of a variety of voices and experiences.

The Mass and Confessing, Revisited[17]

The word "Mass" evokes different feelings among Lutherans. For some, the word implies the heart of the reformers' criticism and thus something to be abolished even from the vocabulary as a Catholic expression of worship and what all that entails. Others use the word, normally, for worship

---

[17]Read AC 24. (Skim Ap. 24.) Recommended SA Part II art. 2, 3. Part III, art. 7, 8.

with the sacrament of the Lord's Supper. The confusion about the word is understandable, given the tumults of the reformations and how the consequences were negotiated. Yet the original documents are quite clear about the Lutheran position on the Mass, referring to a worship where the sacrament is offered.[18]

Article twenty-four seeks to correct any misunderstandings: "Our churches are falsely accused of abolishing the Mass. In fact, the Mass is retained among us and is celebrated with the greatest reverence. Almost all the customary ceremonies are also retained, except that German hymns, add for the instruction of people, are interspersed here and there among the Latin ones" (AC 24:1–2).

The word "Mass" in itself is good and also gives an ecumenically fruitful foundation for discourse on worship matters and the celebration of the sacrament of the Lord's Supper. A Lutheran emphasis can be detected in how the Mass is taught. The confession writers saw in their own eyes how widespread the general ignorance about faith was; thus teaching about religion was named an urgency. It was—and is—especially important to teach about the dignity of the sacrament, "how it offers great consolation to anxious consciences—so that they may learn to believe in God and expect and ask for all that is good from God. Such worship pleases God, and such use of the sacrament cultivates piety towards God" (AC 24:7–9).

This is an important clarification, again to prove the reformers were not wanting to depart from or abolish what for centuries had been central for the faith communities—worship and sacraments. Rather, they sought to purge those practices from misleading teachings and abuses that seemed to work against the very purpose of the sacrament: to offer comfort and consolation and closeness with God. The reformers concluded this from what they heard from the field. One of the major scandals was the association of the sacrament with money. "However, for a long time there has been a serious public outcry by good people that Masses were being shamefully profaned and devoted to profit. It is public knowledge how widely this abuse extends in all places of worship, what kind of people celebrate masses only for a revenue or stipend" (AC 24:10-1). A stern judgment is made against private masses: in a custom that developed in the Middle Ages, priests could perform the Mass by himself, in return for a donation by a patron who did not need to be present. That was not, and is not ever, a Lutheran way. The Mass in Lutheran practice always involves a community of faith present, regardless of how many individuals in addition to the priest.

Next the attention is turned to the bishops who were charged with oversight. They were hardly ignorant of the abuses in the field, the article argues. "If they had corrected them in time there would be less dissension now. By their negligence many vices have been allowed to creep into the

---

[18]Luther attends to the question of the Mass with considerable fury in the SA Part II art. 2.

church" (AC 24: 14–15). Apart from the money issue, the gravest and most urgent matter to correct was people's understanding about what the Mass does for the person and what Christ does. Especially with the private Masses, people had begun to believe that "Christ had by his passion made satisfaction for original sin and had instituted the Mass in which an offering might be made for daily sins, mortal and venial. From this came the common opinion that the Mass is a work which *ex opere operato* blots out the sins of the living and the dead" (AC 24:21–2). In Lutheran view, "Scripture does not allow" any such suggestions that the work of the Mass would justify. Rather, "Scripture teaches that we are justified before God through faith in Christ" (AC 30:28–9).

Given that the rationale for and the effectiveness of the sacrament depends on what Christ has already done—and to avoid any misconceptions that the Mass was in anyway needed for justification—the reformers deemed it unnecessary to celebrate it every day or several times a week. That said, more important than the frequency question is to remember what the sacraments and the Mass are for. They are ways to remember what Christ has done, and sacraments are done in his memory. The Mass itself "was instituted so that the faith of those who use the sacrament should recall what benefits are received through Christ and should encourage and console the anxious conscience. For to remember Christ is to remember his benefits and realize that they are truly offered to us" (AC 24:30–2). Remembering all this is important, and the community of faith has an important role here, also to invite people to actually use the sacrament, for their own benefit. Bottom line: "The Mass is to be used for the purpose of offering the sacrament to those who need consolation" (AC 24:33).

Lutherans' reforms with the Mass, thus, focused on equipping and inviting people to come to worship and to receive the sacrament. Behind the practical reforms was a theological switch with the justification by faith doctrine. The needs of the congregants needed to be met with the proper offering of the Mass, where all are welcome, as they are. These guidelines serve well also contemporary communities of faith, as they deliberate on the frequency, format, and other practical matters with the worship, with or without the sacrament.

Returning to the topic of the article eleven, the document makes another statement on the importance of confession, against false accusations, to make sure it is understood that "[c]onfession has not been abolished in our churches" (AC 25:1). What has changed, though, is that it is no longer considered its own separate sacrament, and the role of the priest-confessor is clarified and expanded to include actually all in the priesthood of believers. For centuries, since 1215, confession has been one of the seven sacraments practiced in the Catholic church, all within the purview of the duly ordained priest. After some deliberation, and focusing their reasoning on theological grounds, reformers deemed the rite as an important aspect of preparing oneself for the Eucharist, and an orientation in life for a Christian, rather than a separate means of grace, a sacrament by itself.

If it was a sacrament on its own, it might lead to a misconception that forgiveness and justification somehow would be contingent on how one performs in confession, in other words, a form of works' righteousness. Namely, in earlier times, "satisfactions were immoderately extolled; nothing was mentioned about faith, the merits of Christ, or the righteousness of faith" (AC 25:5). The way the confession had been practiced in the church, the reformers explained, had been confusing if not abusive: it had become unclear for people who exactly was the one who forgives and what was required for that. The reformers drew attention to God and God's promises and viewed the act of confessing from that starting point. "People are taught to make the most of absolution because it is the voice of God and is pronounced following the command of God" (AC 25:2).

Instead of focusing on enumerating every possible sin committed (AC 25:7)—which would be impossible any way, in the reformers' view—the confessing individual should focus on the promise of forgiveness, one that works even without the act of confessing, actually. At the same time, the so-called power of the keys is highlighted as a real deal: "The power of the keys is praised and remembered for bringing such great consolation to terrified consciences, both because God requires faith so that we believe such absolution as God's own voice resounding from heaven and because this faith truly obtains and receives the forgiveness of sins" (AC 25:4).

In light of how sin is understood, even with the forgiven and justified person, it is impossible to imagine knowing and naming all of one's sins. Furthermore, the most grievous sins may actually be those not regretted or actively remembered, because the human heart is "devious" and "perverse" (Jeremiah 17:9) (AC 25:7). The point of confession is to find peace and forgiveness, not to make one more anxious. Practically speaking, the danger is this: "But if no sins were forgiven except those which are recounted aloud, consciences could never find peace, because many sins cannot be seen or remembered" (AC 25:8–9). The confession therefore must rely on something else but the labor of self-examination and reveling in one's regrets. That something else is God and God's promise.

In other words, people are invited, in the spirit of compassion, to come to confession and not be afraid of the priest or judgment or acts of penance required but rather to seek for consolation and freedom; this is offered by God directly and freely (Psalm 37:5). Stressing God as the "judge" and the one who forgives, the reformers effectively put the priest's role in a new perspective. They also sought to free the act of confession from fear and force, in order for it to effect freedom from what binds, most of all the guilty conscience and personal, unavoidable regrets. Thus, "[f]or even our adversaries are compelled to grant us that the teaching concerning confession has been most carefully treated and brought to light by our people" (AC

25:6). In sum, "confession is retained among us because of the great benefit of absolution and because of other advantages for consciences" (AC 25:13). It is noteworthy that pastoral care issues were in the front burner at the time of writing the confessions. This should not come as a surprise, remembering how vital the question of burdened or free conscience was for Luther in his spiritual journey, which led him to rebel against all that threatens the liberating power of the gospel and to do all in his power to communicate it to his fellow human beings he knew could relate.

Christian Perfection Perspectives[19]

Toward the end of the document, issues on the table are ones that involve the practice of religion in households and personal lives. Tensions are palpable because, unlike with doctrinal debates, critique or changes regarding people's religious habits and value systems touch sensitive nerves. One of the main reformation calls was to purge religious life from teachings and practices that burdened the soul and moved people further from the gospel promises. A distinction was made between what exactly God demands and wants, and what are "human traditions." Fasting and distinguishing between forbidden and allowed foods and other regulations used for penitence and satisfaction had become a distraction if not plain harmful. Imagining that any human traditions would merit any grace was not helpful (AC 26:1–2).

In their zeal to show light on the unconditional gospel promise, the reformers spoke against traditions that had become familiar to people. Three reasons are given, all of which point to the distortion of people trusting human conventions above God and smothering of the Scriptures' communication of grace. First, the medieval confessional practice had effectively

> obscured the teaching concerning grace and the righteousness of faith, which is the chief part of the gospel and which ought to be present and prominent in the church so that the merit of Christ is well-known and that faith, which believes in the forgiveness of sins on account of Christ, may be exalted far above works and other acts of worship. (AC 26:4)

Relatedly, a second point is made about the dangers of human traditions being "preferred" over "the precepts of God" (AC 26:8). For instance, celebrations of holy days, fasting, and other rituals and observances had become the center piece in "spiritual" and "perfect life" (AC 26:9–10). "Meanwhile the commands of God pertaining to one's calling were not

---

[19]Read AC 26. (Skim Ap. 26.) Recommended LC, Commandments and Creed; SA Part III art. 3, 4, 10, 15; Part II art. 1–2.

praised: that the head of the household should rear the children, that a mother should bear them, that a prince should govern his country. These were considered as 'worldly' and 'imperfect works'." The article offers criticism against such dichotomies between what is religious and what is not and points out the consequences: "This error greatly tormented pious consciences" (AC 26:11). While admiring the monks and nuns as if their God had found their observances "more pleasing," people lost the sight of the holiness of their own lives. Rather "they grieved that they were bound to an imperfect kind of life: in marriage, in government, or in other civil functions" (AC 26:11). The reformers' resolute to refute such imaginations rests on the notion of justification by faith making human sinners equally holy, and it expresses a radically inclusive vision of spirituality, vocation, and holiness.

The third point takes the reader back to the fundamental commitment of Luther and his fellow reformers: that the Christian teachings soothe the aching conscience rather than further burden them. Relying on observations of human traditions, no matter how helpful they may be, would be dangerous to the conscience, simply for the reason that nobody could keep all of them. As a fact, the history shows how "many fell into despair, and some even took their own lives because they felt that they could not keep the traditions. Meanwhile, they never heard the consolation that comes from the righteousness of faith and from grace" (AC 26:13). The article wants to readjust the perspective on what matters in religious life and what are "indifferent" things that should not be made a "must" and a law. The only must in teaching and proclaiming Christian faith is the gospel. There are many aspects in Christian life and in religious matters that are negotiable, but one is not: the gospel and its promise of holiness and freedom. Finally, the urgency with the reforms, and with this article, concerns the troubled conscience. "For the gospel compels us to insist in the church on the teaching concerning grace and the righteousness of faith, which can never be understood if human beings think that they merit grace by observances of their own choice" (AC 26:20).

Contemporary Lutherans are exploring the ways to exercise faith with different rituals, including varied forms of fasting. This is done with the understanding that there is no added worth or extra holiness merited in so doing, but rather deepening of one's faith in God and capacity to love one another. "Therefore, fasting itself is not condemned"; it just cannot be prescribed or held as necessary (AC 26:39). In addition to fasting, practices of disciplining one's body and acts of self-mortification as a way of earning merit are condemned in the article. At the same time, it is taught "that all Christians should train and restrain themselves with bodily discipline, or bodily exercise and labors, that neither over-exertion nor idleness may lure them to sin" (AC 26:33). Christians can benefit from spiritual discipline, which is acknowledged, while there is no need for self-inflicted suffering; life brings along suffering no matter what and this is the area where Christians can practice genuine discipline. "For concerning the cross they have always taught that Christians should endure afflictions. To be disciplined by various afflictions and crucified with Christ is a true and serious, not a simulated, mortification" (AC 26:31–32). There is no need for fake crosses; resilience, and mutual support, is needed in bearing the crosses that Christians cannot avoid in any event.

These changes in Luther's time were significant, from the grounds up. It mattered to care for how theology was lived out in ritual and that one's conception of self was to be detached from rituals. The foundation was in a theology highlighting, insisting on, grace alone as the modus that makes one holy and worthy. The theological emphasis was new; there is no question about that. And yet continuity in practice was maintained whenever it was possible. The reformers with the *Augsburg Confession* were consistent with their desire for order and unity. "Nevertheless, many traditions are kept among us, such as the order of readings in the Mass, holy days, etc., which are conducive to maintain good order in the church" (AC 26:40). With the warning to be repeated that none of these traditions and acts would in any way justify person, freedom is the word to take home from this article targeting the value of and flexibility with human traditions in religious life.

Power in the Church and Living in the World

Toward the end of the confession, the articles get longer and longer. The last one, on church and power, has much territory to cover. For starters, it names that in the past there had been issues around the bishop's office and in how those in the office had handled the sword given to them: some, problematically, had mixed the spiritual with the political sword, which had led to troubles of different kind, including violence and excommunications. The article reminds that "according to the gospel, the power of the keys or the power of the bishops is the power of God's mandate to preach the gospel, to forgive sins, and to administer the sacraments" (AC 28:5).

Power in the church is of special kind and its use is measured against the effectiveness with which the gospel message is conveyed to people needing it. "This power is exercised only by teaching or preaching the gospel and by administering the sacraments either to many or to individuals, depending on one's calling." The substance of what is being communicated is of spiritual nature. "For no bodily things but eternal things, eternal righteousness, the Holy Spirit, eternal life, are being given. These things cannot come about except through the ministry of Word and Sacrament, as Paul says [Rom. 1:16]" (AC 28:8). The church and its ministers have a solemn mission with the gospel and a duty that is exclusive to ministry and to the power in the church. Other forms of power, such as civil government, focus on other matters than the gospel.

If taking seriously the church's mission with the gospel about Christ and communicating it to people, there is an endless field of labor and opportunities ahead. Nobody else will do this. "For civil government is concerned with things other than the gospel" (AC 28:11). A clear division is held between what the church offers and what the church's jurisdiction is—spiritual life and matters relating to eternity—and what the state does with its officials. Both areas are considered holy and important. The concern is about mixing the two, thus the clarification of the two realms. "In this way our people distinguish the duties of the two powers, and they command that both be held in honor and acknowledged as a gift and blessing of God" (AC 28:18). This distinction was hardly any clearer then than it is now and continues to be an area of ambiguity and negotiation in different global, and local, contexts.

The question of power in the church involves deliberation specifically on the office of bishops. Historically, that office had been invested with a considerable amount of power, religious and also outside the church, as the medieval bishops could rise to a status akin to a landowning lord and also live accordingly. Reports of the bishops forgetting their primary duties and enjoying their privileges and misusing their authority and involving themselves in the politics did not enhance people's trust in church leadership, neither did the observations of some of the bishops' living lives not in agreement with the vows they had taken. Refocusing their job description, with the gospel, was needed.

> So, when asking about the jurisdiction of bishops, one must distinguish political rule from the church's jurisdiction. Consequently, according to the gospel, or, as they say, by divine right, this jurisdiction belongs to the bishops as bishops (that is, to those to whom the ministry of Word and sacrament has been committed): to forgive sins, to reject teaching that opposes the gospel, and to exclude from the communion of the church the ungodly whose ungodliness is known—doing all this not with human power but by the Word. In this regard, churches are bound by divine right to be obedient to the bishops (Luke 10:16). (AC 28:21–2)

The conviction stands on a long history of the bishop's office as the highest authority in ecclesial affairs and the very office that guarded and steered proper teaching and practice of ministry. The unity of the church at large and the successful spreading of Christianity from the early centuries onward relied on this office with deep roots. Obedience to the bishops entailed adhering to the orthodox teaching of the church with the ecumenical Creeds. The obedience manifests itself in different ways and areas. There are times and situations, however, when bishop's authority can be challenged. That is "when they [the bishops] teach or establish anything contrary to the gospel, church have a command from God that prohibits obedience" (AC 28:23).

In addition to establishing the situation for disobedience in respect to the bishops, and therewith to the highest authority and the teaching authority in the church, parameters are drawn for the limits of the bishop's authority in a variety of matters. It is not at all clear that bishops would have the right to instigate ceremonies and regulations of any kind on their accord. When in doubt, the rule of the thumb would be that "bishops do not have the power to establish anything contrary to the gospel" (AC 28:34). Disobedience would be in order if the bishops were to establish traditions that were against the command of God or when such traditions were required or made conditions for salvation. Several "what if's" are mentioned, asking about the limits of episcopal power and where to draw the line. As long as what is regulated by the bishops is not against the gospel and not deemed as in any way relating to the matters of salvation, then Lutherans could assume a relaxed attitude. "It is fitting for the churches to comply with such ordinances for the sake of love and tranquility and to keep them insofar as they do not offend others" (AC 28:55).

The rule of the thumb is, with offices, teachings, and actions, how it looks in light of the gospel. What would be considered contrary to the gospel can have multiple meanings but basically such a transgression could be anything not in agreement with the proclamation of grace and forgiveness for the sake of freedom of people and any action or teaching that would digress from the meaning of the life, death, and resurrection of Christ as the act of grace that was the sole cause of justification.

For contemporary Lutherans, the question of power is a live one. Global Lutheran communities have different authority invested on the office of the bishop but all have something equivalent in practice in terms of a central office of jurisdiction. Bishop is the shepherd of the shepherds, with slightly different lines of duties in different Lutheran contexts (e.g., in North America, the term "superintendent" has been one of the options in some Lutheran faith communities). While there is no pope, or first among equals, in Lutheran tradition, the hierarchy among the episcopal leaders is organized in a variety of ways. E.g., in the Finnish Evangelical Lutheran Church, the office of the Archbishop is the culmination of episcopal power in a church divided in bishop-led dioceses. In the ELCA in North America, the equivalent is the Presiding Bishop and the central office for all the member churches. In both contexts, the bishops' collegiate is central in negotiating the church's positions and theological directions, while each bishop in their respective synod holds the jurisdiction and implements the shared decisions.

Bishops' leadership is sought after on a broad spectrum of questions: one has been women's role in the church, another the rights of LGBTQIA[20] individuals. Even with the shared standing of the bishops, they each have a substantial amount of power in their respective synods and not just as

---

[20]LGBTQIA refers to persons identifying with the lesbian, gay, bisexual, transgender, queer, intersex, and asexual communities.

a disciplinary force but also in steering the communities theologically. In the matters of women's rights and sexual orientation, many a Lutheran has hoped for bishops taking the lead, collectively or individually. When that has not happened, and when the current practice has been condemned as something contrary to the gospel, Lutherans have taken the right to disobey and demand and implement change. A powerful example of this is the steps taken by individual bishops, synods, and local congregations for hiring a candidate against the standing "official" teaching of the church. Some of the first openly queer pastors in the ELCA were called and ordained through such gospel-driven disobedience.[21]

A related example: the Lutheran church in Finland, per the bishops' decision, does not currently (2020) officially support the marriage of same-sex couples. *Sateenkaaripappeus*, i.e., "rainbow ministry," has developed on the side with pastors willing to officiate in such weddings, even at the risk of losing their calls. The model for gospel-inspired disobedience in church matters comes from the sixteenth-century reformers themselves, the ones who wanted to articulate a Lutheran position at the time when the story was still unfolding and the question of obedience/disobedience was – as it is today – a tender, possibly life-and-death issue.

The Lutheran example is a brave one, when it comes to power and disobedience, ecclesial and civil. The courage draws from the fundamental theological principles. Lutheran position on civil service in the society is based on the doctrine of justification of all by faith, by grace. Another basis is, relatedly, the teaching of priesthood of all believers and the holiness of all vocations. Yet another is the conviction that Christian life of the justified involves engagement. One is freed in love of God to free others, as Luther phrased it in his *The Freedom of a Christian*. Not only is civil engagement appropriate; it is expected and highly encouraged.[22] The famous example of courageous Lutherans such as Dietrich Bonhoeffer and Sophie Scholl embody the theology that calls to stand one's ground and confess for the sake of freedom.[23]

---

[21]In 2009 ELCA decided to ordain openly gay and lesbian persons. The first gay bishop took office in 2013. The first ordination of a transgender person took place in 2014. Before these dates, individual congregations had called pastors who were gay, at the risk, by congregational decision, of potentially finding themselves outside the ELCA.

[22]See Hans J. Hillerbrand, "'Christ Has Nothing to Do with Politics': Martin Luther and the Societal Order" and Carter Lindberg, "Luther on Government Responsibility for the Poor," in Stjerna and Schramm, eds., *Encounters with Luther*.

[23]See, e.g., Eberhard Bethge, *Dietrich Bonhoeffer: A Biography*, transl. Victoria J. Barnett (Minneapolis: Fortress Press, 2000). Hans Scholl, Sophie Scholl, *At the Heart of the White Rose: Letters and Diaries of Hans and Sophie Scholl* (Walden, NY: Plough Publishing, transl., 2017).

According to the *Augsburg Confession*, serving the society in one's place is in sync with God's will, with the focus on involvement and engagement and caring for the sake of the common good. Christians can give oaths and work in courts and law, they can serve in the military and go to justified war, they can serve in any profession as anyone else, they can marry, and all vocations are holy and valued in the sight of God. The article harshly condemns other options, such as the Anabaptists who deliberately did not take oaths or carry arms. Their view of the life of a Christian was different: Christian communities in their view would belong outside the world, be its own entity, dedicated to earnest religious lifestyle in their own community, with regulations that would govern everyone's life more so than the laws of the land. Lutherans, from the start, have operated within or in relation to the laws of the land and found their way there. With the conviction of God's omnipresence and the holiness of all life's corners, and thus with a broad view of spirituality and what is meant with spiritual, Lutherans are called to embrace all there is to living in a society and to attend to issues as needed and knowing that is pleasing to God.

Faithful to Lutheran teaching of justification, no merit is earned with this. Still, the wording "one's own" or "proper righteousness" can be used to talk about one's involvement in the society. A justified person is called, internally compelled, to engage one's neighbor and the issues human beings face. The motivation is in the gospel and the freeing one has experienced first. It is about righteousness but not about the *alien* or earning kind. A life of a Christian, in the world, is the arena for *proper* righteousness. That engagement, without a guarantee of a success, is also the vista for Christian perfection, in Lutheran view. "Because the gospel transmits an eternal righteousness of the heart, they also condemn those who locate evangelical perfection not in the fear of God and in faith but in abandoning civil responsibilities" (AC 16:4–5). Quite the contrary is expected; law and government are required by the ordinances of God, as is "the exercise of love in these ordinances." As with obedience to bishops, obedience to magistrates and authorities is a given, unless one is "commanded to sin." In that case "they owe greater obedience to God than to human beings" (AC 16: 5, 6–7).

Article sixteen is a good way to end the discourse here on the Lutheran grammar of faith. As suggested early on in the book, Lutheran faith language can address real-life issues and freedom questions are at the heart of the urgencies, as we speak. The real test of the relevance of Lutheran theology for today and future is not depending on a nuanced phrasing or defining doctrine. It is rather found in the midst of life where theology either does or does not offer a relevant language and horizons of hope and a stimulus toward social transformation just as much as spiritual renewal. This book has been written with the hope that Lutheran theology bears the test and that the word "Lutheran" continues to be associated with the drive for freedom and justice, for all.

I. Central Topics and Learning Goals

1. Lutheran positions on marriage and sexuality.
2. Lutheran approaches to episcopacy and papacy.
3. Principles of Lutheran spirituality, Christian living and, repentance.
4. Lutheran views on vocation, involvement in the world, and the use of power.

II. Questions for Review, Discussion, and Further Reflection

1. What are the possibilities for Lutheran thinking vis-à-vis matters with sexuality, orientation, and identity?
2. In what ways can Lutheran communities become more inclusive and egalitarian?
3. How do Lutherans' topics of concern relate to those of neighboring Christian traditions?
4. The imagined rationales for disobedience and social action?

III. Keywords

Bishop, Christian life, confession, communion, Lord's Supper, marriage, monastic vows, perfection, spirituality.

IV. Readings with the Chapter

AC 22–8. (Skim Ap. 22–8.) LC, Lord's Prayer.
SA Part II, and Part III, passim.

9

Conclusions—All about Freedom

Having considered the evidence, and looking at the world we live in, the question is: what are the pillars of Lutheran faith that can work across cultural, geographic, and linguistic boarders? Is there a theme or a lens that arises as the most pertinent when moving forward? I would propose "freedom" as the word and as the concern to focus on.

When addressing this question in classroom discussions, when searching, on the one hand, to name the urgent needs for transforming theologies addressing the burning issues of our day and, on the other hand, when considering the central principles on which Lutheran theology at its best has stood on, freedom has arisen as the focal point and as the word of most meaning in contemporary theological discernment.

Freedom is an existential concern that touches upon the central theological categories at play in Christian religious discourse, including Lutheran. Whether articulated or not with the topics treated in this book, the concept of freedom has been the underlying and ultimate point of interest and, I would like to propose, the test for the bearing of Lutheran theology today beyond the church walls and as a transformative force in the world we live in. By now, I hope, it has become evident for the reader of the Lutheran sources that Lutheran theology from its starting point has addressed the dimensions of human freedom from different angles. While the freedom negotiations of the sixteenth-century writers were not identical with those of twenty-first-century persons' concerns, there are important points of connection that are both inspiring and compelling in the task of reconfiguring Lutheran theological language for today.[1]

---

[1] For an example of such transformative theology, see Anna Madsen, *I Can Do No Other. The Church's New Here We Stand Moment* (Minneapolis: Fortress Press, 2020).

Unfolding the meaning of the word "Lutheran," the starting point remains in the story of Luther, where freedom issues feature prominently. His doctrine of justification by faith can be best rearticulated as freedom theology. His pivotal theological insights arose from his experience of freedom of conscience. His central spiritual teaching was that of Christian's existential freedom from proving one's worth and the ensuing freedom-inspired compassionate orientation in life to care for one's neighbors. His reform calls demanded freedom from human-made regulations that compromised Christian freedom. Furthermore, many of the decisions made by Luther when negotiating his realm of operations, his authority and rights, and the moves forward with his peers and followers, inherently entailed the question of freedom. In his case, theology of freedom fueled his personal liberation and the freedoms he took—as a person, as a teacher, as a preacher, as a leader. Coinciding, freedom theology was the undercurrent of his proclamation and reforming acts. With Luther, the freedom of conscience, the core of his doctrine of justification, naturally led to actions – and hopes – toward justice. All this is to say that the word "freedom" is relevant both in the interpretation of Lutheran history and the narrative of what happened in the sixteenth century, as well as in the contemporary theological construction of Lutheran faith language that speaks to real-life issues. For contemporary Lutheran theological imagination, freedom can serve as a most productive lens and criteria, and it offers a concrete aim and a reality check, and motivation to stay theologically engaged in the affairs of our world.

The concept of freedom opens up theological study in ways that connect theory with practice and give helpful criteria for the relevance, or lack, of theological arguments, including the historical Lutheran ones. Freedom is a universal aspiration and it is a human right that continues to be compromised. A theological attention is needed to conquer expressions and experiences of injustice and to find life-giving sources of transformation, personal and social. Luther serves as an important case in point, given his importance as a pivotal Christian theologian of grace, and in light of the role freedom had in his spiritual journey, theological imagination, and reform negotiations. His model and theology has been used toward freedoms and unfreedoms. It has that potential. Globally and locally, Luther and the Lutheran sources deserve further wrestling with to search for the threads in theological argumentation that both reveal the situations and application of Christian sources where freedom is or is not the primary concern or is jeopardized, and, second, give stimulus and hope to work with toward ensuring freedoms. Without going too far on this road, let freedom be understood here to imply all the aspects of life that ensure quality of life, dignity, and emancipation (discussion on this would entail addressing social issues such as racism, poverty, right for education, intellectual and religious freedom, and different forms of bondage that torment and inhibit individuals).

The bottom line is this: if Lutheran theology does not speak to the issues of freedom and of justice as an essential dimension and expression of that, then what is it worth for? For the word "Lutheran" to have a positive "trans" meaning, the primary principle, goal, and experience promoted, protected, and proclaimed need to be something else but a doctrinal detail or worry for orthodoxy. If Lutheran theology, and thus Lutheran expressions of faith, is to play a transformative role in human lives today, reorientation is necessary regarding the parameters for (any) religious orientation and for the chances for (any) religion to be a transformative power in the world, with an actual impact with actual people's lives. Lutheran theology promises this kind of relevance—when considered critically and compassionately, for its good seeds, and while pruning off the tarnished and antiquated ingredients.

To conclude, I wish to invite the readers to engage Luther boldly with the topics they are passionate about and not worry too much about the historical distance or the appropriateness of the questions raised. Some of the best scholarship on Luther has emerged from courageous and authentic examinations by individuals to whom faith and religion matter and who in their own situation have faced urgencies they have felt called to attend to, even at a cost. Some of the best scholars have, like Luther, been passionate seekers of truth and risk-takers, immersed in dangerous or complex situations, suffered persecution and hardship, have broken free from the confines of the tradition or the binds of the academic guild, and more often than not have found themselves working with Luther's theology in the shadow of the cross of suffering in their own lives. Exercising hermeneutical freedoms, seeking for authentic encounters with Luther and for alternative approaches, individuals from vastly different scholarly networks have found Luther a worthy conversation partner,[2] with warts and all, on issues that have timeless relevance.[3] They have modeled how, with Luther, we can address violence and suffering, pray and articulate new visions of hope, engage in the world toward transformation and justice for all while boldly nurturing faith with sacraments and "divine therapy", and, last but not least, embody

---

[2] For example, in *Encounters with Luther*, eds. Kirsi Stjerna and Brooks Schramm, 2016, 74, John Douglas Hall writes, "I have found Luther a trustworthy guide in most things, but my interest in him is not that of a historian, who only wants to know what Luther did and said then; I want him to help me know what to do and say now." And Deanna A. Thompson (ibid., 97), "If Luther's theology of the cross is revisited, feminists will be surprised to meet in Luther and ally for thinking through how theologians re-imagine and reform dominant, abusive forms of Christianity, and move toward a more faithful, liberating portrait of life lived in response to the gospel message."

[3] One of the most exciting paradigm shifts in international and interdisciplinary Luther scholarship is presented in Else Marie Wiberg Pedersen, ed., *The Alternative Luther: Lutheran Theology from the Subaltern* (Lanham, MD and London: Lexington Books/Fortress Academic, 2019), with chapters addressing such questions as gender, violence, race, power, sexuality, ecological issues, and decolonizing with Luther.

love for all life around us in order to leave a free and just world for our children and children's children.[4]

Luther's theology of the cross, often cited and employed, offers a foundation for a theologically guided hope-oriented living in the reality that includes death and suffering. To draw from John Douglas Hall, "[T]he theology of the cross is a theology of faith (not sight), a theology of hope (not consummation), and a theology of love (not power)." As theology of compassion and about God in solidarity with creation, theology of the cross is world oriented and committed to truth-telling.[5] It is extroverted theology that calls to practice and brings justice issues to the center of theological work. In the poetic words of Vitor Westhelle,

> In the cross, in suffering and humiliation, we can only utter the story of this suffering that God will deliver us from, while with the same confidence cry out the lament of forsakenness. The theologian of the cross, from the standpoint of the cross itself cannot speak *about* the cross; she can only speak from the cross in sheer faith without evidence, on complete trust amidst abandonment in her radical refusal to say that evil is good. This location calls us to "simply be honest about the world" and not buffer the cries that come from the crosses even today, not to stifle the "deafening cry" of the oppressed.

Returning to the Easter morning story and the women in the empty tomb, Westhelle writes, "A theology of the cross (*in usus passionis*) is always the other side of a practice of resurrection, and the other way around; a practice of resurrection can only be exercised in the face of the dismal experience of the cross that in the Shabbat of prayer and weeping is remembered and thus brought back."[6] In other words, with Luther, Lutheran theology boldly stands on radical hope, humbly so, with confidence in the source of hope and promise of life.

---

[4]The authors in the *Encounters with of Luther*, eds. Kirsi Stjerna and Brooks Schramm, 2016, each in their own way, have tested this theology from different angles. Their contributions, in each case, first a public lecture and then published, are listed in the bibliography; here authors are named in the order of the chapters: Eero Huovinen, Denis Janz, Volker Leppin, Mickey L. Mattox, Stanley Hauerwas, Douglas John Hall, Vitor Westhelle, Deanna A. Thompson, John Witte Jr., B.A. Gerrish, Kurt K. Hendel, Mary Jane Haemig, Peter D. S. Krey, Hans J. Hillerbrand, Carter Lindberg, Surekha Nelavala, Anna Madsen, and Brooks Schramm. I have had the pleasure of getting to know these individuals, either in the course of my studies in Helsinki and Boston or during the years of leading the Institute for Luther Studies in Gettysburg. These voices continue to shape my thinking with Luther and are very present in my classrooms, where students engage Luther in this precious company.

[5]John Douglas Hall, *Encounters with Luther*, eds. Kirsi Stjerna and Brooks Schramm, 2016, 80, 84.

[6]Vitor Westhelle, in *Encounters with Luther*, Kirsi Stjerna and Brooks Schramm, 2016, 89, 95.

To conclude, Luther's theology of the cross sets a model for Lutheran theology to stand bold with faith, even in situations where hope seems futile and faith ridiculous. Luther's life and theology, as do the Lutheran confessions, give a paradigm to live in this moment, facing the realities of the day, to do what needs to be done, and to speak the truth where so needed. Cross is the starting point for theological conversations, and action, which can be life-giving and lifesaving. The sixteenth-century reformers' compassionate concern for the gospel message about the freedoms the cross of Christ had promised for all gave them the courage to call for changes in practice and in ways of thinking and, also, in the matters of faith. For them, none of that was theory only. Far from it. Lutheran theological tradition is about faith that is a live and changing matter.

BIBLIOGRAPHY

Arand, Charles P., Robert Kolb, and James A. Nestingen, editors. *The Lutheran Confessions: History and Theology of the Book of Concord*. Minneapolis: Fortress Press, 2012.

Barth, Hans-Martin. *The Theology of Martin Luther: A Critical Assessment*. Minneapolis: Fortress Press, 2013.

Bethge, Eberhard. *Dietrich Bonhoeffer: A Biography*. Translated by Victoria J. Barnett. Minneapolis: Fortress Press, 2000.

Bielfeldt, Dennis, editor. "Heidelberg Disputation." In *The Annotated Luther*, Vol. 1, edited by Timothy J. Wengert, (67) 80–120. Minneapolis: Fortress Press, 2015.

Braaten, Carl E. *Principles of Lutheran Theology*. 2nd ed. Minneapolis: Fortress Press, 2007.

Braaten, Carl E., and Robert W. Jenson, editors. *Union with Christ: The New Finnish Interpretation of Luther (Paperback)*. Grand Rapids, MI: Wm. B. Eerdmans, 1998.

Brecht, Martin. *Martin Luther*. Translated by James L. Schaaf. 3 vols. Philadelphia: Fortress Press, 1985.

Burnett, Amy Nelson. *Debating the Sacraments: Print and Authority in the Early Reformation*. Oxford: Oxford University Press, 2019.

Burnett, Amy Nelson. *Karlstadt and the Origins of the Eucharistic Controversy. A Study in the Circulation of Ideas*. Oxford: Oxford University Press, 2011.

Cameron, Euan, editor. *The Annotated Luther*. Vol. 6. 6 vols. Minneapolis: Fortress Press, 2017.

Cameron, Euan, editor. *The European Reformation*. 2nd ed. Oxford: Oxford University Press, 2012.

Cummings, Ryan. *Forgotten Luther II*. Minneapolis: Fortress Press, 2019.

Deifelt, Wanda, editor. "A Brief Introduction on What to Look for and Expect in the Gospels." In *The Annotated Luther*, Vol. 2, edited by Kirsi Stjerna, (25) 28–37. Minneapolis: Fortress Press, 2015.

Dingel, Irene, editor. *Die Bekenntnisschriften der Evangelisch-Lutherischen Kirche*. Göttingen: Vandenhoeck & Ruprecht, 2014.

Eire, Carlos M.N. *Reformations: The Early Modern World, 1450–1650*. New Haven: Yale University Press, 2016.

Evangelical Lutheran Church in America. "We Are Church, We Are Called," 2019. Accessed February 29, 2020. https://www.elca.org/50yearsofordainedwomen.

Fredriksen, Paula. *From Jesus to Christ: The Origins of the New Testament Images of Christ*. 2nd ed. New Haven: Yale University Press, 2000.

Gassmann, Günther, and Scott H. Hendrix. *Fortress Introduction to the Lutheran Confessions*. Minneapolis: Fortress Press, 1999.

Gaventa, Beverly Roberts, and Cynthia L. Rigby, editors. *Blessed One: Protestant Perspectives on Mary*. Louisville, KY: Westminster John Knox Press, 2002.

Gerle, Elisabeth, and Michael Schelde, editors. *American Perspectives Meet Scandinavian Creation Theology*. Aarhus: Church of Sweden Research Department, The Grundtvig Study Center, Aarhus University, 2019.

Gerrish, B.A. "Luther and the Reformed Eucharist: What Luther Said, or Might Have Said, about Calvin." In *Encounters with Luther: New Directions for Critical Studies*, edited by Kirsi Stjerna and Brooks Schramm, 147–60. Louisville, KY: Westminster John Knox Press, 2016.

Godfrejów-Tarnogórska, Agnieszka. "Celebrating 50 Years of Women's Ordination in Estonia." *The Lutheran World Federation*. Last modified September 15, 2017. Accessed February 29, 2020. https://www.lutheranworld.org/news/celebrating-50-years-womens-ordination-estonia.

Grane, Leif. *The Augsburg Confession: A Commentary*. Translated by John H. Rasmussen. Minneapolis: Augsburg Publishing House, 1987.

Gritsch, Eric W. *Fortress Introduction to Lutheranism*. Minneapolis: Fortress Press, 1994.

Gudmundsdottir, Arnfridur. *Meeting God on the Cross: Christ, the Cross, and the Feminist Critique*. Hardcover, 2009.

Haemig, Mary Jane, editor. *The Annotated Luther*. Vol. 4. 6 vols. Minneapolis: Fortress Press, 2016.

Haemig, Mary Jane. "Praying amid Life's Perils: How Luther Used Biblical Examples to Teach Prayer." In *Encounters with Luther: New Directions for Critical Studies*, edited by Kirsi Stjerna and Brooks Schramm, 177–88. Louisville, KY: Westminster John Knox Press, 2016.

Hall, Douglas John. "The Theology of the Cross: A Usable Past." In *Encounters with Luther: New Directions for Critical Studies*, edited by Kirsi Stjerna and Brooks Schramm, 73–84. Louisville, KY: Westminster John Knox Press, 2016.

Hauerwas, Stanley. "Why War Is a Moral Necessity for America, or, How Realistic Is Realism?" In *Encounters with Luther: New Directions for Critical Studies*, edited by Kirsi Stjerna and Brooks Schramm, 59–70. Louisville, KY: Westminster John Knox Press, 2016.

Helmer, Christine, editor. *The Global Luther: A Theologian for Modern Times*. Minneapolis: Fortress Press, 2009.

Hendel, Kurt. "Finitum Est Capax Infiniti: Luther's Radical Incarnational Perspective." In *Encounters with Luther: New Directions for Critical Studies*, edited by Kirsi Stjerna and Brooks Schramm, 161–74. Louisville, KY: Westminster John Knox Press, 2016.

Hendel, Kurt, editor. "Smalcald Articles." In *The Annotated Luther*, Vol. 2, edited by Kirsi Stjerna, (417) 423–77. Minneapolis: Fortress Press, 2015.

Hendrix, Scott H. *Martin Luther: Visionary Reformer*. New Haven: Yale University Press, 2015.

Hendrix, Scott H. *Recultivating the Vineyard: The Reformation Agendas of Christianization*. Louisville, KY: Westminster John Knox Press, 2004.

Hermann, Erik, editor. "On the Babylonian Captivity." In *The Annotated Luther*. Vol. 3, edited by Paul W. Robinson, (9) 13–129. Minneapolis: Fortress Press, 2016.

Hillerbrand, Hans J. "'Christ Has Nothing to Do with Politics': Martin Luther and the Societal Order." In *Encounters with Luther: New Directions for Critical*

Studies, edited by Kirsi Stjerna and Brooks Schramm, 207–19. Louisville, KY: Westminster John Knox Press, 2016.

Hillerbrand, Hans J., editor. *The Annotated Luther*. Vol. 5. 6 vols. Minneapolis: Fortress Press, 2017.

Hillerbrand, Hans J., editor. *The Protestant Reformation. Revised edition.* New York: HarperCollins, 2009.

Huovinen, Eero. "A Common Teacher, Doctor Communis? The Ecumenical Significance of Martin Luther." In *Encounters with Luther: New Directions for Critical Studies*, edited by Kirsi Stjerna and Brooks Schramm, 3–14. Louisville, KY: Westminster John Knox Press, 2016.

Janz, Denis R. "To Hell (and Back) with Luther: The Dialectic of Anfechtung and Faith." In *Encounters with Luther: New Directions for Critical Studies*, edited by Kirsi Stjerna and Brooks Schramm, 17–29. Louisville, KY: Westminster John Knox Press, 2016.

Johnson, Elizabeth A. *She Who Is*. Chestnut Ridge, NY: The Crossroad Publishing Company, 2002.

Kapic, Kelly M., and Hans Madueme, editors. *Reading Christian Theology in the Protestant Tradition*. London and New York: T&T Clark, 2018.

Karant-Nunn, Susan, and Merry Wiesner-Hanks, editors and translators. "Consolation to Those Women Who Have Had Difficulties in Bearing Children" by Martin Luther [WA 53:206.12]. In *Luther on Women: A Sourcebook*, 179–88. Cambridge University Press, 2003.

Kärkkäinen, Veli-Matti. *One with God: Salvation as Deification and Justification*. Collegeville, MN: Liturgical Press, 2004.

Kim, Grace Ji-Sun, and Hilda P. Koestner, editors. *Planetary Solidarity. Global Women's Voices on Christian Doctrine and Climate Justice*. Minneapolis: Fortress Press, 2017.

Kolb, Robert. *Confessing the Faith: Reformers Define the Church, 1530–1580.* St. Louis: Concordia Publishing House, 1991.

Kolb, Robert, editor. "Preface to Luther's Latin Works." In *The Annotated Luther*. Vol. 4, edited by Mary Jane Haemig, (489) 491–503. Minneapolis: Fortress Press, 2016.

Kolb, Robert, and Timothy J. Wengert, editors. *The Book of Concord.* Minneapolis: Augsburg Fortress, 2000.

Kreitzer, Beth, editor. "The Magnificat, 1521." In *The Annotated Luther*, Vol. 4, edited by Mary Jane Haemig, 347–85. Minneapolis: Fortress Press, 2016.

Krey, Peter D. S. "Luther's In-depth Theology and Theological Therapy: Using Self Psychology and a Little Jung." In *Encounters with Luther: New Directions for Critical Studies*, edited by Kirsi Stjerna and Brooks Schramm, 189–204. Louisville, KY: Westminster John Knox Press, 2016.

Leppin, Volker. "Luther on the Devil." In *Encounters with Luther: New Directions for Critical Studies*, edited by Kirsi Stjerna and Brooks Schramm, 30–41. Louisville, KY: Westminster John Knox Press, 2016.

Leppin, Volker, editor. "The Bondage of the Will." In *The Annotated Luther*, Vol. 2, edited by Kirsi Stjerna, (153) 158–258. Minneapolis: Fortress Press, 2015.

Leppin, Volker. *Martin Luther: A Late Medieval Life*. Translated by Rhys Bezzant and Karen Roe. English edition. Grand Rapids, MI: Baker Academic, 2017.

Lindberg, Carter. *The European Reformations*. 2nd ed. Chichester, UK: Wiley-Blackwell, 2010.

Lindberg, Carter. "Luther on Government Responsibility for the Poor." In *Encounters with Luther: New Directions for Critical Studies*, edited by Kirsi Stjerna and Brooks Schramm, 220–31. Louisville, KY: Westminster John Knox Press, 2016.

Lindberg, Carter, and Paul Wee, editors. *Forgotten Luther I*. Minneapolis: Augsburg Press, 2016.

Lobulu, Elizabeth. "More Than 250 Female Pastors and Growing." *The Lutheran World Federation*. Last modified September 23, 2016. Accessed February 29, 2020. https://www.lutheranworld.org/news/more-250-female-pastors-and-growing.

Lohrmann, Martin J. *Book of Harmony: Spirit and Service in the Lutheran Confessions: A Historical Timeline*. Minneapolis: Fortress Press, 2016.

Lohrmann, Martin J., editor. "Invocavit Sermons." In *The Annotated Luther*. Vol. 4, edited by Mary Jane Haemig, (7) 14–45. Minneapolis: Fortress Press, 2016.

Lohrmann, Martin J. *Stories from Global Lutheranism: A Historical Timeline*. Minneapolis: Fortress Press, 2021.

Lohse, Bernard. *Martin Luther's Theology: Its Historical and Systematic Development*. Edited by Roy A. Harrisville. Translated by Roy A. Harrisville. Minneapolis: Fortress Press, 1999.

Luther's Works—American Edition, edited by Jaroslav Pelikan and Helmut T. Lehman, 55 vols. Philadelphia: Fortress Press, 1957.

Luther's Works—American Edition, edited by Jaroslav Pelikan and Helmut T. Lehman, 55. Vols, Philadelphia: Fortress Press, 1957. *The Freedom of a Christian*, LW 31:333–77.

Luthers Werke: Kritische Gesamtausgabe. 65 vols. Weimar: H. Böhlau, 1883.

Luther's Works – American Edition, edited by Jaroslav Pelikan and Helmut T. Lehman, 55. Vols, Philadelphia: Fortress Press, 1957. *Von der Freiheit eines Christenmenschen*, WA 7: 20–38; *De libertate Christiana*, WA 7, 49–73.

Madsen, Anna. *I Can Do No Other. The Church's New Here We Stand Moment*. Minneapolis: Fortress Press, 2020.

Madsen, Anne. "Suffering and the Theology of the Cross from a Feminist Perspective." In *Encounters with Luther: New Directions for Critical Studies*, edited by Kirsi Stjerna and Brooks Schramm, 241–9. Louisville, KY: Westminster John Knox Press, 2016.

Mannermaa, Tuomo. *Christ Present in Faith: Luther's View of Justification*. Translated by Kirsi Stjerna. Minneapolis: Fortress Press, 2005.

Mannermaa, Tuomo. *Two Kinds of Love: Martin Luther's Religious World*. Translated by Kirsi Stjerna. Minneapolis: Fortress Press, 2010.

Mattox, Mickey L. "Warrior Saints: Warfare and Violence in Martin Luther's Readings of Some Old Testament Texts." In *Encounters with Luther: New Directions for Critical Studies*, edited by Kirsi Stjerna and Brooks Schramm, 42–58. Louisville, KY: Westminster John Knox Press, 2016.

McFague, Sallie. *Models of God*. Minneapolis: Fortress Press, 1987.

McGrath, Alister E. *Iustitia Dei: A History of the Christian Doctrine of Justification*. 3rd ed. Cambridge: Cambridge University Press, 2005.

Melloni, Alberto, editor. *Martin Luther: A Christian between Reforms and Modernity (1517–2017)*. 3 vols. Berlin: Walter de Gruyter, 2017.

Moe-Lobeda, Cynthia. *Resisting Structural Evil. Love as an Ecological-economic Vocation*. Minneapolis: Fortress Press, 2013.

Nelavala, Surekha. "Martin Luther's Concept of Sola Scriptura and Its Impact on the Masses: A Dalit Model for Praxis-Nexus." In *Encounters with Luther: New Directions for Critical Studies*, edited by Kirsi Stjerna and Brooks Schramm, 232–8. Louisville, KY: Westminster John Knox Press, 2016.

Nelson, Derek R., and Paul R. Hinlicky, editors. *The Oxford Encyclopedia of Martin Luther*. 3 vols. New York: Oxford University Press, 2017.

Nissinen, Martti. *Homoeroticism in the Biblical World*. Translated by Kirsi Stjerna. Minneapolis: Fortress Press, 2004.

Oberman, Heiko A. *Luther: Man between God and the Devil*. Translated by Eileen Walliser-Schwarzbart. New Haven: Yale University Press, 1989.

Ocker, Christopher. *Luther, Conflict, and Christendom: Reformation Europe and Christianity in the West*. Cambridge: Cambridge University Press, 2018.

Pedersen, Else Marie Wiberg, editor. *The Alternative Luther: Lutheran Theology from the Subaltern*. Lanham, MD and London: Lexington Books/Fortress Academic, 2019.

Pedersen, Else Marie Wiberg, editor. "Two Kinds of Righteousness." In *The Annotated Luther*. Vol. 2, edited by Kirsi Stjerna, (9) 13–24. Minneapolis: Fortress Press, 2015.

Peters, Ted, Martinez Hewlett, Joshua M. Moritz, and Robert John Russell, editors. *Astrotheology: Science and Theology Meet Extraterrestrial Life*. Eugene, OR: Cascade Books, 2018.

Peterson, Cheryl M. *Who Is the Church? An Ecclesiology for the Twenty-First Century* (Minneapolis: Fortress Press, 2013).

Räisänen, Heikki. *The Rise of Christian Beliefs: The Thought World of Early Christian*. Minneapolis: Fortress Press, 2009.

Robinson, Paul W., editor. *The Annotated Luther*. Vol. 3. 6 vols. Minneapolis: Fortress Press, 2016.

Roper, Lyndal. *Martin Luther: Renegade and Prophet*. New York: Random House, 2017.

Ruether, Rosemary Radford. *Sexism and God Talk: Toward a Feminist Theology*. Boston: Beacon Press, 1993.

Saarinen, Risto. *Oppi Toivosta*. Helsinki: Gaudeamus, 2019.

Schaff, Philip. "The Apostles' Creed." In *The Creeds of Christendom*. Vol. 1. 6th edition, by David S. Schaff, 1919. Accessed March 13, 2020. https://www.ccel.org/ccel/schaff/creeds1.iv.ii.html.

Scholl, Hans, and Sophie Scholl. *At the Heart of the White Rose: Letters and Diaries of Hans and Sophie Scholl*. Walden, NY: Plough Publishing, 2017.

Schramm, Brooks, editor. "How Christians Should Regard Moses." In *The Annotated Luther*, Vol. 2, edited by Kirsi Stjerna, (127) 132–51. Minneapolis: Fortress Press, 2015.

Schramm, Brooks. "Like a Sow Entering a Synagogue." In *Encounters with Luther: New Directions for Critical Studies*, edited by Kirsi Stjerna and Brooks Schramm, 250–60. Louisville, KY: Westminster John Knox Press, 2016.

Schramm, Brooks, editor and translator. "On the Schem Hamphoras and on the Lineage of Christ" ["On the Ineffable Name"]. In *The Annotated Luther*, Vol. 5, edited by Hans J. Hillerbrand, (609) 622–66. Minneapolis: Fortress Press, 2017.

Schramm, Brooks, and Kirsi Stjerna, editors. *Martin Luther, the Bible, and the Jewish People*. Minneapolis: Fortress Press, 2010.

Stjerna, Kirsi, editor. *The Annotated Luther*. Vol. 2. 6 vols. Minneapolis: Fortress Press, 2015.

Stjerna, Kirsi. "Freedom of a Christian (1520). Martin Luther (1483–1546)." In *Reading Christian Theology in the Protestant Tradition*, edited by Kelly M. Kapic and Hans Madueme, 335–50. London: T&T Clark, 2018.

Stjerna, Kirsi. "Grief, Glory and Grace: Insights on Eve and Tamar in Luther's Genesis Commentary." *Seminary Ridge Review* 6, no. 2 (Spring 2004), 19–35.

Stjerna, Kirsi, editor. "The Large Catechism (1529) of Dr. Martin Luther." In *The Annotated Luther*, Vol. 2, edited by Kirsi Stjerna, (279) 289–416. Minneapolis: Fortress Press, 2015.

Stjerna, Kirsi. "The Large Catechism (1529), Martin Luther (1483–1546)." In *Reading Christian Theology in the Protestant Tradition*, edited by Kelly M. Kapic and Hans Madueme, 351–61. London: T&T Clark, 2018.

Stjerna, Kirsi. "Law and Gospel." In *Martin Luther in Context*, edited by David Whitford, 272–82. Cambridge: Cambridge University Press, 2018.

Stjerna, Kirsi. "Luther on Marriage, for Gay and Straight." In *Encounters with Luther: New Directions for Critical Studies*, edited by Kirsi Stjerna and Brooks Schramm, 126–44. Louisville, KY: Westminster John Knox Press, 2016.

Stjerna, Kirsi. "Lutheran Faith: Rebellion and Responsibility." In *Forgotten Luther II*, edited by Ryan Cummings, 35–40. Minneapolis: Augsburg Press, 2019.

Stjerna, Kirsi. "A Lutheran Feminist Critique of American Child Protection Laws: Sins of Sexual Nature." In *On Secular Governance: Lutheran Perspectives on Contemporary*, edited by Ronald Duty and Marie Failinger, 141–59. Grand Rapids, MI: Eerdmans, 2016.

Stjerna, Kirsi. *No Greater Jewel: Thinking of Baptism with Martin Luther*. Minneapolis: Augsburg Press, 2010.

Stjerna, Kirsi. "Seeking Hospitable Discourse on the Sacrament of Baptism." *Dialog: A Journal of Theology* 53, no. 2 (2014), 93–100.

Stjerna, Kirsi. "Reformation Revisited: Women's Voices in the Reformation." *The Ecumenical Review*, Vol. 69, no. 2 (July 2017), 201–14.

Stjerna, Kirsi. 'Women Writers of the 16th Century." In *Reading Christian Theology in the Protestant Tradition*, edited by Kelly M. Kapic and Hans Madueme, 387–98. London: T&T Clark, 2018.

Stjerna, Kirsi. *Women and the Reformation*. Malden, MA: Wiley-Blackwell, 2009.

Stjerna, Kirsi, and Brooks Schramm, editors. *Encounters with Luther*. Louisville, KY: Westminster John Knox Press, 2016.

Stjerna, Kirsi, and Brooks Schramm, editors. *Spirituality: Toward a 21st Century Understanding*. Minneapolis: Lutheran University Press, 2004.

Thompson, Deanna A. "Becoming a Feminist Theologian of the Cross." In *Encounters with Luther: New Directions for Critical Studies*, edited by Kirsi Stjerna and Brooks Schramm, 96–108. Louisville, KY: Westminster John Knox Press, 2016.

Tillich, Paul. *The Courage to Be*. 4th ed. New Haven: Yale University Press, 2000.

Tillich, Paul. *The Essential Tillich*. Edited by F. Forrester Church. Chicago: Chicago University Press, 1999.

Tranvik, Mark D., editor. "Concerning Rebaptism." In *The Annotated Luther*, Vol. 3, edited by Paul W. Robinson, 275–316. Minneapolis: Fortress Press, 2016.

Vuola, Elina. *Virgin Mary across Cultures: Devotion among Costa Rican Catholic and Finnish Orthodox Women*. Abingdon; New York: Routledge, 2019.

Wengert, Timothy J. *The Annotated Luther*. Vol. 1. 6 vols. Minneapolis: Fortress Press, 2015.

Wengert, Timothy J., editor. "The Freedom of a Christian." In *The Annotated Luther*, Vol. 1, edited by Timothy J. Wengert, (467) 474–538. Minneapolis: Fortress Press, 2015.

Westhelle, Vitor. "Usus Crucis: The Use and Abuse of the Cross and the Practice of Resurrection." In *Encounters with Luther: New Directions for Critical Studies*, edited by Kirsi Stjerna and Brooks Schramm, 85–95. Louisville, KY: Westminster John Knox Press, 2016.

Wiesner-Hanks, Merry, editor. *Convents Confront the Reformation: Catholic and Protestant Nuns in Germany*. Translated by Joan Skocir. Marquette: Marquette University Press, 1996.

Witte, Jr., John. "The Freedom of a Christian: Martin Luther's Reformation of Law & Liberty." *Evangelische Theologie* 74, no. 2 (2014), 127–35.

Witte, Jr., John. "'The Mother of All Earthly Laws': The Lutheran Reformation of Marriage." In *Encounters with Luther: New Directions for Critical Studies*, edited by Kirsi Stjerna and Brooks Schramm, 111–25. Louisville, KY: Westminster John Knox Press, 2016.

Witte, Jr., John. *From Sacrament to Contract: Marriage, Religion, and Law in the Western Tradition*. Louisville, KY: Westminster John Knox Press, 2012.

"Affirming Women's Ordination as Our Shared Goal." *The Lutheran World Federation*. Last modified June 6, 2016. Accessed February 29, 2020. https://www.lutheranworld.org/news/affirming-womens-ordination-our-shared-goal.

"Celebrating Commitment to Women's Ordination in Mozambique." *The Lutheran World Federation*. Last modified March 7, 2017. Accessed February 29, 2020. https://www.lutheranworld.org/news/celebrating-commitment-womens-ordination-mozambique.

"Mexican Church Marks 10 Years of Women's Ordination." *The Lutheran World Federation*. Last modified April 12, 2019. Accessed February 29, 2020. https://www.lutheranworld.org/news/mexican-church-marks-10-years-womens-ordination.

"Social Statements." *Evangelical Lutheran Church in America*. Last modified 2020. Accessed March 13, 2020. http://www.elca.org/Faith/Faith.and.Society/Social.Statements.

"Thailand: First Lutheran Women Ordained into Ministry." *The Lutheran World Federation*. Last modified February 5, 2018. Accessed February 29, 2020. https://www.lutheranworld.org/news/thailand-first-lutheran-women-ordained-ministry.

INDEX